Crypto-assets
global corporate finance transactions

A comparative and functional analysis of crypto offerings and securities laws

Massimiliano Caruso

Singulab
Law Business

Singulab
Law Business

SINGULANCE's vision is that top tier legal practice and academic research are closely connected. SINGULAB is the SINGULANCE's Law & Business Research Centre and produces cutting-edge research works in the international law-sensitive aspects of business, finance, corporate and securities, aiming at improving the education of young researchers, practicing lawyers and law students.

Copyright © 2019 SINGULANCE
Copyright © 2019 Massimiliano Caruso

ISBN-10: **1796623792**
ISBN-13: **978-1796623796**

Printed in the United States of America
Published in New York
First published 2019

No part of this publication may be reproduced, stored in a retrieval system or transmitted, in any form or by any means, without the prior permission in writing, or as expressly permitted by law, license or under terms agreed with the appropriate reprographics rights organization.

The information provided in this publication does not constitute legal advice. It is for general information and education purposes and may not apply in a specific situation. Legal advice should always be sought before taking any legal action based on the information provided. No offering of securities should be undertaken without taking specific legal advice in each case.

To my family, my friends, and Satoshi Nakamoto

1. SOME BASICS

1.1 The roaring twenties — 1
1.2 The rise of crypto finance transactions — 4
1.3 Jurisdiction shopping and the forfeiture of intellectual capital — 8
1.4 Crypto finance transactions decentralize the process of funding technology — 9
1.5 Any law other than that of the jurisdiction of incorporation? — 9

2. CRYPTO-ASSETS

1.1 Legal nature of the crypto-assets among regulators — 13
1.2 A new taxonomy: speculative and non-speculative crypto-assets — 20
1.3 Benefits and risks of crypto-assets — 22
1.4 Cons of fully open decentralized networks in terms of corporate structure, IP and acquisitions — 23

3. INITIAL COIN OFFERINGS

1.1 ICOs regulatory environments — 24
    1.1.1 Australia — 24
    1.1.2 Canada — 26
    1.1.3 China — 27
    1.1.4 EU, EAA and other European jurisdictions — 29
    1.1.5 Hong Kong — 38
    1.1.6 Israel — 39
    1.1.7 Russia — 40
    1.1.8 Singapore — 41
    1.1.9 United States — 43
1.2 The Simple Agreement for Future Tokens — 61
1.3 A Corporate Crypto Conduct Code for ICOs — 64
1.4 Initial Exchange Offerings — 67

4. SECURITY TOKEN OFFERINGS

1.1 Security crypto-assets — 69

Contents

1.2 Securities regulatory environments — 72
1.2.1 Australia — 72
1.2.2 Brazil — 76
1.2.3 Canada — 79
1.2.4 China — 86
1.2.5 European Union and EAA — 93
    1.2.5.1 Austria — 95
    1.2.5.2 France — 98
    1.2.5.3 Germany — 100
    1.2.5.4 Ireland — 105
    1.2.5.5 Italy — 107
    1.2.5.6 Luxemburg — 110
    1.2.5.7 Netherlands — 114
    1.2.5.8 Norway — 116
    1.2.5.9 United Kingdom — 118
1.2.6 Hong Kong — 122
1.2.7 India — 128
1.2.8 Israel — 131
1.2.9 Japan — 133
1.2.10 Nigeria — 138
1.2.11 Russia — 140
1.2.12 Saudi Arabia — 142
1.2.13 Singapore — 145
1.2.14 South Africa — 148
1.2.15 South Korea — 150
1.2.16 Switzerland — 152
1.2.17 United Arab Emirates — 155
    1.2.17.1 Dubai International Financial Centre — 157
1.2.18 United States — 159
    1.2.18.1 Rule 506 of Regulation D in detail — 165
    1.2.18.2 Regulation S in detail — 166
        1.2.18.2.1 Resales into the United States — 168
    1.2.18.3 Rule 144A in detail — 169
        1.2.18.3.1 Restricted securities — 171

5.
HOW TO REGULATE A MERE MARKET RESPONSE TO OVERREGULATION

1.1 A starting point for regulators to think about ICO regulations — 173
1.1.1 Investor protection — 175
    1.1.1.1 Investor losses — 177
1.1.2 Asymmetric information and moral hazard — 178
    1.1.2.1 ICO rating platforms and secondary sources — 179
    1.1.2.2 Strong corporate governance and ethics count — 180
1.1.3 Some actual proposals to balance support for innovation

and investor protection 182
1.1.4 An International Convention for crypto finance transactions? 187
1.1.5 Should regulators take a proactive approach about crypto finance transactions? 187

6.
THE EVOLVING LANDSCAPE 189

Author

Massimiliano Caruso leads the International Business and Corporate Law Department of SINGULANCE, an award-winning international law firm based in New York, specialized in handling complex multi-jurisdictional business and corporate transactions.

Massimiliano is also Senior Advisory Board Member and Visiting Scholar at the FISF Fintech Research Center, Fanhai International School of Finance, Fudan University.

Massimiliano's researches mainly focus on multi-jurisdictional comparative analyses of business, corporate and securities laws, involving primarily major common law systems (US, UK), major European continental civil law systems (France, Germany, Italy, Netherlands) and European Union law, with references to other jurisdictions such as China, Hong Kong, Singapore and Japan.

Massimiliano is a licensed legal consultant in New York and a lawyer admitted to the practice of law in Italy. Massimiliano's professional expertise includes international law-sensitive aspects of business, finance, corporate and securities. His extensive knowledge of the civil and common law legal systems merges with broad international experience and a truly global perspective of law, business and finance.

Massimiliano's professional affiliations include the New York State Bar Association (NYSBA).

Full profile on *linkedin.com/in/massimilianocaruso*

Preface

The rise of crypto-assets and crypto-assets corporate finance transactions – like Initial Coin Offerings, Security Token Offerings, Initial Exchange Offerings and respective variants – are disrupting the way companies raise funds. At the same time the sudden rise of crypto finance transactions has created unprecedented challenges for regulators, financial market authorities, corporate finance lawyers and professionals.

Crypto-assets corporate finance transactions are essentially borderless, global and interconnected. Their borderless nature was the core inspiration of this work. This book, indeed, is an attempt to address a comparative and functional analysis of crypto-assets corporate finance transactions.

I believe it's neutral, international, functional and short.

It's neutral because while it's true that the variety of crypto-assets necessitates a case-by-case analysis, it's unquestionable that some types and hybrid forms of crypto-assets fall within existing securities laws and regulations. Securities offerings, however, are highly regulated in most developed jurisdictions, while, by contrast, the rapid rise of these crypto-assets corporate finance transactions is very likely nothing else than a mere market response to overregulation. It has to be noted that: (i) regulations should be technologically neutral, and in order to become so, address the actors and not the products themselves; (ii) far too often (non-accredited, non-qualified, non-sophisticated) investors are denied the opportunity to invest in new and promising technologies and in new companies – all which undermine productive capital formation and economic growth; (iii) crypto finance transactions are part of a self-contained system and this unique context requires to carefully weigh competing goals – protecting investors (that can lead to a larger and healthier crypto finance environment) while promoting capital raising and economic liberty. This is why these crypto-assets should be treated as a new type of asset whose use – currently falling within existing regulations – should be governed by new and *ad hoc* regulations, above all in the securities field, in order not to disregard their unique operational and technological features. Existing securities rules and best practices are frequently nonsensical or even counterproductive in the context of many crypto finance transactions. Regulation is certainly necessary to allow crypto-assets and crypto-assets corporate finance transactions to achieve their potential, but the regulatory system should have an appropriate balance and a high degree of clarity. I believe, however, optimal regulatory structures will emerge and converge over time. The final part of the book, then, sketches some proposals for regulators – based on a weighted approach – that, if adopted, would enhance legal certainty and seek to balance support for innovation and investor protection.

It's international because it contains summary information on the securities law regimes in Australia, Brazil, Canada, China, EU / EAA (Austria, France, Germany,

Preface

Ireland, Italy, Luxemburg, Netherlands, Norway, United Kingdom), Hong Kong, India, Israel, Japan, Nigeria, Russia, Saudi Arabia, Singapore, South Africa, South Korea, Switzerland, United Arab Emirates, United States, including the principal prospectus exemptions and private placements rules in each jurisdiction. Securities offerings are highly regulated and significant civil and criminal penalties can be incurred as a result of offerings which are not authorized by the relevant authorities or compliant with the applicable securities regime. There are good reasons why similar measures have arisen in the wider corporate world over time – to ensure a sustainable ecosystem with resources directed at better quality projects, to ensure that bad actors are (to the extent possible) eliminated, and to ensure that legal and professional risks are mitigated by a better balance between the interests of all stakeholders. This is why crypto-assets corporate finance transactions falling within existing securities laws and regulations can't be conducted assuming the law doesn't exist – in the meantime specific regulations arise. Also, while the lack of widely accepted global standards has led to a great deal of regulatory arbitrage, as crypto-assets issuers shop for jurisdictions with the lightest touch (or no touch), I believe they should not attempt to flee from regulation. By contrast, they should talk with financial market authorities.

It's functional because with regard to crypto-assets with real intrinsic usage (non-speculative crypto-assets) this book discusses how a proactive self-regulation, ethical human behaviors, rigorous due diligence, improved governance, disclosure, investors protection and accountability measures could be applied to lead to better quality Initial Coin Offerings, a more sustainable fundraising environment for all the parties involved and mitigate risks due to regulatory uncertainty. At the same I propose (and encourage the adoption of) a Corporate Crypto Conduct Code for businesses in this space.

It's short because my project in writing this book is to give a quick framework for understanding the most important securities law regimes. This book is not intended to be an exhaustive guide to the regulation of crypto-assets corporate finance transaction globally or in any of the included jurisdictions. Instead, for each jurisdiction, I have endeavored to provide a sufficient overview for the reader to understand the current legal and regulatory environment. I hope that it remains short enough to attract the readers I would like to reach: (i) my colleagues in international business and corporate law and related legal fields (who can start from these frameworks to make a more detailed analysis of the securities laws in the core jurisdictions summarized in this book); (ii) regulators and lawmakers (with the hope they will find this book a helpful guide to develop new strategies, policies and regulations); (iii) crypto-assets issuers (with the hope they understand the importance of being compliant with the law – even if and when, on the spot, it seems economically irrational – and the reasons why the current measures have arisen in the wider corporate world over time).

Acknowledgements

The writing of this book has engaged me for a considerable time and has involved several people who, with absolute friendship and spirit of collaboration, have made it possible. Many were those who advised, helped and listened me; who have suggested me to embark on this long journey. To them, my dearest and most heartfelt thank you.

I will be extremely grateful to those readers who will report to me (email: mcaruso@singulance.com) any comments and suggestions or parts of the book that are unclear, inaccurate or contradictory.

Massimiliano Caruso

CHAPTER 1
SOME BASICS

1.1 The roaring twenties • 1.2 The rise of crypto finance transactions • 1.3 Jurisdiction shopping and the forfeiture of intellectual capital • 1.4 Crypto finance transactions decentralize the process of funding technology • 1.5 Any law other than that of the jurisdiction of incorporation?

1.1 *The roaring twenties.* The world's capital markets are today indisputably global and interconnected. Securities markets have experienced unprecedented levels of cross-border activity over the past 20 years. The removal of barriers to free movement of capital, the intermediation of professionals who have the skills and the scale to invest internationally, and the digital interconnection of markets across the globe[1] have broken the link between listing on a particular exchange and having access to the capital base originating in the country where that exchange is located. To some extent, crypto-assets corporate finance transactions ("**crypto finance transactions**") have closed the circle, becoming the pinnacle of the free movement of capital.

When and how did this circle start?

In 1600, a group of London merchants led by Sir Thomas Smythe petitioned Queen Elizabeth I to grant them a royal charter to trade with the countries of the eastern hemisphere. And so, the *"Honourable Company of Merchants of London Trading with the East Indies"* – or East India Company, as it came to be known – was founded. On the cusp of imperialism's high point, it seems like everyone had a stake in the profits from the East Indies and Asia except the people living there. Sea voyages that brought back goods from the East were extremely risky – on top of Barbary pirates, there were the more common risks of weather and poor navigation. To lessen the risk of a lost ship ruining their fortunes, ship owners had long been in the practice of seeking investors who would put up money for the voyage – outfitting the ship and crew in return for a percentage of the proceeds if the voyage was successful. These early limited liability companies often lasted for only a single voyage. They were then dissolved, and a new one was created for the next voyage. Investors spread their risk by investing in several different ventures at the same time, thereby playing the odds against all of them ending in disaster.

---

[1] While technologization has increased the interconnectedness of countries and markets, information markets are not yet fully global, meaning local investors may find it easier to procure accurate information, understand the language of issuers' disclosures, or assess the reputation and credibility of directors and officers who write such disclosures. See, e.g., B. Baik, J.K. Jang & J.M. Kim, *Local Institutional Investors, Information Asymmetries, and Equity Returns*, Journal of Financial Economics 97, 81 (2010).

The East India companies changed the way business was done. These companies issued stock[2] that would pay dividends on all the proceeds from all the voyages the companies undertook, rather than going voyage by voyage.

So, when stocks were introduced in the early 1600s to investors, they were designed to open the company to forms of actual co-ownership, where investors share with the founders (the entrepreneurial risks in exchange of part of the) profits coming from the earnings and growth of the underlying company. After some centuries most companies started not to pay dividends, regardless of their actual earnings, and for many investors the security market became speculation and gambling. The only realistic way investors can make money was by selling their shares to other investors. For many decades – after the 1929 crash – we retreated from that model, focusing on companies' fundamentals. But now, again, investors and traders examine the value of the stock itself, apart from the underlying company. The disaggregation between the market value of the security itself and the intrinsic value of the company is increasingly being recognized.

As Michael Lewis writes: *"the line between gambling and investing is thin and artificial. The soundest investment has the defining trait of a bet (you losing all of your money in hopes of making a bit more), and the wildest speculation has the salient characteristic of an investment (you might get your money back with interest). Maybe the best definition of "investing" is "gambling with the odds in your favor"*[3].

Trading, technically, is associated with short term profit seeking, in which securities are bought and sold with a quick turnover. By contrast investing is conceptually associated to long terms buy and hold strategies.

The current model doesn't work.

In 2014 just 14% of families in the US held shares in individual stocks, as Apple and Amazon. 48% of adults have money invested in the stock market, directly or indirectly, through pooled-investment vehicles, such as mutual funds and ETFs. As a result, institutional investors[4] dominate the market.

---

[2] In 1602, the Dutch East India Company (VOC) became the first publicly traded company when it sold shares on its own Amsterdam Stock Exchange (the first stock market). However, while the Dutch East India Company was the first modern company to issue stock to the public, and the first to create a modern public stock exchange, they weren't the first entity to issue stock in general. Modern forms of stocks arise in the trading centers of the Italian Maritime Republics around 1150.
[3] M. Lewis, *The Big Short: Inside the Doomsday Machine*, W. W. Norton & Company (2011).
[4] Among institutions, hedge funds – organizations that pool and manage securities for wealthy groups of investors – are at the forefront.

Jack Favilukis asserts *"Wall Street played a major role in the surging income gap over the last 30 years. Through 2007 the wealthiest 10% owned 72% of the market's total equity"*[5].

Today, you could say almost the same things with regard to crypto-assets and crypto finance transactions. The first adopters of crypto-assets were not just driven by the potential financial upside, but really believed in the technology and want to prove that the technology works. Then, crypto-assets started to be associated with a pricing discovery phase, that suddenly became "irrational exuberance" that led to speculation that continued to drive further interest and raise awareness among a larger portion of market participants. Because crypto-assets investing had become popular, investors relinquished their tried and true fundamentals in order to get in on the next big thing[6]. Today, about 40 percent of Bitcoin is held by perhaps 1,000 owners[7] and there are evidences of wealth concentration and income inequality amongst participants within crypto-assets.[8]

The story of crypto-assets resembles in many ways the story of securities. The 1920s, for example, were a period of strong economic growth and swift technological change, especially in the US[9]. That led to a speculative boom in

---

[5] J. Favilukis, *Inequality, Stock Market Participation, and the Equity Premium*, The London School of Economics (2012).

[6] An empirical study that finds evidence that the long-term fundamental value of Bitcoin is statistically indistinguishable from zero. See E. Cheah, J. Fry, *Speculative bubbles in Bitcoin markets? An empirical investigation into the fundamental value of Bitcoin*, Economics Letters 130, 32-36 (2015); see also D. Yermack, *Is Bitcoin a Real Currency: An Economic Appraisal*, in David Lee Kuo Chuen (ed) Handbook of Digital Currency 31-36 (2015); S. Athey, I. Parashkevov, V. Sarukkai, J. Xia, *Bitcoin Pricing, Adoption, and Usage: Theory and Evidence*, Stanford University Graduate School of Business Research Paper No. 16-42 (Aug. 1, 2016). In fundamental valuation, the fundamental value of an asset is usually defined as the discounted expected future cash flow that the asset delivers to its holder (See B. Cornell, A. Damodaran, *Tesla: Anatomy of a Run-Up Value Creation or Investor Sentiment?*, Working Paper (April 26, 2014); A. Damodaran, *Living with Noise: Valuation in the Face of Uncertainty*, CFA Institute Conference Proceedings Quarterly 30, 22 (2013)). While the market value of Bitcoin is obviously far above zero, the study suggests that the price volatility of Bitcoin implies that its "true", fundamental value is zero. This is different with shares in most companies, partnerships or other entities that, unless in times of extreme crisis, have positive fundamental value.

[7] See O. Kharif, *The Bitcoin Whales: 1,000 People Who Own 40 Percent of the Market*, Bloomberg Businessweek (Dec. 8, 2017), available at: https://www.bloomberg.com/news/articles/2017-12-08/the-bitcoin-whales-1-000-people-who-own-40-percent-of-the-market.

[8] M. Novak, *The Implications of Blockchain for Income Inequality* (2018).

[9] Between 1860 and 1920, the economy changed from "agricultural to industrial to financial". At that time, New York was already battling with London for the throne as the world's financial capital. The New York Stock Exchange ("**NYSE**") today is the largest and, arguably, most powerful stock exchange in the world. The Nasdaq has more companies listed, but the NYSE has a market capitalization – US$30.1 trillion – that is larger than Tokyo, London and the Nasdaq exchanges combined. The history of the NYSE begins with the signing of the Buttonwood Agreement by twenty-four New York City stockbrokers and merchants on May 17, 1792, outside at 68 Wall Street under a Buttonwood tree. In the beginning there were five securities traded in New York City with the first listed company on the NYSE being the Bank of New York. The NYSE passed the milestone of 1 million shares traded in a day in 1886. In 1987, 500 million shares were trading hands on the NYSE during a normal business day. By

stock prices during much of the 1920s decade, similar to the recent bull market in crypto-assets. Much like how blockchain and the crypto-assets are fueling market speculation today, the relatively new communication medium of radio, and the stock of Radio Corporation of America helped drive the 1920s rally[10]. The dominant theme at that time was centralization, while the dominant theme today is decentralization (quite the opposite). Aside that, anyway, the similarities are evident. At that time there were no laws governing trading in securities. At this time there are no specific laws governing crypto finance transactions. At that time companies issued stock and enthusiastically promoted the value of their company to induce investors to purchase those securities. At this time crypto-assets startups issue crypto-assets and enthusiastically promoted the value of their projects to induce investors to purchase those crypto-assets. In many cases, the promises made by companies had little or no substantive basis or were wholly fraudulent. Same situation today with crypto finance transactions.

The invention of financial products or asset classes has always been a complex art. Their adoption and growth very often is the story repeating itself.

1.2 *The rise of crypto finance transactions*. Regulations and governance measures generally struggle to keep up with technological advancements. In finance, in particular, technology and innovation have a habit of reshaping the financial industry faster than the legal and regulatory framework can meaningfully adapt. The rise of crypto-assets[11] and crypto finance transactions – like Initial Coin Offerings ("**ICOs**"), Security Token Offerings ("**STOs**"), Initial Exchange Offerings ("**IEOs**"), and respective variants – are disrupting the way companies[12] raise funds. At the same time the sudden rise of crypto finance transactions has created unprecedented challenges for regulators, financial market authorities, corporate finance lawyers and professionals. Even sophisticated investors are starting to be attracted to this market. By April 2018 there were about 250 funds – mainly hedge and venture funds – investing in crypto-assets[13]. Some commentators have expressed enthusiasm about the rise of crypto finance transactions, noting their potential to energize and democratize start-up funding by offering retail investors the opportunity to participate in the early-stage funding of new

---

1997, the shares traded daily were 1 billion. See. C.R. Geisst, *Wall Street: a history: from its beginnings to the fall of Enron*, Oxford University Press (1997).
[10] L. Bumgardner, *A Brief History of the 1930s Securities Laws in the United States – And the Potential Lessons for Today*, The Journal of Global Business Management, 4-1 (2008).
[11] Few financial assets have generated in the history of finance returns comparable to those of crypto-assets. Bitcoin, for instance, has risen over 500,000,000% in value between its creation (in January 2009) and January 2018.
[12] Especially early stages startups.
[13] See *Initial Coin Offerings: 1Q 2018 in review*, Autonomous Next (April 2018), available at: https://next.autonomous.com/thoughts/initial-coin-offerings-1q-2018-in-review.

businesses[14]. Other observers have expressed skepticism, raising concerns about fraud[15], market manipulation[16], and cybersecurity[17].

In a typical ICO[18], a company (generally the issuing entity) receives fiat currencies, such as US dollars or Euro, or crypto-assets, such as Bitcoin or Ether, in exchange for certain rights embodied in crypto-assets (whose nature and treatment are generating controversy among financial market authorities and regulators around the world). Contrary to traditional Initial Public Offerings ("**IPOs**"), crypto-assets typically do not represent an ownership interest (or dividend right) in the issuing entity.

Unlike ICOs, crypto-assets in STOs are backed by real assets – equity, debts/loans, or investment funds, for instance. As such, security tokens fall within existing securities laws and regulations. As we will see hereinafter, securities definitions are similar in spirit around the world, but vary from jurisdiction to jurisdiction. Securities in the EU are mainly (i) shares in companies ("equity securities") and (ii) bonds issued by companies ("debt securities"), which are (in both cases) negotiable on the capital market, or (iii) other securities which give a right to acquire such said securities or give rise to a cash settlement (besides payment instruments). In the US, the definition is wider and puts more weight on (i) the purpose of the investment and (ii) what the entrepreneurs are doing with the invested funds, rather than on the actual instruments the investors are receiving in return for their money. Stocks, bonds, notes, investment contracts, security future, participation in profit-sharing agreements are some of the financial instruments defined as securities in the Securities Act of 1933. This master list included both the obvious (e.g. stocks, bonds), along with the not so obvious (e.g. investment contracts), but unfortunately didn't entire solve the puzzle. In 1946, the US Supreme Court weighed in and created the famous *Howey Test*, the *de facto* standard for analyzing many securities issues today. Under the *Howey Test*, a

---

[14] J. Preston, *Initial Coin Offerings: Innovation, Democratization and the SEC*, Duke Law & Tech. Review. 16, 318-331 (2018).

[15] See S. Shifflett, C. Jones, *Buyer Beware: Hundreds of Bitcoin Wannabes Show Hallmarks of Fraud*, Wall Street Journal (May 17, 2018), available at: https://www.wsj.com/articles/buyer-beware-hundreds-of-bitcoin-wannabes-show-hallmarks-of-fraud-1526573115; D. Z. Morris, *The Rise of Cryptocurrency Ponzi Schemes*, The Atlantic (May 31, 2017), available at: https://www.theatlantic.com/technology/archive/2017/05/cryptocurrency-ponzi-schemes/528624/.

[16] See J. Clayton, *Governance and Transparency at the Commission and in Our Markets*, Remarks at the PLI 49th Annual Institute on Securities Regulation – New York (Nov. 8, 2017), available at: https://www.sec.gov/news/speech/speech-clayton-2017- 11-08.

[17] See EY Research: *Initial Coin Offerings (ICOs)*, EY (Dec. 2017), available at: https://www.ey.com/Publication/vwLUAssets/ey-research-initial-coin-offerings-icos/$File/ey-research-initial-coin-offerings-icos.pdf.

[18] The most disruptive feature of the technology underpinning ICOs is that it genuinely removes the need for intermediary institutions to be involved in the financing process. It also removes all jurisdictional and temporal boundaries. The blockchain enables funds to be securely transferred in a peer-to-peer manner almost instantaneously. This process contrasts dramatically to that endured by companies raising capital by traditional means.

financial instrument qualifies as an "investment contract" for the purposes of the Securities Act of 1933, if a buyer (i) invests money, (ii) in a common enterprise, (iii) expecting a profit, (iv) predominantly from the effort of others.

Contrary to ICOs and STOs, IEOs[19] are administered by a crypto-assets exchange[20] on behalf of the companies that seek to raise funds with their newly issued crypto-assets. As the crypto-assets sale is conducted on the exchange's platform, issuers have to pay a listing fee along with a percentage of the crypto-assets sold during the IEO. In return, the crypto-assets are sold on the exchange's platform, and listed just after the IEO is over. IEO participants do not send fiat currencies or crypto-assets such as Bitcoin or Ether to a smart contract governing the ICO. Instead, they have to create an account on the exchange's platform where the IEO is conducted, fund their exchange wallets with US dollars or Euro, or crypto-assets, such as Bitcoin or Ether, and use those funds to buy the company's crypto-assets[21].

Currently, main entities conducting ICOs, STOs and IEOs are:

(i) Venture entities. Issuers are small venture companies with limited access to incumbent capital market, or venture capitals, while potential purchasers are investors who are looking for high-risk, high-return investment opportunities other than common equities.
(ii) Ecosystem entities. Issuers are companies (or alliances of companies) that are making concerted efforts to form a new market through an ecosystem, while potential purchasers are companies that wish to participate in an ecosystem when the market is formed (companies which own crypto-assets are entitled to receive an option to participate in the ecosystem with advantageous terms).
(iii) Large entities. Issuers are companies that operate high-risk businesses for which feasibility is difficult to evaluate, or those that try to find ways to vitalize buried in-house assets such as technologies, while potential purchasers are investors who expect to receive special offer from companies or those who want to express their support or sympathy for projects.

---

[19] IEO's nature and treatment are controversial. IEOs could make the underlying crypto-assets more likely to be deemed securities.
[20] The crypto-assets exchange basically act as a form of underwriter.
[21] An increasing number of crypto-assets exchanges have started to embrace IEOs. The first was Binance, which launched its IEO platform Binance Launchpad. In January 2019, BitTorrent – that was bought by TRON – conducted a crypto-assets sale on Binance Launchpad and raised $7.2 million in less than 15 minutes, hitting the hard cap. Following the success of Binance Launchpad, other notable crypto-assets exchanges announced launches of their own IEO platforms – Bitmax Launchpad, Bittrex IEO, OK Jumpstart (OKEx), KuCoin Spotlight, and Huobi Prime. $180 million has been raised in 23 offerings so far.

ICOs, STOs and IEOs are still in their infancy and there are no industry practices yet. Appropriate rules must be set to enable ICOs and IEOs (and to some extent STOs) to obtain public trust and to expand as a sound and reliable financing method. While no measure will ever entirely stamp out bad actors, or the risk of projects failing due to any number of often uncontrollable factors[22], specific corporate crypto financing regulations can be a step in the right direction. In order to maintain investor confidence, an adult environment, and, as a consequence, a healthy financial system, regulators worldwide must proactively put in place regulatory frameworks, based upon global accepted common principles. ICOs, STOs and IEOs, in fact, are additional channels for entrepreneurs to access to finance[23] – and better financial systems drastically improve the probability of successful innovation (thereby accelerating economic growth). La Porta, Lopez-de-Silanes, Shleifer and Vishny argue that investors protection in particular determines the development of the capital market[24]. In this regard, it has been noted many times that most financial problems are caused by unethical human behaviors (that are not going to be solved by technology). Therefore, investors protection can lead to a larger and healthier crypto finance environment. These crypto-assets, however, should be treated as a new type of asset whose use should be governed by *ad hoc* regulations, above all in the securities field, in order not to disregard the unique operational and technological features of crypto-assets[25]. Existing securities rules and best practices are frequently nonsensical or even counterproductive in the context of many crypto finance transactions[26].

---

[22] 75% of venture-backed US companies fail to return invested capital to their investors. See D. Gage, *The Venture Capital Secret: 3 Out of 4 Start-Ups Fail*, The Wall Street Journal (Sept. 20, 2012), available at: https://www.wsj.com/articles/SB10000872396390443720204578004980476429190.

[23] See A. Tapscott, D. Tapscott, *How Blockchain Is Changing Finance*, Harvard Business Review (Mar. 1, 2017), available at: http://hbr.org/2017/03/how-blockchain-is-changing-finance.

[24] R. La Porta, F. Lopez-de-Silanes, A. Shleifer, R. Vishny, *Investor protection and corporate governance*, Journal of Financial Economics 58, 3-27 (2000).

[25] Regardless of the fact that currently some crypto-assets unquestionably fall within existing assets and regulations. As, for instance, the US Supreme Court noted, the usual characteristics of stocks include voting rights, the capacity to appreciate in value and the right to receive dividends, i.e., future cash flows. See Landreth Timber Co. v. Landreth, 471 U.S. 681, 686 (1985). Most crypto-assets do fulfil these criteria and often even crypto-assets that do not necessarily represent shares in companies could be meaningfully compared to them under a functional analysis.

[26] In this context, on December 13, 2018 Basis, an apparently legitimate $133 million project financed by some of the largest venture capital firms in the world, such as Andreessen Horowitz and Bain Capital Ventures, announced that it will shut down operations and return $133 million in capital to investors due to the difficulty – if not impossibility – of complying with securities regulations given the team's vision for the project. As per the official statement, available at: https://www.basis.io: *"as regulatory guidance started to trickle out over time, our lawyers came to a consensus that there would be no way to avoid securities status for bond and share tokens (though Basis would likely be free of this characterization). Due to their status as unregistered securities, bond and share tokens would be subject to transfer restrictions, with Intangible Labs responsible for limiting token ownership to accredited investors in the US for the first year after issuance and for performing eligibility checks on international users"*. See *Cryptocurrency project Basis to shut down and return funding to investors*, Reuters (Dec. 13, 2018), available at: https://www.reuters.com/article/us-crypto-currency-basis/cryptocurrency-project-basis-to-shut-down-and-return-funding-to-investors-idUSKBN1OC2OV.

Crypto-assets global corporate finance transactions

1.3 *Jurisdiction shopping and the forfeiture of intellectual capital.* The following chart shows the significant change in country of issuance of crypto-assets between 2017 and 2018[27].

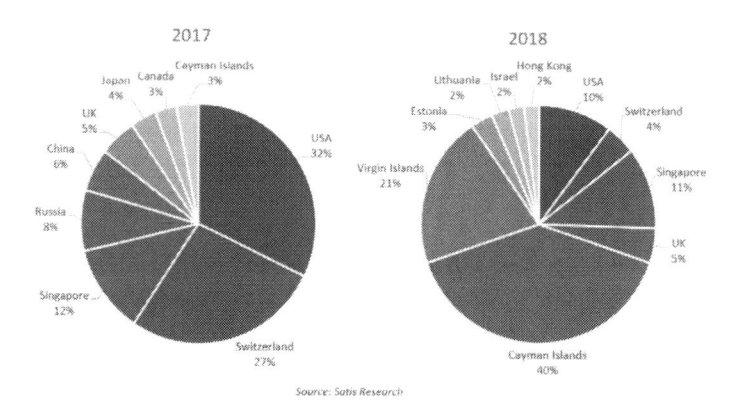

[Pie charts comparing 2017 and 2018 country of issuance of crypto-assets]

2017: Cayman Islands 3%, Japan 4%, Canada 3%, UK 5%, China 6%, Russia 8%, Singapore 12%, Switzerland 27%, USA 32%

2018: Hong Kong 7%, Lithuania 2%, Israel 2%, USA 10%, Estonia 3%, Switzerland 4%, Virgin Islands 21%, Singapore 11%, UK 5%, Cayman Islands 40%

Source: Satis Research

The way governments and regulators decide to behave towards this new technological wave will have a huge impact on where this new generation of wealth creators will choose to base themselves. Crypto-assets issuers are not longstanding, well-established companies. They do not have strong links with any jurisdiction and sometimes are not even incorporated. As a result, they can be incorporated virtually anywhere around the world, depending on the most advantageous regulation (also in terms of taxation). This has to be taken into account by regulators. Implementing harsh frameworks (complete ban of ICOs or STOs for instance) will not be a working regulatory strategy. It will only intensify the impetus behind the mass exodus of crypto-assets issuers to foreign jurisdictions. In many cases projects based originally and organically in ICO banned or ICO unfriendly countries have made the difficult decision to relocate the project to foreign jurisdictions with proactive approach. This is not only a loss of intellectual capital for the countries which seek to lead the world in technology innovation – while the economies and businesses of other competing countries exposed to these technologies first will begin to wield greater advantages over the ICO banned or ICO unfriendly countries' economies and their businesses – but a problem for creators[28], investors[29] and users[30]. Well-developed domestic standards for crypto-assets corporate finance transactions could provide the certainty that keeps innovators at home.

In Europe, Switzerland has become one of the main crypto-hubs on the continent, while Malta is attempting to position itself as the most crypto-

---
[27] Satis group July 2018, Crypto-asset market coverage initiation: network creation.
[28] Creators feel themselves forced to leave.
[29] Investors seeking to fund these projects are usually excluded.
[30] Early adopting users are shut out entirely.

friendly jurisdiction in the world, attracting talent from all over the world, such as Asian crypto giants like Binance, Tron and OKEx to make the long journey to set up shop there. Binance, for instance, announced it is funding the world's first decentralized bank based on the island – a bold experiment which could have profound implications for the future.

Another surprising and very sophisticated example of accommodating attitude towards crypto-assets corporate finance transactions can be seen in the US surprisingly accommodating attitude towards blockchain projects. The Federal Reserve, notoriously protective of US dollar and its influence across the globe, has not yet pushed for the sort of draconian legislation which many expected to come from Washington. While certain restrictions like those pertaining to ICOs remain in effect, many prominent exchanges are based in the US. The US Securities and Exchange Commission has determined that Bitcoin and Ether are not securities and actually is effectively promoting entrepreneurship in a context in which it must weigh competing policy goals – protecting investors (in case of clearly fraudulent or not really functional projects) while promoting capital raising.

1.4 *Crypto finance transactions decentralize the process of funding technology.* Because ICOs and STOs can occur in any country, the importance of going to the US in general, or Silicon Valley / Wall Street in particular, to raise financing will drop. Silicon Valley will likely remain the world's leading technology capital, but it will not be necessary to physically travel to the US as it was for a previous generation of technologists to raising investment capital[31] or generating a dedicated community. Some of the most successful ICOs, by amount raised, have been orchestrated by decentralized teams with members around the globe. In this context, approximately one third of all ICO funding went to US-based teams[32].

1.5 *Any law other than that of the jurisdiction of incorporation?* A question frequently asked is whether any law other than that of the jurisdiction of incorporation of the entity generating or offering the crypto-assets needs to be considered in relation to ICOs or STOs.

The short answer is yes. Crypto-assets offerings are typically international affair, with transfers coming in from all over the world. Therefore, in addition to the laws of the jurisdiction in which the entity issuing or generating the crypto-assets is incorporated or established, the laws of each jurisdiction within which the crypto-assets could be considered to be offered or sold, or

---

[31] A recent study found that US investors allocated 77 per cent of their traditional equity investments to domestic stocks, even though the US only represents 33 per cent of global market capitalization. See N. Coeurdacier, H. Rey, *Home Bias in Open Economy Financial Macroeconomics*, Journal of Economic Literature, American Economic Association 51, 63 (2013).
[32] C. Catalini, J.S. Gans, *Initial Coin Offerings and the Value of Crypto Tokens*, MIT Sloan School of Management working paper 5347-18 (2018).

in which a regulated activity may be deemed to be carried out, will also be relevant[33].

The international reach of ICOs, which frequently is an inevitable consequence of the application of blockchain technology, has likely prompted a number of national regulators to step up oversight of the crypto finance transactions market. Transactions on the blockchain are immutable, frequently do not involve any intermediary subject to regulation by a national or other governmental authority and do not recognize any kind of political border.

In addition, it should be noted that while crypto-assets transactions are a global phenomenon, a huge fraction of startups, founders, institutional participants, investors, developers, and exchange volume is based in the US[34]. The vast majority of non-US ICOs, furthermore, do not bar US investors[35]. This exposes the industry to US securities law[36]. US regulators and law enforcement are not afraid to exert their influence on a global basis[37].

---

[33] One of the most complex frictions related to global transactions is, indeed, adhering to all the applicable regulations. It is complex because regulations generally vary along multiple dimensions such as asset type, investor type, buyer jurisdiction, seller jurisdiction, and issuer jurisdiction. Each of these dimensions has numerous regulatory permutations and multiple regulatory agencies.

[34] Historically, the competitive advantage in capital markets of the US started after World War II since its economic infrastructure was undamaged, and it did not face real competition until the 1980s. See D. C. Langevoort, *U.S. Securities Regulation and Global Competition*, 3 Virginia Law & Business Review 191, 193-96 (2008).

[35] One study that looked at 453 completed ICOs with tokens that traded on an exchange for at least 90 days found that only 19% claimed to bar US investors. *See* Sabrina T. Howell, M. Niessner, D. Yermack, *Initial Coin Offerings: Financing Growth with Cryptocurrency Token Sales* (July 2018).

[36] Experience shows that the standard of the most powerful player is often the one that dominates in a network (R. Bollen, *International Standard-Setting and the Regulation of Hedge Funds: Part II*, Company and Securities Law Journal 28, 370-377 (2010)). In international financial markets this is usually the United States. The reason is that this economic area had the best-developed capital markets in the 1990s, when the internationalization and standardization of the capital markets gained momentum.

[37] Historically, the US Securities and Exchange Commission has actually brought prosecutions against defendants who, because of their international domicile, are unknown. In 2008, for example, when the US Securities and Exchange Commission filed insider trading charges against unknown individuals accused of making suspiciously well-timed purchases of call options in two companies before the companies announced multibillion-dollar mergers. The matter involved certain suspicious trading by "*one or more unknown purchasers*", including the purchase of call option contracts to buy shares of defense company DRS Technologies and American Power Conversion Corp, a power and cooling services company. DRS was in a pending deal to be acquired by Italy's Finmeccanica Spa for $3.94 billion, while American Power was bought by French engineering group Schneider Electric SA for $6.1 billion. Through an account at UBS AG in Zurich, the US Securities and Exchange Commission alleged that the purchasers made "well-timed purchases" of call options of DRS and American Power that yielded profits of about $3.3 million. The US Securities and Exchange Commission ultimately identified the defendant as a resident of Rome (Italy). Toni Chion, who led the US Securities and Exchange Commission investigation, proclaimed boldly after the US Securities and Exchange Commission filing: "*in today's global markets, we will act quickly and decisively against violations of the US securities laws, no matter where that conduct occurs, to protect our securities markets and investors*". The international flair of the US Securities and Exchange Commission continued in late 2010, when the US

Decisions made by the US Securities and Exchange Commission tend to have global knock-on effects[38]. The literature on comparative financial supervision and enforcement places the US as both a global leader and a global outlier. For example, both the number of enforcement actions by the public regulator and the dollar amount of assessed sanctions has been found to be significantly higher in the US than in the UK and Germany[39]. For a full picture, private sanctions should also be considered, but there is little doubt that the US leads the way also in this respect[40]. It has been suggested that these disparities in enforcement activity could make it difficult for other countries to be considered equivalent to the US under a substituted compliance approach[41]. Therefore, US securities law should be taken in serious account when dealing with ICOs[42].

Securities and Exchange Commission obtained an asset freeze and other relief against unnamed investors who bought Wimm-Bill-Dann Foods stock, in the days before PepsiCo agreed to buy the Russian beverage maker. The US Securities and Exchange Commission noticed that the investors' stock purchases *"were highly profitable and suspicious"* and obtained an asset freeze on the proceeds of the relevant trades. The US Securities and Exchange Commission's asset freeze order secured more than $6 million dollars, which the US Securities and Exchange Commission eventually kept as part of a settlement from one of the defendants, who was ultimately identified as a British Virgin Islands corporation. Specifically, the unknown buyers acquired 400,000 American depositary receipts in Wimm-Bill- Dann from Nov. 29 to Dec. 1. Pepsi announced the deal, in which it paid $3.8 billion for a 66 percent stake, on Dec. 2. The Russian company's shares spiked 28 percent on the day of the announcement. As a result, the unknown purchasers were in a position to realize total profits of approximately $2.7 million from the sale of the ADRs. The shares were purchased in an account maintained at SG Private Banking, the Swiss banking unit of Societe Generale, and the trade orders were routed through Instinet Europe, and Brown Brothers Harriman & Co. was the custodian of the shares. Though challenging and resource-intensive, the US Securities and Exchange Commission, then, does have options for filing charges against internationally orchestrated ICOs. For instance, with respect to offshore ICOs, the US Securities and Exchange Commission can easily assert jurisdiction, seek asset freezes of any related US funds, and work with criminal authorities to obtain extradition and arrest of culprits in cooperating countries. Thus, foreign ICO firms, marketers and promoters should at least be prepared for how they will respond to a cross-border regulatory SEC investigation, whether in the form of an SEC subpoena (or, an asset freeze order from a US federal court) by carefully analyzing the intersection of a foreign request or court order with local banking, privacy and consumer protection laws in the various jurisdictions in which they operate.

[38] The SEC oversees approximately $90 trillion in annual securities trading, the disclosures of approximately 4,300 exchange-listed public companies valued at some $32 trillion, and the activities of over 27,000 registered entities such as investment advisers, broker-dealers, and self-regulatory organizations. See SEC, *Annual Report 2018 – Division of Enforcement* (Nov. 2, 2018), available at: https://www.sec.gov/files/enforcement-annual-report-2018.pdf.

[39] H. E. Jackson, *Variation in the Intensity of Financial Regulation: Preliminary Evidence and Potential Implications*, Yale Journal on Regulation 24, 253, 281-85 (2007).

[40] J. C. Coffee Jr., *Law and the Market: The Impact of Enforcement*, University of Pennsylvania Law Review 156, 229 (2007).

[41] J. C. Coffee Jr., *Law and the Market: The Impact of Enforcement*, University of Pennsylvania Law Review 156, 229 (2007).

[42] Within the context of an ICO, for example, the SEC can prosecute a US or foreign issuer who offers or sells its crypto-assets to persons in the US or to an "identifiable group of US persons abroad, without first registering with the SEC or qualifying for a registration exemption. The mere advertisement of an ICO in a publication with a general circulation in the United States is potentially sufficient to subject the foreign ICO issuer to the federal registration requirements. In addition, all security transactions (including exempt transactions) are subject to the antifraud provisions of the

Especially since the financial crisis, the US and the EU have made certain aspects of financial regulation applicable on an extraterritorial basis. This means that the rules apply to the activity in question wherever located in the world, and not just in US or EU territories, respectively. Extraterritoriality, which goes against principles of international comity, has been justified in these instances by the need to maintain financial stability. These rules apply to aspects of the activity of firms that could have a systemic impact in the US or the EU. In the US, for example, systemic risk was a key rationale for the introduction under the Dodd-Frank Act of 2010 of new frameworks for financial market utilities (systems for transfer, clearing, and settlement), disclosure requirements on investment advisers to private funds, the orderly liquidation of systemically important broker-dealers, and the Volcker rule that prohibits banks from engaging in proprietary trading[43].

---

federal securities laws. Section 17(a) – a key antifraud provision in the Securities Act – makes it unlawful to "employ any device, scheme, or artifice to defraud" or "obtain money or property" by using material misstatements or omissions or to "engage in any transaction, practice, or course of business which operates or would operate as a fraud or deceit upon the purchaser". Therefore, ICO issuers who would qualify for an exemption from the registration requirements may nonetheless still be liable for materially false and misleading statements made in connection with their fundraising efforts.

[43] See M.J. White, Testimony on *"Mitigating Systemic Risk in the Financial Markets through Wall Street Reforms"* before the United States Senate Committee on Banking, Housing, and Urban Affairs (July 30, 2013).

Chapter 2
CRYPTO-ASSETS

1.1 Legal nature of the crypto-assets among regulators • 1.2 A new taxonomy: speculative and non-speculative crypto-assets • 1.3 Benefits and risks of crypto-assets • 1.4 Cons of fully open decentralized networks in terms of corporate structure, IP and acquisitions.

1.1 *Legal nature of the crypto-assets among regulators*. In 1983 David Chaum conceived of *"an anonymous cryptographic electronic money"*[44] referred to as eCash, subsequently implemented through Digicash in 1995[45]. In 2009, in the dark days of a growing global financial market crisis, Satoshi Nakamoto famously created Bitcoin[46]. Fundamental to this innovation was the distributed ledger[47] on which it ran, known as a blockchain. When this crypto-currency first emerged, those studying and using it realized that blockchain

---

[44] See D. Chaum, *Blind signatures for untraceable payments*, available at: http://www.hit.bme.hu/~buttyan/courses/BMEVIHIM219/2009/Chaum.BlindSigForPayment.1982.PDF

[45] J. Pitta, *Requiem from a bright idea*, Forbes (Nov. 1, 1999) available at: https://www.forbes.com/forbes/1999/1101/6411390a.html#67b1b3ed715f.

[46] See S. Nakamoto, *A Peer-to-Peer Electronic Cash System* (October 31, 2018), available at: https://bitcoin.org/bitcoin.pdf.

[47] Whenever a transaction occurs in the economy, proof of the transaction is tracked in various accounting ledgers. These ledgers, which reference an enormous mass of data, are maintained and controlled by central institutions. For instance, when Ben pays James for his advice, Ben's bank updates its ledger to reflect this payment, whilst James's bank does the same. This occurs for the billions of transactions that occur every day. Centralized ledgers have many weaknesses. They are vulnerable to attack, prone to error, time consuming, and expensive. A blockchain is a digital ledger that records digital currency transactions chronologically and publicly. A public blockchain has several important characteristics that differentiate it from a traditional ledger. First, the blockchain ledger is distributed. Rather than being stored with and maintained by one central institution, the ledger is distributed and synchronized across many computers (nodes). This makes it incredibly difficult to attack because a hacker would need access to every computer. This feature in turn makes blockchain incredibly secure. Second, public blockchains are not operated by an organization or other familiar entity, but by the participants of the system itself. This means that any entity or individual can submit information to it. In order to be sure of the author's trustworthiness, information must be reviewed and confirmed before being accepted as a new block. The way that distributed operators of the blockchain evaluate and agree the data is true is through the process of consensus. This consensus actually refers to sophisticated cryptography which prohibits Ben from spending crypto-assets he doesn't hold or spending his crypto-assets twice, and is a key reason why fraudulent transactions are kept out of the ledger. It is also difficult to falsify entries because new blocks can only ever be added to the chain, meaning that once a record is on the blockchain, it cannot be deleted or modified. Every record can be viewed by any member of the public, allowing for any person to individually verify the authenticity of each transaction recorded for any single entry. This transparency means that blockchains are auditable. Whilst a blockchain is a public record of each transaction that has taken place, individual privacy is maintained. Only a string of numbers (known as an individual's public key) is published, which is nearly impossible to link to any particular identity. In summary, a blockchain can serve as an open, distributed ledger that can record transactions between two parties efficiently and in a verifiable and permanent way. Many blockchains now exist which record a large variety of different types of data.

was a technology that would revolutionize not only the economy, but in fact the whole world[48]. The rest is history[49].

As Van Valkenburgh says, "*[cryptocurrencies] present an arrangement of technological components that is so novel as to defy categorization as any traditional asset, commodity, security, or currency*".

At root, crypto-assets are exchangeable numerically limited items that have value despite the fact they have no institutional issuer or legally-promised redemption. In this sense, crypto-assets are valuable commodities, like gold (but at the same time, unlike gold, entirely non-tangible).

Bitcoin, the first decentralized crypto-asset, was conceived simply as a decentralized currency[50], operating via peer-to-peer transactions[51]. More

---

[48] Given the size of investments and the speed of developments in this new technology, blockchain is often described as a fundamental feature of the fourth industrial revolution. See World Economic Forum, *Centre for the Fourth Industrial Revolution*, available at: https://www.weforum.org/centre-for-the-fourth-industrial-revolution/areas-of-focus; J. Czarnecki, *Blockchain, Smart Contracts and DAO*, Wardynski & Partners (2016).

[49] In January 2009, New Liberty Standard opened the first Bitcoin trading platform (the initial exchange rate was 1,309.03 Bitcoin for one US$) and in February 2010, the first payment in Bitcoin was processed to buy two pizzas at a price of 10,000 (more than US$34 million at today's exchange rate). In the 2010s, Bitcoin started gaining attention. The first large company to accept Bitcoin was the WordPress online publishing platform. Overstock.com, Zynga, and TigerDirect followed swiftly. Today, hundreds of large companies worldwide accept Bitcoin for their services, including Amazon, Bloomberg, Microsoft, PayPal, Subway, Target, and Tesla. A comprehensive list of companies accepting payment in Bitcoin is published in S. Walters, *100 Companies That Accept Bitcoin Payments*, unblock (Oct. 29, 2018), available at: https://unblock.net/companies-that-accept-bitcoin/.

[50] Several cryptocurrencies, including Bitcoin, focus primarily on payments for goods and services, akin to fiat currencies. A merchant may therefore accept payment in Bitcoin in lieu of dollars. Such cryptocurrencies enable that exchange in a decentralized manner, such that one individual can transfer payment directly to another without processing by a central bank, unlike fiat currencies.

[51] Bitcoin uses the blockchain to solve, among the others, faith in the stability of the monetary supply, harmonization of ledger records, accuracy of recordation of ownership of money. Blockchains, anyway, are now beginning to be used for securely and verifiably transferring other financial assets (by, e.g., Nasdaq), identity credentials (by e.g. Blockstack), automobile loans (by e.g. Visa), document notarizations (by e.g. Proof of Existence), machine-to-machine messages on the Internet of Things (by e.g. IBM), and more. The first State in implementing blockchain technology was Delaware. In May 2016 the Delaware General Corporation Law was amended in order to make it legal for entities incorporated in Delaware to use blockchain technology for recordkeeping and administration of stock ledgers. The State of Delaware has also partnered with a startup called Symbiont to develop a blockchain and smart contract layer technologically capable of distributing corporate shares (see C. Long and A. Tinianow, *With Blockchain, the Early Lawyer Gets the Worm*, LAW360 (Oct. 4, 2017), available at: https://www.law360.com/articles/970948/with-blockchain-the-early-lawyer-gets-the-worm). This is important since Delaware is regarded as one of the most important states for corporate law in the world. In 2015, 86% of all IPOs chose to incorporate in Delaware; more than half of all United States publicly traded companies and 66% of Fortune 500 companies are incorporated in Delaware as well. The German car manufacturer Daimler AG successfully tested the use of blockchain technology to issue corporate bonds and, once allowed by regulators, intends to adopt blockchain debt issuances as a corporate practice (see N. Trentman, *Daimler Uses Blockchain to Issue Bonds*, Wall Street Journal (July 12, 2017), available at: https://blogs.wsj.com/cfo/2017/07/12/daimler-uses-blockchain-to-issue-bonds/).

recent crypto-assets[52], instead, go beyond the functionality of traditional currencies. Some facilitate the automatic execution of contracts using computerized protocols ("smart contracting")[53]; others support decentralized applications[54]; still others are issued as a means of fundraising in lieu of an offering[55]. The latter use[56] has caught the attention of regulators and financial market authorities worldwide.

Part of the legal complexity surrounding crypto-assets stems from the simple fact that crypto-assets are truly innovative. This is why since agencies, regulators and financial market authorities started looking at crypto-assets more closely, sometime around 2013, there have certainly been seemingly contradictory definitions. For example:

(i) In 2015 the US Commodity Futures Trading Commission ("**CFTC**") qualified Bitcoin as commodity[57] (this qualification does not apply to

---

[52] There are 2119 cryptocurrencies identified in CoinMarketCap as of January 28, 2019.

[53] A smart contract is a computerized transaction protocol that executes terms of a contract. The general objectives of smart contract design are to satisfy common contractual conditions (such as payment terms, liens, confidentiality, and even enforcement), minimize exceptions both malicious and accidental, and minimize the need for trusted intermediaries. Related economic goals include lowering fraud loss, arbitrations and enforcement costs, and other transaction costs. Thus, the purpose is to facilitate peer-to-peer transactions, but with added automation to exclude middlemen and transaction fees and risks associated with middlemen, as well as standardize contractual language.

[54] For instance, the Ethereum blockchain is open source, meaning the underlying code is freely available and licensed to the public for use in applications created by the public. It thus supports a variety of applications, including prediction markets, banking services, investment or venture capital, and web browsing. Ether, the primary cryptocurrency token issued on the Ethereum blockchain, can either be used either directly within such applications or indirectly as payment for other cryptocurrencies built on the Ethereum blockchain that can be used in such applications.

[55] Such fundraising frequently occurs in the form of an ICO, whereby a promoter makes an initial issuance of a newly-created crypto-asset. The largest ICOs to date have been those of EOS ($4.2 billion in June 2017), Telegram ($1.7 billion raised from an invite-only private sale in April 2018), Filecoin ($257 million in September 2017) and Tezos ($232 million in July 2017). Other notable examples include Sirin Labs ($158 million in December 2017), Bancor ($153 million in June 2017) and Polkadot ($145 million in October 2017). Notably, Kik, a company that has raised over $120 million in traditional venture capital, also conducted an ICO to raise roughly $100 million in September 2017 in lieu of an initial public offering.

[56] The practical "how it is employed" question is more significant to any regulator than the abstract "what is it" question.

[57] See *In the Matter of Coinflip, Inc., d/b/a Derivabit, and Francisco Riordan*, CFTC Docket No. 15-29 (September 17, 2015), available at: https://www.cftc.gov/PressRoom/PressReleases/pr7231-15 (the "**Derivabit Order**"). The Derivabit Order finds that Coinflip and Riordan operated Derivabit as an online trading platform that offered to connect buyers and sellers of Bitcoin option contracts. Derivabit designated numerous put and call options for the delivery of Bitcoins as eligible for trading on the Derivabit platform, allowing its approximately 400 users to post bids and offers for the Bitcoin option contracts, 4 which were confirmed by Coinflip by communicating the bids and offers to all users through its website. In the Derivabit Order, the CFTC defines virtual currencies, such as Bitcoin, as "*a digital representation of value that functions as a medium of exchange, a unit of account, and/or a store of value, but does not have legal tender status in any jurisdiction*". The Derivabit Order distinguishes these virtual currencies from "real" currencies, defined as "*the coin and paper money of the United States or another country that are designated as legal tender, circulate, and are customarily used and accepted as a medium of exchange in the country of issuance*". Without providing a detailed

other crypto-assets, in relation to which an individual analysis is needed). In 2017 the US Securities and Exchange Commission ("**SEC**") qualified the crypto-assets of an unincorporated organization called the DAO as securities in application of the *Howey Test* pattern[58]. US Financial Crimes Enforcement Network ("**FinCEN**") regards developers as well as exchanges of ICO crypto-assets as "money transmitters" for the purposes of the US Bank Secrecy Act, and so crypto-assets as money[59]. The Board of Governors of the Federal Reserve System ("**Fed**")[60], the Office of the Comptroller of the Currency ("**OCC**")[61], the Federal Deposit Insurance Corporation ("**FDIC**")[62] and the Consumer Financial Protection Bureau ("**CFPB**")[63], instead, have

---

legal analysis, the CFTC holds that Bitcoin and other virtual currencies fall within the definition of "commodity" under section 1a(9) of the Commodity Exchange Act ("**CEA**"), which definition includes, among other things, "all services, rights, and interests in which contracts for future delivery are presently or in the future dealt in". The Derivabit Order is available at: https://www.cftc.gov/sites/default/files/idc/groups/public/@lrenforcementactions/documents/legalpleading/enfcoinfliprorder09172015.pdf.

[58] See SEC, *Report of Investigation Pursuant to Section 21(a) of the Securities Exchange Act of 1934: The DAO*, (July 25, 2017), available at: https://www.sec.gov/litigation/investreport/34-81207.pdf.

[59] See FinCEN, *Application of FinCEN's Regulations to Persons Administering, Exchanging, or Using Virtual Currencies*, (March 18, 2013), available at: https://www.fincen.gov/sites/default/files/shared/FIN-2013-G001.pdf.

[60] In a press conference in late 2017, the former Chair of the Fed, Janet Yellen, responded to a question regarding the Fed's policy regarding Bitcoin as follows: "*it is a highly speculative asset, and the Fed doesn't really play any role – any regulatory role with respect to Bitcoin other than assuring that banking organizations that we do supervise are attentive, that they're appropriately managing any interactions they have with participants in that market and appropriately monitoring anti-money laundering Bank Secrecy Act, you know, responsibilities that they have*" (see J. Yellen, *Transcript of Chair Yellen's Press Conference December 13, 2017*, (Dec. 13, 2017), available at: https://www.federalreserve.gov/mediacenter/files/FOMCpresconf20171213.pdf). Chair Yellen confirmed, in short, that the Fed does not have any direct role in regulating Bitcoin, and by implication the class of other crypto-assets with similar features. Nonetheless, the Fed continues to monitor the use and development of crypto-assets and the role of Fed-regulated financial institutions in crypto-assets activities through a working group that includes the CFTC, the SEC and FinCEN.

[61] The OCC has published little guidance regarding the role of national banks in crypto-assets ecosystems, taking the position that the nascent market, and the role of national banks in the market, is not yet sufficiently developed to warrant regulatory intervention. However, on 31 July 2018, the OCC announced it will make available a special-purpose national bank charter, generally known as a FinTech charter, that may be owned by certain types of non-bank financial services companies. A FinTech charter permits a company to operate on a national basis under the OCC's supervision and thereby bypass multi-state licensing and supervision, and certain types of state regulation. The OCC has stated that applicants and licensees will be held to the same standards as national banks, suggesting that even if the FinTech charter is an avenue for certain crypto-assets activities, only certain industry participants may be in a position to meet the applicable regulatory requirements.

[62] The FDIC has publicly stated that it is actively studying the potential effects of crypto-assets on the banking system and banks under its jurisdiction through an internal working group, the Financial Technology Working Group (see FDIC, *2017 Annual Report*, (Feb. 15, 2018), available at: https://www.fdic.gov/about/strategic/report/2017annualreport/contents.html).

[63] The CFPB's focus with respect to crypto-assets has been on ensuring that consumers are adequately informed of the characteristics and risks of crypto-assets before engaging in crypto-assets transactions. In this regard, in 2014 the CFPB issued a public warning to consumers regarding the risks of transacting and investing in crypto-assets and began accepting consumer complaints regarding crypto-assets matters, a potential first step towards regulation or enforcement (see Consumer Fin.

largely adopted a more limited "wait and see" approach. New York regulations[64] define virtual currencies as *"any type of digital unit that is used as a medium of exchange or a form of digitally stored value"* and includes both centralized and decentralized currencies[65].

(ii) Canadian's Financial Market Authorities concluded that many crypto-assets, including crypto-assets sales through ICOs, are to be qualified as securities[66].

(iii) The European Securities and Markets Authority ("**ESMA**") stated that crypto-assets, depending on their structure, may be classified as transferable securities or financial instruments[67]. Despite the high harmonization of EU financial markets regulations, the legal qualification of crypto-assets differs among EU member states:

> (iii)(a) In France whether (and if so, how) crypto-assets would be deemed a "financial instrument" or an "other regulated asset", and therefore fall within the scope of French financial regulations, needs to be considered on a case-by-case basis.

Protection Bureau, *CFPB Warns Consumers About Bitcoin*, (Aug. 11, 2014), available at https://www.consumerfinance.gov/about-us/newsroom/cfpb-warns-consumers-about-bitcoin/). In 2016, however, after taking public comments on its expansion of Regulation E to cover prepaid products (Prepaid Rule), the CFPB declined to bring crypto-assets within the scope of the Prepaid Rule or to take a position concerning whether virtual currencies are otherwise subject to Regulation E.

[64] Given that New York is the epicenter of US financial markets and services, New York, through rulemaking by the New York Department of Financial Services ("**NYDFS**"), has been the earliest the states in regulating virtual currencies. Under New York law, a license referred to as a BitLicense is broadly required to engage in any virtual currency business activity. Virtual currency business activity, the activity that gives rise to the licensing requirement, broadly entails any of the following: (i) receiving a virtual currency for transmission or transmitting a virtual currency; (ii) storing, holding or maintaining custody or control of a virtual currency on behalf of others; (iii) buying and selling a virtual currency as a customer business; (iv) performing exchange services; and (iv) controlling, administering or issuing a virtual currency. Virtual currency business activities do not include use of a virtual currency by merchants or consumers to purchase goods or services, investment by merchants and consumers, and the development and issuance of software.

[65] Excluded from the definition of virtual currencies are prepaid cards that are issued or redeemable in legal tender; digital units that are part of a customer affinity or rewards programme that cannot be converted into legal tender or a virtual currency; and digital units used within gaming platforms that have no real-world value or market outside the gaming platform, and cannot be converted into real-world value or a virtual currency.

[66] See CSA, *CSA Staff Notice 46-307 Cryptocurrency Offerings*, (Aug. 24, 2017), available at: http://www.osc.gov.on.ca/documents/en/Securities-Category4/csa_20170824_cryptocurrency-offerings.pdf.

[67] See ESMA, *Alerts Firms Involved in Initial Coin Offerings to the Need to Meet Relevant Regulatory Requirements*, (Nov. 13, 2017), available at: https://www.esma.europa.eu/sites/default/files/library/esma50-157-828_ico_statement_firms.pdf.

(iii)(b) The German Financial Supervisory Authority ("**BaFin**") qualified crypto-assets as units of account and thus considered them financial instrument[68].

(iii)(c) In 2017 the United Kingdom Financial Conduct Authority ("**FCA**") held that, depending on the structure of the individual crypto-asset, it may fall into the regulatory perimeter[69]. Crypto-assets that grant a holder some or all of the rights that would typically be enjoyed by a shareholder (for example, entitlements to dividends declared, profits or the proceeds of the assets of an insolvent company), a bondholder (for example, a right to the repayment of a sum of money), or a participant in a fund (for example, to profits or income from the acquisition, holding, management or disposal of the fund property), are likely to be considered "specified investments".

(iv) In Honk Kong, crypto-assets are not legal tender[70], and form no part of the traditional banking system[71]. Moreover, they are not transmitted via the traditional banking system. The Hong Kong Monetary Authority has consistently emphasized that crypto-assets are merely a type of virtual commodity[72]. On September 5, 2017[73] and March 28, 2019[74] the Hong Kong Securities and Futures Commission ("**SFC**") held that crypto-assets could constitute securities (and in some

---

[68] See BaFin, *Virtual Currency (VC)*, available at https://www.bafin.de/EN/Aufsicht/FinTech/VirtualCurrency/virtual_currency_node_en.html.

[69] See FCA, *Distributed Ledger Technology Feedback Statement on Discussion Paper 17/03*, (Dec. 2017), available at: https://www.fca.org.uk/publication/feedback/fs17-04.pdf.

[70] In Hong Kong, a vendor is not obliged to accept crypto-assets as payment for goods and services rendered by him or her, since crypto-assets are not legal tender. However, if he or she voluntarily accepts crypto-assets as payment, it could be enforceable based on principles of Hong Kong contract law, absent any public policy issues. In this regard, if the use of crypto-assets in this manner becomes sufficiently widespread, the Hong Kong Monetary Authority could designate it as a medium of exchange, thereby requiring its issuer or operator to obtain a license under the Anti-Money Laundering and Counter-Terrorist Financing Ordinance.

[71] In Hong Kong, the issuance of legal tender currency is regulated by the Legal Tender Notes Issue Ordinance (see Chapter 65 of the Laws of Hong Kong).

[72] See Hong Kong Monetary Authority, *The HKMA reminds the public to be aware of the risks associated with Bitcoin*, (Feb. 11, 2015), available at: https://www.hkma.gov.hk/eng/key-information/press-releases/2015/20150211-3.shtml.

[73] See SFC, *Statement on initial coin offerings*, (Sept. 5, 2017), available at: https://www.sfc.hk/web/EN/news-and-announcements/policy-statements-and-announcements/statement-on-initial-coin-offerings.html.

[74] See SFC, *Statement on Security Token Offerings*, (Mar. 28, 2019), available at: https://www.sfc.hk/web/EN/news-and-announcements/policy-statements-and-announcements/statement-on-security-token-offerings.html.

cases are likely to be securities)[75] subject to regulation under the Securities and Futures Ordinance ("**SFO**").

(v) In the United Arab Emirates, the Abu Dhabi Global Markets Financial Services Regulation Authority ("**ADGM FSRA**") has backed the commodity-categorization of crypto-assets, while individual crypto-assets, issued in connection with ICOs, may be regarded as securities, depending on the specific structure of such crypto-assets. The ADGM FSRA has, however, indicated that where crypto-assets do not have the features and characteristics of "securities" such as shares, debentures or units in a fund, the trading of such crypto-assets is unlikely to constitute a regulated activity[76]. In January 2017, the Central Bank issued the regulatory framework for stored values and electronic payment systems ("Stored Value Regulation")[77] to regulate different types of electronic payments and stored value[78]. The Regulation defines virtual currencies as *"any type of digital unit used as a medium of exchange, a unit of account, or a form of stored value"*.

(vi) In Singapore[79] and Australia[80], crypto-assets are qualified as securities, provided that the crypto-assets feature additional rights, as ownership or voting rights.

---

[75] Security crypto-assets – i.e. digital representations of ownership of assets (e.g., gold or real estate) or economic rights (e.g., a share of profits or revenue) utilizing blockchain technology – are likely to be securities under the SFO (see, in particular, SFC, *Statement on Security Token Offerings*, (Mar. 28, 2019), available at: https://www.sfc.hk/web/EN/news-and-announcements/policy-statements-and-announcements/statement-on-security-token-offerings.html).

[76] See ADGM, *Guidance – Regulation of Crypto Asset Activities in ADGM*, (June 25, 2018), available at: https://www.adgm.com/media/304701/guidance-regulation-of-crypto-asset-activities-in-adgm-25th-june-2018-2.pdf; ADGM, *Supplementary Guidance – Regulation of Initial Coin/Token Offerings and Virtual Currencies under the Financial Services and Markets Regulations*, (Oct. 10, 2017), available at: https://www.adgm.com/media/192772/20171009-fsra-guidance-for-icos-and-virtual-currencies.pdf.

[77] The Stored Value Regulation applies in the UAE, but does not apply in the Dubai Financial Services Authority ("**DIFC**") and the Abu Dhabi Global Market ("**ADGM**").

[78] UAE Central Bank, *Regulatory Framework for Stored Values and Electronic Payment Systems* (Jan. 1, 2017), available at: https://www.centralbank.ae/en/pdf/notices/Regulatory-Framework-For-Stored-Values-And-Electronic-Payment-Systems-En.pdf.

[79] See MAS, *A Guide to Digital Token Offerings*, (Nov. 20, 2017), available at: http://www.mas.gov.sg/~/media/MAS/Regulations%20and%20Financial%20Stability/Regulations%20Guidance%20and%20Licensing/Securities%20Futures%20and%20Fund%20Management/Regulations%20Guidance%20and%20Licensing/Guidelines/A%20Guide%20to%20Digital%20Token%20Offerings%20%2014%20Nov%202017.pdf.

[80] See ASIC, *Initial Coin Offerings and Crypto-Currencies*, (May 2018) available at: https://asic.gov.au/regulatory-resources/digital-transformation/initial-coin-offerings-and-crypto-currency/. The Reserve Bank of Australia ("**RBA**"), Australia's principal payments system regulator, has stated, instead, that it does not consider virtual currencies to be part of the Australian payments system because: (i) they are not widely accepted or used as a payment method; (ii) they are not an effective store of value due to large fluctuations and strong speculative influences; and (iii) they are not commonly used as a unit of account: goods and services in Australia continue to be priced overwhelmingly in Australian dollars. The RBA consequently has limited concerns regarding virtual currencies with respect to competition, efficiency or risk to the financial system warranting urgent

It's clear from the above that regulators and agencies are looking at how a crypto-asset is employed and what it accomplishes – rather than what they really are – regulating activities they have always regulated in a situation where the activity is suddenly being performed using crypto-assets.

In practice, the regulatory status of crypto-assets largely depends on the rights associated with the crypto-assets, how they are employed and the jurisdiction of the issuance.

1.2 *A new taxonomy: speculative and non-speculative crypto-assets*. "Digital currency" is a term commonly employed by regulators. Actually, since the vast majority of fiat currencies are held and transmitted digitally, they could be defined as digital currency as well. At the same time, while some crypto-assets are designed explicitly as currencies, their real nature more closely aligns with property or a scarce asset like gold.[81] Crypto-assets basically do not circulate, but their ownership does. There are a finite number in

---

regulatory intervention, even in the event of token valuation losses. The RBA has indicated that regulatory intervention can be expected once virtual currencies mature beyond speculative mania to become an efficient or widely used payment method to mitigate any payments system stability risks (see P. Lowe, *Address to 2017 Australian Payment Summit*, (Dec. 13, 2017), available at: https://www.rba.gov.au/speeches/2017/sp-gov-2017-12-13.html.

[81] Crypto-currencies probably sit between order and bearer instruments: like with order instruments, a register exists (the blockchain); however, it does not contain real identities, but only pseudonymized information about public keys and signatures stemming from private keys. Like with bearer instruments, the true identity of crypto-currencies holders is not registered on the blockchain (or anywhere else); rather, they may be used for payments purposes by whoever presents the right combination of public and private key to cryptographically unlock them. However, the purpose of cryptographically securing crypto-currencies via public and private key is precisely to ensure that only the legitimate owner (the holder of the private key) can use them. If private keys are kept truly private, crypto-currencies can only be transferred by the legitimate owner. This, in turn, does liken them to order instruments which are transferred by indorsement of the registered owner. What differentiates crypto-currencies from both bearer and order instruments, and from electronic money more generally (see M. Lerch, *Bitcoin als Evolution des Geldes: Herausforderungen, Risiken und Regulierungsfragen*, Zeitschrift für Bankrecht und Bankwirtschaft (ZBB) / Journal of Banking Law and Banking (JBB), RWS Verlag 27(3), 190-204 (2015)), however, is that they do not embody a claim against an issuing entity (such as a bank) to make a payment to the claimant. In this sense, they resemble pieces of gold, or cash, rather than cheques (see G. Spindler, M. Bille, *Rechtsprobleme von Bitcoins als virtuelle Währung*, WM 1357-1360 (2014). One may, however, argue that holders of crypto-currencies have at least an implicit claim against core developers, and potentially miners, to adequately maintain and develop the respective blockchain, and its payment capabilities, for example as a result of fiduciary duties (see A. Walch, *In Code(rs) We Trust: Software Developers as Fiduciaries in Public Blockchains*, in G. Dimitropoulos, S. Eich, P. Hacker, I. Lianos (eds), The Blockchain Revolution: Legal & Policy Challenges (2018 Forthcoming)). While most scholars reject the classification of Bitcoin as electronic money (see M. Lerch, *Bitcoin als Evolution des Geldes: Herausforderungen, Risiken und Regulierungsfragen*, Zeitschrift für Bankrecht und Bankwirtschaft (ZBB) / Journal of Banking Law and Banking (JBB), RWS Verlag 27(3), 190-204 (2015)), the developing discussing on fiduciary duties of core developers vis-à- vis crypto-currencies owners could throw a different light on this discussion. At the end of the day, pure crypto-currencies share a number of important characteristics, such as significant liquidity and lack of the registration of the "true owner", with bearer payment instruments. This is why recent legislation in Japan has treated crypto-currencies not as legal tender, but as means of payment similar to prepaid payment instruments.

circulation. Therefore, their exchange rate is a function of scarcity. Crypto-assets are programmable. Crypto-currency (or even better crypto-assets) is, then, a better definition than digital currency. However, as highlighted, the majority of crypto-currencies are neither designed nor function as currencies. Burniske and Tatar[82] categorize those crypto-assets (as just said crypto-currencies that are neither designed nor function as currencies) into crypto-commodities and crypto-tokens. Crypto-commodities are the value units of blockchain providing basic digital goods, such as compute power, storage capacity, and network bandwidth (easily compared to physical commodities like gasoline or corn). Ether in theory is a crypto-commodity[83]. Crypto-tokens are tokens connected to "finished product" digital networks. Typically, they do not operate on their own blockchain. Instead, they are built on top of a crypto-commodity's blockchain. These native crypto-tokens will then use a crypto-commodity to pay the crypto-commodity it is built upon to execute certain transactions[84].

The division between crypto-commodities and crypto-tokens is a grey area, though. Crypto-assets like Ether have the same basic structure based on the relation buy a token/participate in a decentralized network. Thus, we believe it makes more sense to categorize crypto-assets only into non-speculative crypto-assets (crypto-assets with real intrinsic usage[85]) and speculative crypto-assets. Speculative crypto-assets are issued speculatively (with little backing, no community backing, and no viable product, often by un-transparent teams, with corporate structures in tax havens) and represent significant risks for non-sophisticated investors (investors with no depth of experience and market knowledge)[86]. Currently the vast majority of crypto-assets are speculative crypto-assets. Speculative crypto-assets, regardless of any possible intrinsic usage, should be treated as securities[87] (until when

---

[82] C. Burniske, J. Tatar, *Cryptoassets: The Innovative Investor's Guide to Bitcoin and Beyond*, McGraw-Hill Education (2017).

[83] Bitcoin is certainly not a security due to the lack of identifiable common enterprise (counterparty) upon on whom the holder of the crypto-asset would rely upon for the expectation of profit. Ethereum could be potentially classified as securities at the time of its ICO, but no more now because it is *de-facto* decentralized.

[84] These crypto-tokens are easy to create and this is why they have contributed significantly to the proliferation of crypto-assets on crypto-assets exchanges globally.

[85] As a recent study highlighted, 68% of crypto-assets did offer (at least formally) access to platform services, and 16% even endowed holders with the right to shape the design of the services Importantly, access to platform services seems to be valued by investors, being one of the strongest predictors of the success of an ICO. See S. Adhami, G. Giudici, S. Martinazzi, *Why Do Businesses Go Crypto? An Empirical Analysis of Initial Coin Offerings*, Journal of Economics and Business (Jan. 6, 2018).

[86] It is arguable that the proliferation of thousands of crypto-assets has changed their status from a technical protocol for distributed networks to a vehicle for potential financial speculation.

[87] The main reason why instruments of payment are excepted from securities regulation is that they pertain to an adjacent, but substantially different regulatory area: banking and (freedom of) payment services regulation. Due their liquidity, pure crypto-currencies share the key characteristic of crypto-assets with real intrinsic usage: typical financial risks of investments are not at stake. There are some notable exceptions, though: exchange rate risks, introduced by the high volatility of exchange rates

regulated properly) on the base of the specific jurisdiction applicable to investors, in order to protect them and make possible well-informed investment decisions (investors protection can lead to a larger and healthier financial environment on the long term).

1.3 *Benefits and risks of crypto-assets*. Crypto-assets have both tremendous potential benefits and risks.

(i) Cryptocurrencies (i.e. payment crypto-assets) may inspire conventional payment methods to increase efficiency in respect of cost, speed, user-friendliness and security and therefore be highly beneficial. The open-source network approach empowers individuals as it provides open access to businesses and services without institutional barriers. For people lacking a bank account it may facilitate financial inclusion. Risks on the other hand are various: (a) new types of fraud could be developed; (b) cryptocurrencies, being based on anonymity of its users, could be used for money laundering or other criminal purposes; (c) there is a custody risk; (d) cryptocurrencies, in this very first stage, seem not to be really used as payment instruments but as speculative investments, creating additional investor protection problems (since no Central Bank can intervene to smooth extreme price fluctuations, cryptocurrencies volatility will be potentially always higher than fiat); (e) there is also a risk of market abuse.

(ii) Crypto-assets with real intrinsic usage representing services may facilitate trading in such services. They have a business dimension: by issuing those crypto-assets the issuer creates a network of users, which further increases the value of the business. They also present an alternative source of early stage funding to traditional venture capital funding for innovative projects. They allow prefunding of a future business without diluting ownership. The main risk of crypto-assets with real intrinsic usage is a performance risk (the issuer of the crypto-asset may not deliver the service as expected, or may go out of business, making the crypto-asset useless). In case of secondary market, there is also a risk of market abuse, in addition to the actual risk of it being actually purchased as a speculative investment.

(iii) Crypto-assets representing physical goods. If the underlying assets are commodities these crypto-assets share characteristics with commodity derivatives or with securitized commodities, such as a

---

between crypto-currencies and regular currencies (see D. Yermack, *Is Bitcoin a Real Currency: An Economic Appraisal*, in David Lee Kuo Chuen (ed) Handbook of Digital Currency 31-44 (2015)) and the residual "default risk" of the entire crypto-currency blockchain, flowing from unresolved governance problems in the various communities. Furthermore, default risks exist with respect to intermediaries. These conditions generate operational, credit and liquidity risks for users of crypto-currencies tokens (see European Central Bank, *Virtual Currency Schemes* (2012)).

commodity ETF. They may facilitate trading in such goods, without the good physically changing hands. It can furthermore make it easier to use the underlying physical goods as collateral to secure payment. Crypto-assets representing physical goods also function as a digital identifier for the underlying physical asset. If a physical object has its own ID, it can record its own history of origin. The digital ID linked to products could solve problems of counterfeiting and product piracy as well. Crypto-assets representing physical goods could facilitate trade and documentary credit operations. They could be used to represent title and title transfer could be recorded on a blockchain making it secure and accessible by all relevant parties. Crypto-assets representing a monetary claim on the issuer share characteristics with securities or derivatives. They may therefore have similar benefits: facilitating financing and risk-transfer. Risks of crypto-assets representing physical goods on the other hand are various: (a) they may facilitate trading for speculative purposes; (b) the use of encryption would diminish supervisory oversight, which may result in increased market abuse; (c) since crypto-assets representing a monetary claim on the issuer resemble securities, they pose much the same risk, including counterparty risk and dilution risk if there's not issuance control, as well as custody risk; (d) in relation to crypto-assets resembling securities there is also the risk that investors trust blindly the system; (e) in case of secondary market there is a market abuse risk (insider dealing and market manipulation).

1.4 *Cons of fully open decentralized networks in terms of corporate structure, IP and acquisitions*. Fully open decentralized networks, lacking corporate structure and binding developer agreements, cannot be acquired. Intellectual property is generally nonexistent, aside from open-source licensing constraints. The vast majority of fully open decentralized projects boasts no physical assets. Fully open decentralized networks are managed in many cases by foundations. Therefore, acquisitions are largely foreign to the space. Since these fully open decentralized networks projects generally focus around incentivizing a network to adopt their platform, they are poorly transferable. Acquisitions do occasionally occur, labeled coin swaps. The difference between a coin swap and a codebase hard fork is subtle – the former is done with the asset of the crypto-assets holders being acquired, the latter involves copy-pasting existing code and attempting to coax an existing community to the new project. Swaps generally involve maintaining the existing blockchain, while "repository forks" take existing code and relaunch it under a new name, with the crypto-assets holders receiving no preferential treatment. Given the difficulty involved in benignly commandeering an existing community or crypto-asset, repository forks are more common than coin swaps.

Chapter 3
INITIAL COIN OFFERINGS

1.1 ICOs regulatory environments: 1.1.1 Australia; 1.1.2 Canada; 1.1.3 China; 1.1.4. EU, EAA and other European jurisdictions; 1.1.5 Hong Kong; 1.1.6 Israel; 1.1.7 Russia; 1.1.8 Singapore; 1.1.9 United States • **1.2 The Simple Agreement for Future Tokens** • **1.3 A Corporate Crypto Conduct Code for ICOs** • **1.4 Initial Exchange Offerings**.

1.1 *ICOs regulatory environments*. Regulators have been evaluating possible risk factors (especially for retail investors) associated with ICOs since the inception of ICOs[88]. There are many reasons. While in the traditional corporate infrastructure shareholders are able to appoint directors and vote for or against them, ICO investors have no control over the founders of the project whatsoever. ICO investors have no preemptive rights or other anti-dilution protections. The only real control ICO investors have to protect themselves is to sell their crypto-assets post-ICO (ICOs provide the highest possible liquidity for investors at the earliest possible time in the lifecycle of the issuer). The context, however, is subject to very high volatility. ICO investors typically do not receive a liquidity preference that would protect them in the case of termination of the project in which they invested. In contrast, in a typical venture capital seed stage investment, the venture capital fund obtains at least a simple liquidity preference. This allows venture capital funds to reclaim their initial seed investment before other creditors are satisfied.

Below a quick analysis of the current regulatory environment for some of the most important jurisdictions.

1.1.1 **Australia**. The Australian Securities and Investment Commission ("**ASIC**") has provided general guidance[89] for determining whether its

---

[88] In 2013, J.R. Sweezy introduced MasterCoin (later rebranded as OMNI), a protocol built on top of Bitcoin. Unlike earlier crypto-assets, units of MasterCoin were created by a fundraiser in the month of August 2013, during which, interested parties could send Bitcoins to an account and receive MasterCoins back at a pre-established exchange rate. The fundraiser collected approximately $500,000 worth of Bitcoin which was to be used for development and payment of bounties for important tasks. Other cryptocurrencies started using the fundraiser model for the creation of cryptocurrencies, with Ethereum raising over $15 million in August 2014. In 2015, Ethereum's introduction of a standard for implementing tokens (ERC20) further streamlined the ICO process. In 2015, there were 9 such offerings, 74 in 2016, and more than 1000 ICOs in 2017. So far ICOs have raised $22 billion. For a comprehensive list of completed, ongoing and upcoming crypto-assets sales see SMITH + CROWN, *ICO/Token Sales*, available at: https://www.smithandcrown.com/sale/.
[89] See ASIC, *Information Sheet 225*, (May 2018), available at: https://asic.gov.au/regulatory-resources/digital-transformation/initial-coin-offerings-and-crypto-currency/.

Corporations Act applies to ICOs and crypto-assets[90]. If a crypto-asset falls under the Corporations Act[91], additional disclosures are triggered[92]. For instance, an ICO might trigger a disclosure requirement if the ICO is a managed investment scheme[93]. A few other possible triggers of the Corporations Act involve, for instance, whether the ICO is being offered as a share of a company, as a derivative, or as a non-cash payment[94]. Australia has also implemented an Innovation Hub ("**Hub**") to help blockchain companies comply with and navigate the regulatory world[95]. Through the Hub, eligible businesses can request to receive informal guidance from ASIC on the licensing process and key regulatory issues[96] that should be considered[97].

---

[90] Chapters 6D and 7 of the Corporations Act, which regulate fundraising and financial services markets respectively, are the main aspects of the Corporations Act that could potentially apply to ICOs.

[91] The Corporations Act operates on a technology-neutral basis and has not been changed to specifically accommodate or prohibit ICOs. Whether crypto-assets and ICOs are caught by the Corporations Act turn principally on whether they are financial products (see Corporations Act Chapter 7, Part 7.1 Division 3).

[92] If the crypto-asset is a financial product, then the Corporations Act will apply, and the company must comply with strict disclosure obligations (for example, issuing a prospectus or a product disclosure statement). The Act also prohibits misleading and deceptive conduct. If companies do not make sufficient disclosure or includes false statements in their whitepaper, they would be breaking the law, and investors could either: (i) recover their investment; (ii) take action against the company; or (iii) refer the matter to ASIC for investigation.

[93] A managed investment scheme, also known as pooled or collective investments, in particular, is a type of Australian investment scheme where pooled contributions produce financial benefits for scheme members (see Corporations Act Section 9). A managed investment scheme, must be registered, and cannot be operated unless it is registered, if it meets certain criteria (e.g., it has more than 20 members). A managed investment scheme does not need to be registered if all interests issued would not have required a product disclosure statement had the scheme been registered. Rights granted to crypto-assets holders described in whitepapers can potentially constitute a managed investment scheme. This is particularly the case where issuers seek to tokenize certain assets or create exposure to a certain asset class or trading activity, such as a venture capital fund or hedge fund, through issuing a bundle of rights using a blockchain.

[94] Crypto-assets and ICOs can be financial products:
(i) where crypto-assets have the characteristics of a security, such as linking to an underlying asset granting rights to voting, dividends or distribution of capital in a body corporate;
(ii) where crypto-assets may be used as a payment method that makes it a non-cash payment facility – a non-cash payment ("**NCP**") is a payment made without physically delivering Australian or foreign currency, made through an NCP facility (See Corporations Act Section 763D(1)) (although in May 2018, ASIC stated that a virtual currency or ICO token itself is unlikely to be an NCP facility, a crypto-asset or ICO may be an NCP facility in certain circumstances, unless an existing exemption applies or ASIC grants relief from the operation of these provisions);
(iii) where crypto-assets exchange transactions do not settle immediately, or the price or a requirement to provide consideration is derived from another asset or index, in a way that makes it a derivative;
(iv) where entities that are currently licensed to provide financial services or a financial market in respect of a financial product expand their offering to incorporate crypto-assets or ICOs.

[95] See https://asic.gov.au/for-business/your-business/innovation-hub/.

[96] If the crypto-asset isn't a financial product, Australian Consumer Law ("**ACL**") applies. Australia's consumer watchdog, the Australian Competition and Consumer Commission ("**ACCC**") delegated its powers to ASIC to take action against ICOs that breach the ACL. This means ASIC can take action against a company for misleading and deceptive conduct connected to an ICO regardless of whether it's a financial product. This action may include: (i) seeking an injunction to stop the ICO from

1.1.2 **Canada**. The Canadian Securities Administration ("**CSA**")[98] is the relevant regulatory authority in Canada. The CSA applies a four-factor test[99] in determining whether a crypto-asset should be qualified as a security[100]. The factor test considers substance over form when considering: (i) soliciting a broad base of investors, including retail investors; (ii) using the internet, including public websites and discussion boards, to reach a large number of potential investors; (iii) attending public events, including conferences and meetups, to actively advertise the sale of the crypto-asset; and (iv) raising a significant amount of capital from a large number of investors[101]. The CSA has also developed a regulatory sandbox specifically for blockchain companies to stay in compliance[102]. All the applications are considered on a case-by-case basis, in a procedure managed — at least in its early stages — by the local securities regulators

---

proceeding; or (ii) pursuing damages if the investor has suffered a loss because of the offeror's misleading statements.

[97] ASIC urges all eligible businesses with innovative financial business models in areas including marketplace lending, crowd-funding, robo-advice, payments and blockchain technology to connect with.

[98] The CSA is an umbrella organization of Canada's provincial and territorial securities regulators whose objective is to improve, coordinate and harmonize regulation of the Canadian capital markets.

[99] The definition of security in Canada includes, among other things, an investment contract. The leading case in Canada for determining whether an investment contract exists is Pacific Coast Coin Exchange v. Ontario (Securities Commission) (Pacific Coast Coin Exchange v. Ontario (Securities Commission), [1978] 2 SCR 112) where the Supreme Court of Canada identified the four central attributes of an investment contract, namely: (i) an investment of money; (ii) in a common enterprise; (iii) with the expectation of profit; and (iv) which profit is to be derived in significant measure from the efforts of others. If an instrument satisfies the Pacific Coin test, the instrument will be considered an investment contract and, therefore, a security under Canadian securities laws.

[100] See *CSA Staff Notice 46-307 Cryptocurrency Offerings*, (Aug. 24, 2017), available at: http://www.osc.gov.on.ca/documents/en/Securities-Category4/csa_20170824_cryptocurrency-offerings.pdf.

[101] Other circumstances may cause a crypto-assets to be considered an investment contract are:
(i) the underlying blockchain technology or platform has not been fully developed;
(ii) the crypto-asset is immediately delivered to each purchaser;
(iii) the stated purpose of the offering is to raise capital, which will be used to perform key actions that will support the value of the crypto-asset or the issuer's business;
(iv) the issuer is offering benefits to persons who promote the offering;
(v) the issuer's management retains a significant number of unsold crypto-assets;
(vi) the crypto-asset is sold in a quantity far greater than any purchaser is likely to be able to use;
(vii) the issuer suggests that the crypto-assets will be used as a currency or have utility beyond its own platform, but neither of these things is the case at the time the statement is made;
(viii) management represents or makes other statements suggesting that the crypto-assets will increase in value;
(ix) the crypto-asset does not have a fixed value on the platform;
(x) the number of crypto-assets issuable is finite or there is a reasonable expectation that access to new crypto-assets will be limited in the future;
(xi) the crypto-asset is fungible;
(xii) the crypto-assets are distributed for a monetary price; and
(xiii) the crypto-asset may be reasonably expected to trade on a trading platform or otherwise be tradeable in the secondary market.

[102] See CSA, *The Canadian Securities Administrators launches a regulatory sandbox initiative*, (Feb. 23, 2017), available at: https://www.securities-administrators.ca/aboutcsa.aspx?id=1555.

in order to achieve a faster and more flexible process than through a standard application process[103]. After many months of experimentation with the sandbox, the CSA has been able to publish more precise guidelines — for instance, defining the concrete elements which classify a token as a security or a non-security[104].

1.1.3   ***China***. On September 4, 2017[105], seven government agencies of China, i.e. the People's Bank of China ("**PBOC**"), the Central Cybersecurity and Information Technology Lead Group of the Communist Party of China, the Ministry of Industry and Information Technology, the State Administration for Industry and Commerce, China Banking Regulatory Commission, China Security Regulatory Commission and China Insurance Regulatory Commission, jointly issued the Notice regarding Prevention of Risks of Token Offering and Financing ("**Notice**")[106]. The Notice banned all ICOs in China, the operation of crypto-currencies trading platforms and ordered that any organizations or individuals who had previously completed an ICO to make arrangements including the return of token assets to investors to protect investor rights[107]. Shortly thereafter,

---

[103] The attitude of the Canadian authorities is to affirm the need to apply the fundamentals of security law (prospectus and registration) to new fintech businesses, recognizing the possibility, however, that such a new industry may require some exceptions, at least on a temporary basis.

[104] See *CSA Staff Notice 46-308 Securities Law Implications for Offerings of Tokens*, (June 11, 2018), available at https://www.bcsc.bc.ca/Securities_Law/Policies/Policy4/PDF/46-308_CSA_Staff_Notice_June_11_2018/.

[105] The Beijing Internet Finance Association estimated that 65 ICO transactions were completed in the first seven months of 2017 (just before China's ICO ban kicked in), netting a combined 2.6 billion yuan (US$398 million). More than 105,000 individual investors took part in the deals.

[106] See the English translation of the statement in W. Zhao, *China's ICO Ban: A Full Translation of Regulator Remarks*, Coindesk (Sept. 5, 2017), available at: https://www.coindesk.com/chinas-ico-ban-a-full-translation-of-regulator-remarks.

[107] Interestingly, it is not illegal to hold Bitcoins and other crypto-assets, or even to buy or sell them in China. Indeed, there is no PRC law or regulation that prohibits Chinese investors from holding cryptocurrencies, or from trading cryptocurrencies. This has been confirmed by the Shenzhen Court of International Arbitration in a ruling in favor of an unnamed plaintiff in an equity transfer dispute, in which the defendant failed to return holdings of Bitcoin, Bitcoin Cash ("**BCH**") and Bitcoin Diamond ("**BCD**") as had been agreed upon in a contractual agreement. The defense had attempted to argue that the contractual equity transfer agreement was invalid, pointing to the fact that cryptocurrencies are not recognized as legal tender in China, and that their circulation is subject to severe restrictions in the country. The defendant cited the Notice, stating that ICOs that raise *"so-called virtual currencies"* such as BTC and Ether *"through the irregular sale and circulation of tokens"* are engaging in *"unauthorized"* public financing, which is *"illegal"* and that the central bank had also determined that crypto *"cannot and should not be circulated nor used in the market as currency"*. The Shenzhen Court of International Arbitration, however, found that the contractual obligation under dispute did not fall under the relevant provisions as outlined in the Notice, stating that: *"there is no law or regulation that explicitly prohibits parties from holding bitcoin or private transactions in bitcoin, [only warnings to] the public about the investment risks. The contract in this case stipulates the obligation to return the bitcoin between two natural persons, and does not belong to the [Sept. 2017 ban]"*. The arbitrator thus concluded that the contract was legally binding, adding that: *"Bitcoin has the nature of a property, which can be owned and controlled by parties, and is able to provide economic values and benefits"*. The arbitration award is available (only in Chinese) at: https://mp.weixin.qq.com/s/U_qDgQN9hceLBbpQ13eEdQ. The Chinese government also encourages

crypto-currency exchanges discontinued their operations in China[108]. In the Notice, an ICO was described as a process by which fundraisers distribute digital tokens to investors who make financial contributions in the form of cryptocurrencies, such as Bitcoin and Ether. The Notice further pointed out: *"by nature, it is an unauthorized and illegal public financing activity, which involves financial crimes such as illegal distribution of financial tokens, illegal issuance of securities and illegal fundraising, financial fraud and pyramid scheme"*. Among the crimes mentioned in the notice, illegal fundraising, which generally means raising funds without government approval, is a crime that has been widely used in cracking down on undesirable financial activities, as the scope of the crime can be interpreted very broadly. It should be noted that even ICOs outside China are not completely safe if they target Chinese investors. According to article 6 of the PRC Criminal Law, if any of the criminal activities or results of such activities occurred in China, the crime is deemed to have occurred in the territory of China. Therefore, if the ICO involves financial crimes as per the PRC Criminal law, the promoters or organizers of those ICOs – even if they are not Chinese citizens – may potentially be subject to criminal liabilities in China. In November 2018 Huo Xuewen, chief of Beijing Bureau of Financial Work, issued a warning against STOs saying: *"I want to warn those who are promoting STO fundraising in Beijing. Don't do it in Beijing. You will be kicked out if you do it"*. In December 2018 Pang Gongsheng, a deputy governor of the People's Bank of China, the country's central

---

the development and application of blockchain technology, but has made it clear that blockchain technology must service the real economy. In recent years, indeed, various guidelines and papers issued by the government have endorsed blockchain technology and even placed blockchain technology in the same category of big data and artificial intelligence.

[108] The Notice also targeted crypto-assets exchanges and ordered that any so-called fundraising and trading platforms must not:
(i) Offer exchange services between fiat currency and crypto-assets;
(ii) Buy or sell crypto-assets, or buy or sell crypto-assets as a central counterparty ("**CCP**"); or
(iii) Provide price determination or information intermediary services for crypto-assets.
In the several months following the notice, most of the crypto-assets exchanges closed down their platforms in China, but continued exchange business through platforms registered in more favorable foreign jurisdictions. They also made adjustments to their business models. To avoid direct confrontation with Chinese monetary authorities, some exchanges no longer provided exchange services between fiat currency and crypto-assets. Some chose to introduce a new token (such as USDT, QC, etc.) to their platforms, which have value equivalent to the value of fiat currency, as an intermediary between fiat currency and crypto-assets. Investors may use fiat currency to buy this new crypto-asset and then use this new crypto-asset to buy other crypto-assets. Further, many exchanges launched peer-to-peer trading platforms that support direct transactions between investors without the exchange acting as a CCP. On those platforms, one investor can buy crypto-assets from another investor and pay the seller via bank transfers, Alipay or Wechat pay. These modified business models are not safe from Chinese criminal law perspective. Although major exchanges have been relocated overseas, they may still be subject to criminal liabilities in China. If the founders or managers of an exchange are Chinese nationals, or they make decisions in China to operate the overseas exchange, or the investors are in China, or if the exchange performs prohibited functions, Chinese justice authorities will still have jurisdiction over them.

bank, speaking at an internet finance forum in Beijing, said that *"the STO business that has surfaced recently is still essentially an illegal financial activity in China"*[109].

1.1.4 ***EU, EAA and other European jurisdictions***. The European Securities and Markets Authority ("**ESMA**") took the view that depending on how the ICO is structured[110], the crypto-asset could, potentially, fall within the definition of a transferable security[111]. The ESMA has also warned that certain crypto-assets may constitute financial instruments. An ICO with crypto-assets that can be considered to be transferable securities[112] would require compliance with the following regimes and obligations:

---

[109] See D. Ren, *Central bank deputy governor: STO business 'essentially an illegal financial activity in China'*, South China Morning Post (Dec 9, 2018), available at: https://www.scmp.com/business/banking-finance/article/2177134/central-bank-deputy-governor-sto-business-essentially.

[110] While ESMA has not specifically considered the free transfer of crypto-assets in airdrops, it has outlined helpful guidance with regard to free offers of shares (free public offerings) in its Questions and Answers on the regulation of prospectuses (see ESMA, *Questions and Answers Prospectuses*, (Jan. 2019), available at: https://www.esma.europa.eu/sites/default/files/library/esma31-62-780_qa_on_prospectus_related_topics.pdf). Two of the issues discussed in the document appear to be particularly relevant:
(i) In situations of allocations of securities where there is no element of choice on the part of the recipient (including no right to repudiate the allocation), there is no offer of securities to the public within the meaning of the Prospectus Directive. In the context of airdrops, this would mean that crypto-assets distributions conducted without the knowledge of the recipients do not constitute offers of securities to the public even if the allocated crypto-assets are found to be securities.
(ii) On the other hand, if the recipient of the free securities decides to accept the offer, the public offering can be properly regarded as an offer for zero consideration which is entitled to qualify for exclusions established by the Prospectus Directive (the exclusion primarily refers to the absence of a requirement to issue a prospectus and make it available to the public if the total value of the securities on the basis of the issue price or selling price does not exceed €1,000,000). This exclusion also appears to work in favor of airdrop organizers.
Therefore, it is possible that in at least some circumstances, airdrop organizers will not be subject to public offering regulations even if the allocated crypto-assets constitute securities. However, it has to be noted that these conclusions are based on regulatory bodies' interpretations from 2012, primarily related to employee share schemes.

[111] Thus, the question is whether crypto-assets are "transferable securities" within the meaning of the uniform definition under EU financial regulation. It is obvious from the wording that the definition is based on the transfer of units in the secondary market, not the underlying investment characteristics. This is a major deviation from the US approach which focuses on the "investment contract".

[112] Generally:
(i) crypto-assets are transferable unless they have a permanent lockup function;
(ii) crypto-assets are negotiable unless there are elements that make listing at an exchange platform impossible;
(iii) the blockchain technology allows secure transactions, which would be sufficient if an increased form of negotiability was necessary;
(iv) crypto-assets are countable and thus traded anonymously, making them sufficiently standardized; therefore, most of the crypto-assets commonly described as "security tokens" would be considered as "transferable securities" pursuant to Art. 4(1)(44) MiFiD II.

(i) Prospectus Directive[113]: publication of an approved prospectus when securities are offered to the public with exceptions for offers (a) to qualified investors (as defined in the Prospectus Directive), (b) to fewer than 150 natural or legal persons, (c) of at least €100,000 per investor and (d) with a minimum denomination of €100,000.

(ii) Markets in Financial Instruments Directive ("**MiFID**"), as amended: licensing requirements, product governance rules, pre- and post-trading transparency requirements, requirements for adequate systems and controls, organizational requirements for trading platforms, requirements for companies active in algorithmic and/or high frequency trading, among others.

(iii) The Market Abuse Regulation: regulation of insider dealing, unlawful disclosure of inside information, market manipulation.

(iv) Alternative Investment Fund Manager Directive: licensing requirements, conduct of business and transparency requirements, prospectus and disclosure requirements, mandatory appointment of depositories and custodians, restrictions on the use of leverage, among others.

(v) The 4th Anti-Money Laundering Directive: due diligence on customers and ongoing monitoring of customer relationships, requirements regarding systems and controls and record-keeping, reporting on suspicious activities and co-operation with any investigations by relevant public authorities.

That being said, it is possible to identify certain comparable characteristics which suggest applicability of relevant legislation:

(i) Cryptocurrencies (i.e. payment crypto-assets) are not currently covered by MiFID II, nor the Prospectus Directive or the Market Abuse Regulation. Since a number of cryptocurrencies, such as Bitcoin, are, however, increasingly considered as investment

---

[113] The Prospectus Directive and all related level 2 measures will be replaced by the Prospectus Regulation (Regulation (EU) 2017/1129) on July 21, 2019. The Prospectus Regulation will provide a common legal basis for securities offerings in the European Union and its rules will be binding and directly applicable in all EU member states. The Prospectus Regulation aims to: (i) make it easier and cheaper for smaller companies to access capital; (ii) introduce simplification and flexibility for all types of issuers, in particular for secondary issuances and frequent issuers which are already known to capital markets; (iii) improve prospectuses for investors by introducing a retail investor-friendly summary of key information, catering for the specific information and protection needs of investors. The new prospectus regime will ensure that appropriate rules cover the full life-cycle of companies from start-up until maturity as frequent issuers on regulated markets.

objects, risks arise that are very similar to risks on the capital markets (investor protection and market abuse concerns).

(ii) Crypto-assets with real intrinsic usage are currently not covered by the financial regulation. If they are only usable in relationship with the issuer, and not transferable, they should not be covered by MiFID II, the Prospectus Directive or the Market Abuse Regulation. If they are, on the contrary, transferable, they have the potential to become investment objects. In such a case, risks arise that are very similar to risks on the capital markets (investor protection concerns and market abuse concerns).

(iii) Crypto-assets representing physical goods. In order to determine whether those crypto-assets are covered by MiFID II, the Prospectus Directive, and the Market Abuse Regulation, it should be determined whether they are financial instruments (for MiFID purposes and the Market Abuse Regulation) and transferable securities (for purposes of the Prospectus Directive). Many crypto-assets, however, exhibit components of all three of the archetypes. Generally, the touchstone for the applicability of EU securities regulation should be whether crypto-assets promise their holders the participation in future cash flows generated by the ongoing (or liquidated/sold) project. Where this is not the case, the mere possibility of an appreciation in value should not suffice to equate these crypto-assets with either shares, securitized debt, or options, i.e., with securities.

>(iii)(i) If these crypto-assets give right to a financial entitlement, they represent the features of either bonds (if the entitlement is a predetermined cash flow) or shares (if the entitlement is a share of profit). If those crypto-assets are transferable, they share important characteristics with transferable securities under MiFID, and are therefore subject to MiFID II and the Prospectus Directive.

>(iii)(ii) If crypto-assets representing physical goods give right to an entitlement in kind, and the holder gets decision power into the project, these crypto-assets share important characteristics with shares. If they are transferable, there are good arguments to consider them transferable securities subject to MiFID II and the Prospectus Directive.

>(iii)(iii) If crypto-assets representing physical goods give right to an entitlement in kind, without giving the

holder decision power, and the crypto-asset is not transferable, these crypto-assets share much characteristics with prepaid assets. They currently do not fall under the scope of application of financial regulation.

(iii)(iv) If crypto-assets representing physical goods give right to an entitlement in kind, without giving the holder decision power, but the crypto-asset is transferable, a distinction should be made in respect of (a) the way the token is structured and (b) the nature of underlying asset.

> A number of such crypto-assets will share characteristics with asset-linked notes, in which case there are good arguments to consider them transferable securities subject to MiFID II and the Prospectus Directive.

> Other such crypto-assets may rather share characteristics with derivatives, in which case the following distinction should be made. If the underlying asset is no commodity, they are not financial instruments, since they cannot be related to any of the categories of Annex I C of MiFID II. If the underlying asset is a commodity, they share important characteristics with derivative contracts relating to commodities. If they are settled in cash, there are good arguments to consider them as covered by MiFID as financial instruments under Annex I, Section C (5). If they are physically settled, they could only be covered by MiFID as derivative products under Annex I, Section C (6) of MiFID II, if they are tradable on a regulated market.

In respect of each jurisdiction of EU, EEA and other European jurisdiction like Gibraltar, Switzerland, Jersey, Guernsey and Isle of Man, countries have either taken a nuanced approach or not expressed a clear / definite approach to the evolving nature, typography or offer of ICOs and crypto-assets. While nearly all securities' agencies have published warnings to the public about investment risks inherent to ICO and crypto-assets, no jurisdiction appears to have imposed severe limitations or outright bans for ICOs and crypto-assets

Initial Coin Offerings

initiatives or offerings within its territory. These countries can be broadly classified into three categories:

(i) Proactive approach: Malta[114], Switzerland[115], France[116], Lithuania[117], Gibraltar[118], Jersey[119] and Isle of Man[120] have expressly legislated or specifically developed methodologies.

---

[114] Initial Virtual Financial Asset Offerings (e.g. ICO) are regulated by virtue of a new law – Virtual Financial Assets Act ("**VFA Act**"). The law regulates the field of Initial Virtual Financial Asset Offerings ("**IVFAO**") and Virtual Financial Assets ("**VFA**") and makes provision for matters ancillary or incidental thereto. IVFAO means a DLT-enabled method of raising funds whereby an issuer is issuing virtual financial assets and is offering them to the public in exchange for funds. To offer legal clarity the Malta Financial Services Authority ("**MFSA**") created the Financial Instrument Test ("**Test**"). The Test must be applied to each DLT asset to determine its nature and the respective applicable legal framework based on the crypto-asset's features. The VFA Act provides that a DLT asset may be classified as one of these four types: electronic money, a financial instrument, a virtual token or a VFA. Once the type of DLT asset is determined, the following legal regime will be applicable: (i) virtual tokens are not regulated by any specific body of law in Malta; (ii) financial instruments are defined as set out in the MiFID and thus regulated by financial services legislation; (iii) electronic money is regulated in Malta by the Financial Institutions Act; and (iv) VFAs are regulated by the VFA Act. If a DLT asset is considered to be a financial instrument by the Test, then it is to be regulated by financial services legislation. In this case, rather than conducting an IVFAO or ICO, the issuer would need to conduct an initial public offering in line with the Prospectus Directive or consider the applicability of exemptions. On the other hand, if a service provider offers services in or from Malta in relation to a DLT asset that qualifies as a financial instrument, this would require a license under the Maltese Investment Services Act.

[115] The Swiss Financial Market Supervisory Authority ("**FINMA**") has published market guidance in September 2017. Depending on the structure of an ICO, FINMA determined, among others, that supervisory regulations, collective investment scheme legislation and banking law provisions may be applicable to specific ICOs. Notably, FINMA determines the applicability of regulation to crypto-assets on a case-by-case basis, focusing on the "*economic function and purpose of the tokens*". The key factors are the underlying purpose of the crypto-assets and whether they are already tradeable or transferable. FINMA outlined three categories of crypto-assets – while acknowledging that hybrids are possible – and set out the likely regulatory stance for each as follows. These include "payment tokens", "utility tokens" and "asset tokens". Payment tokens are synonymous with crypto-currencies and have no further functions or links to other development projects (these crypto-assets may in some cases only develop the necessary functionality and become accepted as a means of payment over a period of time). For ICOs where the crypto-asset is intended to function as a means of payment and can already be transferred, FINMA will require compliance with anti-money laundering regulations. Utility tokens are crypto-assets intended to provide digital access to an application or service. These crypto-assets do not qualify as securities only if their sole purpose is to confer digital access rights to an application or service and if the utility token can already be used in this way at the point of issue. If a utility token functions solely or partially as an investment in economic terms, FINMA will treat such tokens as securities (i.e. in the same way as asset tokens). Asset tokens represent crypto-assets such as participations in real physical underlyings, companies, or earning streams, or an entitlement to dividends or interest payments. In terms of their economic function, these crypto-assets are analogous to equities, bonds or derivatives, which means that there are securities law requirements for trading in such tokens, as well as civil law requirements under the Swiss Code of Obligations (e.g. prospectus requirements).

[116] The Autorite Des Marchés Financiers ("**AMF**") is France's regulatory authority on the matter of crypto-assets. ICO regulations will be drafted in 2019. The proposed regulation would introduce a new chapter to Book V, Title V of the French Monetary and Financial Code ("**CMF**"), which will be renamed "Intermediaries in Miscellaneous Property and Token Issuers". Chapter 2 of Title V will be titled "Token Issuers", will detail the rules applicable to ICOs and in particular will provide a definition of tokens, indicating that a token is intangible property representing, in numerical form, one or more rights that can be issued, registered, conserved or transferred using a shared electronic registration

Crypto-assets global corporate finance transactions

(ii) Wait-and-see approach: Austria[121], Belgium[122], Bulgaria[123], Denmark[124], Estonia[125], Finland[126], Germany[127], Italy[128],

mechanism that facilitates the identification, directly or indirectly, of the owner of said property. It also will define an ICO as any offer to the public, in any shape or form, to purchase tokens. However, it will exclude offers made to a small number of buyers. Under the proposed legislation, the issuer should notify token buyers of the status of the project the ICO funds were used to finance, and of the establishment of any secondary market for the tokens. The AMF will be authorized to approve ICOs, but AMF approval will be not necessary to proceed. The AMF may simply require heightened disclosure, so investors may make a more informed decision.

[117] The national regulatory and legal regime may apply to specific ICO models. Entities are required to observe parameters and restrictions outlined in the position of the Bank of Lithuania on virtual currencies and initial coin offering approved by the board of Bank of Lithuania at the meeting of 10 October 2017.

[118] As of 1 January 2018, any firm carrying out by way of business, in or from Gibraltar, the use of distributed ledger technology ("**DLT**") for storing or transmitting value belonging to others needs to be authorized by the Gibraltar Financial Services Commission as a DLT Provider.

[119] The Jersey Financial Services Commission does not regulate ICOs and will impose minimum standards. ICO issuers will be required to be administered by a trust and company service provider licensed by the Jersey Financial Services Commission.

[120] Crypto-assets issued through an ICO do not fall within the definition of "investments", and therefore these crypto-assets are not regulated investments and the protections afforded to investors of traditional investment products regulated under the Financial Services Act 2008 do not apply.

[121] The Austrian Financial Market Authority ("**FMA**") states that as the design of ICOs varies in terms of technical, functional and economic terms, an assessment would need to be done in accordance prevailing supervisory rules on a case-by-case basis. Crypto-assets may constitute financial instruments if their respective underlying rights are comparable to mainstream categories of investments. Therefore, both the Austrian Alternative Investment Fund Managers Act ("**AIFMG**") and the Austrian Capital Markets Act ("**KMG**") are potentially applicable to crypto-assets and ICOs. In accordance with Section 2 (1)(1) of the AIFMG, any collective investment undertaking (including its sub-funds) that collects funds from a number of investors to invest them for the benefit of those investors in accordance with a specified investment policy shall be deemed to be an Alternative Investment Fund ("**AIF**") as long as the funds directly serve the operational activity and the fund is not an Undertaking for Collective Investments in Transferable Securities ("**UCITS**") pursuant to the UCITS Directive. The management of an AIF requires a license as alternative investment fund manager ("**AIFM**") to be issued by the FMA. According to Section 2 of the KMG, the public offering of securities or investments is only permitted if a prospectus has been published, at the latest one banking day prior to the launch of the offer. With respect to securities as qualified by the KMG, the European and national legislators understand transferable securities in accordance with the MiFID II. These mainly include equities and equity-type securities, as well as non-equity securities such as debt securities and other securitized debt securities. If taking the crypto-asset is not to be qualified as securities, it is still necessary to assess whether they may constitute investments. Differences between securities and investments basically only exist with regard to which specifications a prospectus must be prepared to. Otherwise, the differences are negligible. In accordance with Section 1 (1)(3) KMG, investments are uncertificated property rights (rights to claims, membership rights or rights in rem) for the direct or indirect investment of several investors who carry the risk, either alone or jointly with the issuer, and that investors do not administer themselves. The term investment includes uncertificated profit participation rights, limited partnerships and silent participations. Prospectuses for investments do not follow the scheme of the Prospectus Directive, but those according to the annexes provided in the KMG.

[122] The Financial Services and Markets Authority identified a number of national laws which, in addition to European laws, apply depending on how ICOs are structured. Each case is examined on a case-by-case basis. The Belgian legislation on financial instruments consists of the Act of 21 November 2017 regarding the infrastructures of the market for financial instruments, which transposes Directive 2014/65 into national law ("**Act on Financial Instruments**"), and the Act of 25 October 2016 on access to investment services companies, and on the legal status and supervision of portfolio management

and investment advice companies ("**Act on Investment Services**"). The Act on Financial Instruments and the Act on Investment Services are the national laws implementing the second Markets in Financial Instruments Directive (MiFID II). This MiFID-based legal framework aims to foster investor protection and to cope with new trading technologies, practices and activities. The legal framework governing investment instruments consists of the Prospectus Act of 2006 ("**Prospectus Act**"), implementing the provisions of the Prospective Directive. The Prospectus Act requires that a prospectus for a public offer of investment instruments be drafted. A list of such instruments can be found in Article 4, Section 1 of the Prospectus Act. Its scope of application is very broad because investment instruments cover a catch-all category of *"all other instruments that enable carrying out a financial investment, regardless of the underlying assets"*. Because crypto-assets are all traded on exchange platforms, and because their highly volatile nature leads to market speculation, it could be argued that crypto-assets would all fall under the scope of investment instrument within the meaning given to the term under the Prospectus Act. Hence, companies offering these crypto-assets to the public and certain intermediaries that act on their behalf would have to comply with the prospectus requirement under certain circumstances. It should be emphasized that the legal framework applying to prospectus duties will be amended by the time the new Prospectus Regulation enters into force on 29 July 2019. The Belgian Act of 11 July 2018 has been adopted to replace the Prospectus Act of 2006 once the Prospectus Regulation enters into force.

[123] The Financial Services Commission monitors the market for crypto-assets and ICOs on the Bulgarian market with a view to undertaking specific measures related to money laundering and abuse stemming from their trade.

[124] No specific rules but current laws remain applicable subject to design of ICO. Crypto-assets that resemble financial instruments could potentially fall under one or more EU laws, and therefore within scope of relevant regulations. The Danish rules on offering securities to the public or having securities admitted to trading are mainly regulated in the Danish Capital Markets Act ("**CMA**"), which implements the Prospectus Directive and certain aspects of MiFID II and the Market Abuse Regulations.

[125] Crypto-assets considered depending on their design and scope of issue. ICO may also be governed by the Credit Institutions Act if they are akin to loans.

[126] Different current national rules may apply depending on the ICO design.

[127] ICOs are covered by the applicable regulatory requirements depending on the configuration of the crypto-asset, and assessed by BaFin on a case-by-case basis with respect to the language of the statutory provisions under securities law. Hence, the BaFin determines the applicability of the German Banking Act (Kreditwesengesetz), the German Securities Prospectus Act (Wertpapierprospektgesetz), the German Capital Investment Code (Kapitalanlagegesetzbuch), the German Capital Investment Act (Vermögensanlagegesetz) and the Payment Services Supervisory Act (Zahlungsdiensteaufsichtsgesetz) on individual basis. A prospectus for the marketing of the crypto-assets may be required where crypto-assets resemble participations rights which might be classified as securities under the German Securities Prospectus Act (Wertpapierprospektgesetz) or capital investments under the German Capital Investment Act (Vermögensanlagegesetz). Any act of trading, including an arrangement for acquisition, sale or purchase of crypto-assets, when qualified as units of account, would, as a general rule, require a license by the BaFin.

[128] While Italy was the first European country to create legislation for crypto-assets through defining the virtual currency exchanger – the legislative decree on the 25th March 2017, that implemented the IV directive of European anti-money laundering, came into effect on the 4th July in 2017 and has introduced the concept of cryptocurrencies into Italian legislation, classifying in particular those who habitually use cryptocurrencies for work purposes – it does not currently have a specific law regulating the issuance of ICOs. Hence, depending on the characteristics of the offer, it may constitute a regulated activity that must be carried out according to regulations on financial investments (the Prospectus Directive, MiFID, AIFMD and the Anti-Money Laundering Directive). On December 27, 2018, the Italian Ministry of Economic Development appointed a panel of experts to develop the country's blockchain strategy. On March 19, 2019, Consob (the Italian Companies and Exchange Commission) published a discussion paper ("**Discussion Paper**") about ICOs and crypto-assets exchanges, that may lead to the introduction of a specific regulation (See CONSOB, *Initial Coin Offerings and Crypto-Assets Exchanges*, (Mar. 19, 2019), available at:

Luxembourg[129], Netherlands[130], Portugal[131], Spain[132], United Kingdom[133], Lichtenstein[134] and Guernsey[135] do not specifically

---

http://www.consob.it/documents/46180/46181/doc_disc_20190319_en.pdf/e981f8a9-e370-4456-8f67-111e460610f0). The Discussion Paper attempts to identify the defining elements of crypto-assets and the interactions with the category of financial products, that comprises financial instruments as well as "any other form of investment having a financial nature" (i.e. any form of financial investment which involves three elements: (i) the use of capital; (ii) an expectation of a future financial return; (iii) the assumption of a risk linked to the use of that capital). Consob highlights that it is undisputable that at least certain types of crypto-assets (investment crypto-assets or security-like-crypto-assets) qualify as financial instruments and/or as financial products because of their characteristics. At the same time Consob embraces the definition of crypto-assets as "digital registrations which incorporate rights connected to investments in entrepreneurial projects" and suggests the application of a new special financial regulatory regime for them. This approach would have the advantage of avoiding the burden of conducting every time a case-by-case analysis for identifying whether a crypto-asset qualifies or not as a financial product and it would potentially allow issuers and offerors to be exempted from the rules concerning financial products, to the extent that certain safeguards are put in place (such as the supervision of Consob over the platform for the offerings of crypto-assets, defined by Consob as the "online platform whose exclusive purpose is the promotion and realization of offerings of newly issued crypto-assets"). However, Crypto-assets clearly and undoubtedly qualifiable as financial instruments or investment products would remain subject to the current EU regulations.

[129] Despite the lack of specific regulations that applies to ICOs, the activities related thereto or implied through the creation of crypto-assets, the collection and raising of funds may, depending on their characteristics, be subject to certain legal provisions in Luxembourg and thus to certain supervisory requirements. An ICO could fall, among others, within the remit of the Law of 5 April 1993 on the financial sector, the Law of 30 May 2018 on markets in financial instruments, the Law of 17 December 2017 relating to undertakings for collective investment and the Law of 10 July 2005 on prospectuses for securities.

[130] Potential issuers need to properly analyze the extent of any overlap with financial regulation and supervision before launching their ICO. If a crypto-asset qualifies as a security, a prospectus is compulsory.

[131] FinTech business models (which include ICOs) are varied and may be subject to legislation and Portuguese Securities Market Commission's supervision. The few Portuguese legal academics that have addressed this topic have concluded that security crypto-assets are likely to be deemed atypical securities, and that some hybrid crypto-assets (those that also have the characteristics of security tokens) may also be deemed atypical securities pursuant to Portuguese law. A case-by-case assessment must, however, be carried out to conclude whether a specific virtual currency qualifies as an atypical security. The classification of a crypto-asset as an atypical security has very important consequences as, for instance: (i) the public offerings framework would apply to the ICO (to assess whether an exclusion may apply or, even if that is not the case, whether the issuance of the crypto-asset could be exempt from the obligation to publish and file a prospectus); (ii) specific transparency and fiduciary obligations would apply in the context of the ICO and to the issuer and the members of its corporate bodies; (iii) some intermediaries providing services to the issuer of such crypto-assets would need to obtain a license as financial intermediaries (e.g., broker-dealer, custodians); (iv) exchanges where the crypto-asset is listed would need to obtain a license to trade securities (e.g., regulated markets or multilateral trading facilities); and (v) specific restrictions may apply to sales in a secondary market, etc.

[132] The National Securities Market Commission considers that a good number of operations structured as ICOs should be treated as issues or public offerings of transferable securities in terms of Spanish law. If ICOs qualify as financial instruments, then the regulation contained in, relating to or arising from MiFID II, the Prospectus Directive and the Alternative Investment Fund Managers Directive should apply to them.

[133] In September 2017 the Financial Conduct Authority ("**FCA**") stated that many ICOs could fall outside the scope of existing regulation. Additionally, it recognized lack of jurisdiction when the ICO is based overseas, although its objective is to regulate the outcome rather than the process. Therefore, it is required a case-by-case analysis of facts. Consequently, an ICO could be considered as deposit-taking,

restrict or prohibit ICOs or crypto-assets initiatives but have taken a measured approach on a case by case basis and in full consideration of legislative instruments in force within their territory and, where applicable, in the EU.

(iii) Undefined approach: Croatia[136], Czech Republic[137], Greece[138], Hungary[139], Ireland[140], Latvia[141], Poland[142], Republic of Cyprus[143], Romania[144], Slovakia[145], Slovenia[146], Sweden[147], Norway[148] and

---

e-money issuance, contract for difference, derivative or a collective investment scheme. For instance, the FCA issued a statement that firms conducting regulated activities in crypto-assets derivatives must comply with all applicable rules in the FCA's Handbook and any relevant provisions in directly applicable European Union regulations. Crypto-assets that grant a holder some or all of the rights that would typically be enjoyed by a shareholder (for example, entitlements to dividends declared, profits or the proceeds of the assets of an insolvent company), a bondholder (for example, a right to the repayment of a sum of money), or a participant in a fund (for example, to profits or income from the acquisition, holding, management or disposal of the fund property), fall with the regulatory perimeter as "specified investments". The UK is currently a member of the EU. Therefore, EU-wide rules regulating the provision of financial services apply to the regulation of virtual currencies in the UK, whether through the direct application of EU regulations or under UK legislation implementing the requirements of EU directives. For instance, the UK has implemented into national law requirements of: (i) the recast Markets in Financial Instruments Directive (MiFID II), which regulates investment services and activities relating to financial instruments; (ii) the Prospectus Directive, which regulates public offerings of securities; (iii) the Capital Requirements Directive and Regulation, which regulate the activities of credit institutions, including deposit taking; and (iv) the revised Electronic Money Directive and the revised Payment Services Directive, which regulate activities relating to the issuance of electronic money and the provision of payment services, respectively. These EU regulatory requirements may be integrated into or sit alongside domestic UK regulatory requirements, such as those under the Financial Services and Markets Act 2000 ("**FSMA**"), the Electronic Money Regulations 2011 ("**EMRs**") and the Payment Services Regulations 2017 ("**PSRs**"). At the time of writing, the UK is due to leave the EU on 29 March 2019. This follows the outcome of the Brexit referendum vote in June 2016 and service of notice of the UK's intention to leave the EU under Article 50 of the Treaty on European Union on 29 March 2017. However, the government has committed to preserve and onshore most existing EU and EU-derived legislation as it stands immediately before the UK's departure through the European Union (Withdrawal) Act 2018. Therefore, the analysis of whether crypto-assets are regulated in the UK (including under applicable EU-wide regulatory frameworks) should not be affected by Brexit, at least in the short term.

[134] Depending on their specification, crypto-assets may constitute financial instruments subject to financial market law.

[135] Cautious approach if approached with applications involving ICOs that could be traded on secondary market.

[136] No specific position on ICOs appears to be available.
[137] No specific position on ICOs appears to be available.
[138] No specific position on ICOs appears to be available.
[139] No specific position on ICOs appears to be available.
[140] No specific position on ICOs appears to be available.
[141] No specific position on ICOs appears to be available.
[142] No specific position on ICOs appears to be available.
[143] No specific position on ICOs appears to be available.
[144] No specific position on ICOs appears to be available.
[145] No specific position on ICOs appears to be available.
[146] No specific position on ICOs appears to be available.
[147] No specific position on ICOs appears to be available.
[148] No specific position on ICOs appears to be available.

Crypto-assets global corporate finance transactions

Iceland[149] do not appear to provide clear information as to their stance in these areas.

1.1.5   **Hong Kong**. While it is part of the People's Republic of China, Hong Kong maintains its own domestic legal system by virtue of its status as a special administrative region. Chinese laws do not apply in Hong Kong, save as expressly listed in Annex III of the Basic Law. Accordingly, while China has recently moved towards an outright ban on offerings of crypto-assets, the position in Hong Kong is a little more nuanced. Reliance has been placed on existing laws, notably the Securities and Futures Ordinance ("**SFO**"), to police crypto finance transactions. On September 5, 2017[150] the Hong Kong Securities and Futures Commission ("**SFC**") issued an official statement urging the public to exercise caution in their dealings with crypto-assets. The SFC also confirmed that such products could constitute securities[151] subject to regulation under the SFO.

As a rule, if a crypto-asset represents an ownership stake in its issuer's assets, or provides rights to dividends or similar payments, it could be regarded as a security in the form of a share. Similarly, if a crypto-asset creates or evidences a debt payable to its holder, it could constitute a security in the form of a debenture. Most importantly, as a number of initial coin offerings in Hong Kong have previously purported to do, if a person is entitled to a share of economic returns from investments funded by the proceeds of a crypto-asset, then that crypto-asset could well represent an investment in a collective investment scheme[152]. To the extent a crypto-asset constitutes a security, the conduct of various activities relating to it (including dealing in, advising on or managing them as assets) could constitute regulated activities under Schedule 5 to the SFO, for which a license would generally be required[153]. A person

---

[149] No specific position on ICOs appears to be available.
[150] See SFC, *Statement on initial coin offerings*, (Sept 5, 2017), available at: https://www.sfc.hk/web/EN/news-and-announcements/policy-statements-and-announcements/statement-on-initial-coin-offerings.html. See also SFC, *Statement on Security Token Offerings*, (Mar. 28, 2019), available at: https://www.sfc.hk/web/EN/news-and-announcements/policy-statements-and-announcements/statement-on-security-token-offerings.html).
[151] Securities (as defined in Schedule 1 of the SFO) include shares, stocks, debentures, loan stocks, funds, bonds or notes of, or issued by, a body, whether incorporated or unincorporated, or a government or municipal government authority, rights, options or interests, or interests in any collective investment scheme.
[152] Collective investment schemes (as defined in Schedule 1 of the SFO) are composed of four elements: (i) they involve arrangements in respect of any property; (ii) participants do not have day-to-day control over the management of the property; (iii) the property is managed as a whole by or on behalf of the person operating the arrangements, the contributions of the participants and the profits or income from which payments are made to them are pooled, or both; (iv) and the purpose or effect of acquiring the right and interest in the property is to enable participants to participate in or receive profits, income or other returns arising or likely to arise from the acquisition of the property.
[153] Under the SFO, regulated activities that must be carried out with a license are:

who carries on business in a regulated activity (or who holds him or herself out as doing so) without an appropriate license[154] is liable to a fine of up to HK$5 million and to imprisonment for up to seven years[155].

1.1.6   *Israel*. The first time the Israeli legislator referred to crypto-assets was in 2016 when the Knesset passed into law the Financial Services Supervision (Regulated Financial Services) 2016 ("**Financial Services Law**"). Section 1 of the Financial Services Law provides a list of assets that are defined as financial assets. In this list, both securities and virtual currencies are listed as separate types of assets: therefore, a claim can be made that the implicit intention of the legislator is to exclude virtual currency from the definition of securities. In March 2018, the Israel Securities Authority ("**ISA**") released a detailed interim report by the Committee to Examine the Regulation of the Issuance of Decentralized Cryptographic Currency to the Public [156]. In its report, the ISA identifies three subcategories of crypto-assets: (i) currency tokens, which are intended to be used as a method of payment; (ii) security tokens, which confer a right of ownership, membership or participation; (iii) utility tokens, which confer a right to access or use a service or product. The determination of whether a crypto-asset is a security[157] is dependent

---

Type 1: dealing in securities;
Type 2: dealing in futures contracts;
Type 3: leveraged foreign exchange trading;
Type 4: advising on securities;
Type 5: advising on futures contracts;
Type 6: advising on corporate finance;
Type 7: providing automated trading services;
Type 8: securities margin financing;
Type 9: asset management;
Type 10: providing credit rating services;
Type 11: dealing in over-the-counter (OTC) derivative products or advising on OTC derivative products;
Type 12: providing client clearing services for OTC derivative transactions.

[154] It is relatively easy to establish whether or not a person is appropriately licensed as the SFC maintains a public register of licensed persons, available at: https://www.sfc.hk/web/EN/regulatory-functions/intermediaries/licensing/register-of-licensees-and-registered-institutions.html.
[155] Section 114(8), SFO.
[156] See ISA, *The Committee to Examine the Regulation of Decentralized Cryptographic Currency Issuance to the Public – Interim Report*, (March 19, 2018), available at: http://www.isa.gov.il/sites/ISAEng/1489/1511/Pages/eitinot220318.aspx.
[157] Section 1 of the Israeli Securities Law 1968 ("**Securities Law**") defines securities as *"certificates issued in series by a company, a cooperative society or any other corporation conferring a right of membership or participation in them or claim against them, and certificates conferring a right to acquire securities, all of which whether registered or bearer securities, excluding securities issued by the Government or by the Bank of Israel which comply with one of the following:*
(i) they do not confer a right of participation or membership in a corporation and are not convertible into, or realizable for, securities conferring such a right;
(ii) they are issued under special legislation".
This definition is broad, and when taken at face value would seemingly include almost all forms of crypto-assets without taking into account the underlying differences therein. However, case law has ruled that the intention of the legislator was clearly not to paint such a broad stoke. The Israeli

upon the nature of the transaction. The ISA currently views that a crypto-asset is a prima facie security where it confers similar rights to those conferred by traditional securities[158], including the right to profits or income; a right to receive payments, whether by the distribution of additional crypto-assets or cashing crypto-assets into fiat currency; and ownership or participation rights in enterprises whose purpose is to yield financial profit[159]. Anyway, the ISA proposes the following considerations when determining whether a crypto-asset qualifies as a security token: the purpose for which the purchasers of the crypto-asset acquired it; the level of the crypto-asset's functionality during the offering, meaning to what degree can crypto-assets purchasers use them for the purpose for which they was created; and representations and warranties made by the issuer, including a promise to yield profits and create or work towards creating a secondary market for the trade of such crypto-assets.

1.1.7 **Russia**. The initial approach of the Ministry of Finance[160] initially was to prohibit crypto-assets transactions and to impose fines, as well as to equate Bitcoin with money substitutes, the use of which is contrary to the Constitution of the Russian Federation, which declares that the ruble is the only legal means of payment in the territory of Russia. As crypto-assets, and particularly Bitcoin, have gained popularity around the globe, the Russian authorities have modified their strategy, although the Central Bank of the Russian Federation[161] has indicated that regulation of crypto-assets transactions is premature. In the last months, indeed, several Russian ministries[162] have brought forth regulations pertinent to

---

Supreme Court has further backed this position by quoting the landmark decision in US, *SEC v. W.J. Howey Co., 328 U.S. 293, 301 (1946)*. However, in a 2015 case before the Supreme Court of Israel (Appeal of Administrative Petition 7313/14 Israel Security Authority v. Kvutzat Kedem Chizuk V'Chidush Mivnim Ltd.) the Honorable Elyakim Rubenstein noted as obiter dictum that the Israeli definition of securities is inherently different from that in the United States, and stated that *"in any case, it is doubtful whether an analogy should be derived from American law to the Israeli one on this issue"*.

[158] So, generally, crypto-assets would not be considered a security, as long as they do not confer any other rights, including a right to profits or participation from a company that is the offeror or issuer of the crypto-tokens.

[159] Although it may seem that crypto-assets conferring a purely functional right are a security under the Securities Law, as they include a future claim against the issuer, the ISA reiterates that an investment in the acquisition of a product or service, whether future or current, may not be considered an investment in a security under the Securities Law, and that crypto-assets purchased for consumer-related purposes will not necessarily be classified as securities. Moreover, the mere transferability of a crypto-asset does not contribute to its qualification as a security.

[160] See the letter entitled *"On the regulation of the Issue and turnover of cryptocurrency"* published by the Ministry of Finance in October 2017.

[161] The Central Bank of the Russian Federation (Bank of Russia) has a special legal status and the exclusive right to issue currency, protect the ruble and ensure its stability.

[162] In March 2017, Prime Minister Dmitry Medvedev instructed the Ministry of Communications and the Ministry of Economic Development to consider the use of technology in the areas of public administration and Russia's economy in preparation for the Digital Economy plan, which forms part of the government's action plan for 2017 to 2025.

the space. The Ministry of Finance has presented a draft of regulation with regard to digital financial assets[163] which contains a proposal for defining and establishing a regulatory system for crypto-currencies, ICOs, mining, and trading[164], while the Ministry of Communications and Mass Media has published a document proposing licensing rules for ICO projects[165]. In future, accredited Initial Coin Offerings on Russian territory will only be possible with the help of the ruble (i.e. for successful accreditation, ICOs on Russian territory will in future only be able to be operated using the national currency). The guidelines are part of a larger crypto regulatory package aimed at "legalizing" crypto-currencies[166] to be passed by the Russian State Duma[167].

1.1.8 **Singapore**. In August of 2017, the Monetary Authority of Singapore ("**MAS**") released guidance on how it plans to approach regulation of crypto-assets. MAS stated that it regulates crypto-assets if they fall under the Securities and Futures Act ("**SFA**")[168]. The SFA has extraterritorial application. Under the SFA, where acts are carried out partly in and partly outside of Singapore, such acts would be treated as being committed wholly in Singapore, and where an act is carried out wholly outside Singapore, it would be treated as being carried on in Singapore if it has a substantial and reasonably foreseeable effect in Singapore.

Crypto-assets fall under SFA when linked to an ownership or security interest in the issuer's assets or property[169]. If this is the case the issuer

---

[163] The draft law *"On digital financial assets"*.

[164] A digital financial asset is defined as property in electronic form created using encryption means, the ownership of which is certified by making digital entries in the register of digital transactions. Digital financial assets are not a legal means of payment. The distinction between a crypto-currency and a token is made in accordance to three criteria: (i) the method of accounting (a cryptocurrency can be taken into account only in the distributed registry, while in the case of tokens the registry properties are not specified); (ii) the issuer (a token is issued by a legal entity or individual entrepreneur, while a cryptocurrency is created by an undefined set of network members who support the work of the distributed registry); (iii) the objectives of creating an asset (tokens are issued to attract financing, while the purpose of creating a cryptocurrency is not specified). The bill does not directly answer the question of whether a token is a security.

[165] Under the proposed rules, companies who hold ICOs will have to guarantee that investors can sell back their crypto-assets. Additionally, crypto-assets issuing entities will be required to prove that they control a minimum of RUB100 million (just under €1.4 million) of "authorized capital" in a Russian bank account.

[166] In May 2018, the State Duma adopted in the first reading several draft laws that could become the basis for regulating the digital (virtual) economy: the draft law *"On digital financial assets"*, the draft law on crowdfunding (draft law *"On Alternative Methods of Fundraising (Crowdfunding)"*) and the draft law *"On amending the Civil Code of the Russian Federation"*. The draft law on mining (draft law *"On the system of distributed national mining"*) has also been submitted to the State Duma.

[167] The State Duma is the lower house of the Federal Assembly of Russia (Parliament) which is the legislature of the Russian Federation.

[168] Securities and Futures Act, Chapter 289 of Singapore.

[169] For instance, a crypto-asset may constitute;

must register with the MAS, unless exempted, and there is a triggering of conduct rules which concern fair dealing. Offers of crypto-assets which constitute securities or units in a collective investment scheme are in particular subject to the same regulatory regime under Part XIII of the SFA, as offers of securities or units in a collective investment scheme respectively made through traditional means. A person may only make an offer of crypto-assets which constitute securities or units in a collective investment scheme, if the offer complies with the requirements under Part XIII of the SFA 11 including requirements that the offer must be made in or accompanied by a prospectus that is prepared in accordance with the SFA and is registered with MAS[170]. An offer may nevertheless be exempt from the prospectus requirements where, amongst others:

> (i) the offer is a small offer of securities of an entity, or units in a collective investment scheme, that does not exceed S$5 million (or its equivalent in a foreign currency) within any 12-month period, subject to certain conditions;
> (ii) the offer is a private placement offer made to no more than 50 persons within any 12-month period, subject to certain conditions;
> (iii) the offer is made to institutional investors only;
> (iv) the offer is made to accredited investors, subject to certain conditions.

The exemptions for a small offer, a private placement offer and an offer made to accredited investors, are respectively subject to certain conditions which includes advertising restrictions.

In addition, where an offer is made in relation to units in a collective investment scheme, the collective investment scheme is subject to authorization or recognition requirements. An authorized collective investment scheme or a recognized collective investment scheme under

---

(i) a share, where it confers or represents ownership interest in a corporation, represents liability of the crypto-asset holder in the corporation, and represents mutual covenants with other crypto-asset holders in the corporation inter se;
(ii) a debenture, where it constitutes or evidences the indebtedness of the issuer of the crypto-asset in respect of any money that is or may be lent to the issuer by a crypto-asset holder; or
(iii) a unit in a collective investment scheme, where it represents a right or interest in a collective investment scheme, or an option to acquire a right or interest in a collective investment scheme.
[170] Issuers and distributors of security crypto-assets who advise or promulgate research analyses and reports could be subject to the licensing requirements of the Financial Advisers Act ("**FAA**"). Operators of platforms or exchanges that facilitate secondary trading of these security crypto-tokens that are or have characteristics of derivatives contracts, securities or units in collective investment schemes would need to be approved or recognized by MAS, as an approved exchange or recognized market operator, respectively, under the SFA.

Initial Coin Offerings

1.1.9 **United States**. The applicability of federal securities laws to ICOs[171] depends on the classification of the crypto-assets. The SEC[172] determined that crypto-assets may be qualified as securities as a result of the *Howey Test*[173].

The DAO investigation report (hereinafter **"the DAO report"**)[174] indicates, how we are going to see in detail, that crypto-assets offered in connection with an ICO should be classified as securities if the ICO, implicitly or explicitly, is presented to purchasers as an investment opportunity[175]. The DAO was an example of a decentralized autonomous organization, a term used to describe a virtual organization embodied in computer code and executed on a distributed ledger or blockchain. The DAO operated as a for-profit entity[176] to create and hold Ether

---

[171] With regard to the application of US securities laws to cross-border ICOs see J. Debler, *Foreign Initial Coin Offering Issuers Beware: The Securities and Exchange Commission is Watching*, Cornell International Law Journal 51(1), 245-272 (2018), available at: https://www.lawschool.cornell.edu/research/ILJ/upload/Debler-note-final.pdf.

[172] Prior to mid-2017 and the DAO investigation report, the SEC had been largely silent with respect to directly regulating the purchase or sale of cryptocurrencies. Most of its regulation in this area had, instead, solely attempted to protect the public from issuers or exchanges which operate cryptocurrency-related businesses and offer conventional securities. The SEC regulated online exchanges that use cryptocurrencies to trade in securities (BTC Trading Corp., Exchange Act Release No. 73783, 110 SEC Docket 8 (Dec. 8,2014)), redemptions of shares in a trust that held cryptocurrencies as its sole assets (Bitcoin Investment Trust, Exchange Act Release No. 34-78282, 114 SEC Docket 11 (July 11, 2016)), issuers selling shares in themselves in exchange for cryptocurrencies (Erik T. Voorhees, Securities Act Release No. 9592, 109 SEC Docket 1 (June 3, 2014)), and issuers holding cryptocurrency assets or operating cryptocurrency-related businesses that did not disclose sufficient information about such assets (Sunshine Capital Inc., Exchange Act Release No. 80435, 116 SEC Docket 10 (Apr. 11, 2017)) or made fraudulent representations, including operation of Ponzi schemes (SEC v. Homero Joshua Garza, Civil Action No. 3:15-CV-01760 (D. Conn. filed Dec. 1, 2015); SEC v. Trendon T. Shavers, Civil Action No. 4:13- CV-416 (E.D. Tex. filed July 23, 2013)). In 2017, the SEC's Division of Enforcement formed a Cyber Unit, which it stated would focus on the following: (i) market manipulation schemes involving false information spread through electronic and social media; (ii) hacking to obtain material non-public information and trading on that information; (iii) violations involving distributed ledger technology and ICOs; (iv) misconduct perpetrated using the dark web; (v) intrusions into retail brokerage accounts; and cyber-related threats to trading platforms and other critical market infrastructure.

[173] In April 2019, the SEC issued more extended guidance for analyzing whether a digital asset is offered and sold as an investment contract, and, therefore, is a security (see SEC, *Framework for "Investment Contract" Analysis of Digital Assets*, (April 3, 2019), available at: https://www.sec.gov/corpfin/framework-investment-contract-analysis-digital-assets). It's pretty much straight the *Howey test*, with a nod to relevant legal precedents and the DAO report (it does not replace or supersede existing case law, legal requirements, or statements or guidance from the SEC).

[174] See SEC, *Report of Investigation Pursuant to Section 21(a) of the Securities Exchange Act of 1934: The DAO*, (July 25, 2017), available at: https://www.sec.gov/litigation/investreport/34-81207.pdf.

[175] ICOs are not, by default, securities because they are not included within the statutory definition of a security, but they often fall within the category of an investment contract.

[176] The DAO was created by a German corporation named Slock.it UG.

(hereinafter "**ETH**") through the sale of DAO tokens, which ETH would then be used to fund projects. The holders of DAO tokens were to share in earnings from these projects by voting on the projects and earning rewards. They could also re-sell DAO tokens on a number of web-based platforms. In the DAO Report, the SEC analyzing the DAO tokens under the *Howey Test*, found that they were a form of investment contract, and thus securities. An investment contract is an investment of money in a common enterprise with a reasonable expectation[177] of profits[178] to be

---

[177] Although no one of the following characteristics is necessarily determinative, the more the following characteristics are present, the more likely it is that there is a reasonable expectation of profit:
(i) The crypto-asset gives the holder rights to share in the enterprise's income or profits or to realize gain from capital appreciation of the crypto-asset.
  (i)(i) The opportunity may result from appreciation in the value of the crypto-asset that comes, at least in part, from the operation, promotion, improvement, or other positive developments in the network, particularly if there is a secondary trading market that enables crypto-asset holders to resell their crypto-asset and realize gains.
  (i)(ii) This also can be the case where the crypto-asset gives the holder rights to dividends or distributions.
(ii) The crypto-asset is transferable or traded on or through a secondary market or platform, or is expected to be in the future.
(iii) Purchasers reasonably would expect that the promoter's efforts will result in capital appreciation of the crypto-asset and therefore be able to earn a return on their purchase.
(iv) The crypto-asset is offered broadly to potential purchasers as compared to being targeted to expected users of the goods or services or those who have a need for the functionality of the network.
  (iv)(i) The crypto-asset is offered and purchased in quantities indicative of investment intent instead of quantities indicative of a user of the network. For example, it is offered and purchased in quantities significantly greater than any likely user would reasonably need, or so small as to make actual use of the asset in the network impractical.
(v) There is little apparent correlation between the purchase/offering price of the crypto-asset and the market price of the particular goods or services that can be acquired in exchange for the crypto-asset.
(vi) There is little apparent correlation between quantities the crypto-asset typically trades in (or the amounts that purchasers typically purchase) and the amount of the underlying goods or services a typical consumer would purchase for use or consumption.
(vii) The promoter has raised an amount of funds in excess of what may be needed to establish a functional network or crypto-asset.
(viii) The promoter is able to benefit from its efforts as a result of holding the same class of crypto-asset as those being distributed to the public.
(ix) The promoter continues to expend funds from proceeds or operations to enhance the functionality or value of the network or crypto-asset.
(x) The crypto-asset is marketed, directly or indirectly, using any of the following:
  (a) The expertise of the promoter or its ability to build or grow the value of the network or crypto-asset.
  (b) The crypto-asset is marketed in terms that indicate it is an investment or that the solicited holders are investors.
  (c) The intended use of the proceeds from the sale of the crypto-asset is to develop the network or crypto-asset.
  (d) The future (and not present) functionality of the network or crypto-asset, and the prospect that the promoter will deliver that functionality.
  (e) The promise (implied or explicit) to build a business or operation as opposed to delivering currently available goods or services for use on an existing network.
  (f) The ready transferability of the crypto-asset is a key selling feature.

derived from the entrepreneurial or managerial efforts of others[179]. The SEC determined that: (i) investors in The DAO invested money in the

---

(g) The potential profitability of the operations of the network, or the potential appreciation in the value of the crypto-asset, is emphasized in marketing or other promotional materials.

(h) The availability of a market for the trading of the crypto-asset, particularly where the promoter implicitly or explicitly promises to create or otherwise support a trading market for the crypto-asset.

In evaluating whether a crypto-asset previously sold as a security should be reevaluated at the time of later offers or sales, there would be additional considerations as they relate to the "reasonable expectation of profits", including but not limited to:

(i) Purchasers of the crypto-asset no longer reasonably expect that continued development efforts of the promoter will be a key factor for determining the value of the crypto-asset.

(ii) The value of the crypto-asset has shown a direct and stable correlation to the value of the good or service for which it may be exchanged or redeemed.

(iii) The trading volume for the crypto-asset corresponds to the level of demand for the good or service for which it may be exchanged or redeemed.

(iv) Whether holders are then able to use the crypto-asset for its intended functionality, such as to acquire goods and services on or through the network or platform.

(v) Whether any economic benefit that may be derived from appreciation in the value of the crypto-asset is incidental to obtaining the right to use it for its intended functionality.

(vi) No promoter has access to material, non-public information or could otherwise be deemed to hold material inside information about the crypto-asset.

See on the point, in particular, SEC, *Framework for "Investment Contract" Analysis of Digital Assets*, (April 3, 2019), available at: https://www.sec.gov/corpfin/framework-investment-contract-analysis-digital-assets.

[178] Profits can be, among other things, capital appreciation resulting from the development of the initial investment or business enterprise or a participation in earnings resulting from the use of purchasers' funds. Price appreciation resulting solely from external market forces (such as general inflationary trends or the economy) impacting the supply and demand for an underlying asset generally is not considered "profit" under the *Howey test*.

[179] Although no one of the following characteristics is necessarily determinative, the stronger their presence, the more likely it is that a purchaser of a crypto-assets is relying on the "efforts of others":

(i) The promoter is responsible for the development, improvement (or enhancement), operation, or promotion of the network, particularly if purchasers of the crypto-asset expect the promoter to be performing or overseeing tasks that are necessary for the network or crypto-asset to achieve or retain its intended purpose or functionality.

(i)(i) Where the network or the crypto-asset is still in development and the network or crypto-asset is not fully functional at the time of the offer or sale, purchasers would reasonably expect the promoter to further develop the functionality of the network or crypto-asset (directly or indirectly). This particularly would be the case where the promoter promises further developmental efforts in order for the crypto-asset to attain or grow in value.

(ii) There are essential tasks or responsibilities performed and expected to be performed by the promoter, rather than the decentralized network (an unaffiliated, dispersed community of network users).

(iii) The promoter creates or supports a market for, or the price of, the crypto-asset. This can include, for example, a promoter that: controls the creation and issuance of the crypto-asset; or takes other actions to support a market price of the crypto-asset, such as by limiting supply or ensuring scarcity, through, for example, buybacks, burning, or other activities.

(iv) The promoter has a lead or central role in the direction of the ongoing development of the network or the crypto-asset. In particular, the promoter plays a lead or central role in deciding governance issues, code updates, or how third parties participate in the validation of transactions that occur with respect to the crypto-asset.

(v) The promoter has a continuing managerial role in making decisions about or exercising judgment concerning the network or the characteristics or rights the crypto-asset represents including, for example:

form of ETH[180], which constituted a contribution of value as contemplated by *Howey*; (ii) investors who purchased the DAO tokens

---

(a) Determining whether and how to compensate persons providing services to the network or to the entity or entities charged with oversight of the network.

(b) Determining whether and where the crypto-asset will trade. For example, purchasers may reasonably rely on the promoter for liquidity, such as where the promoter has arranged, or promised to arrange for, the trading of the crypto-asset on a secondary market or platform.

(c) Determining who will receive additional crypto-asset and under what conditions.

(d) Making or contributing to managerial level business decisions, such as how to deploy funds raised from sales of the crypto-asset.

(e) Playing a leading role in the validation or confirmation of transactions on the network, or in some other way having responsibility for the ongoing security of the network.

(f) Making other managerial judgements or decisions that will directly or indirectly impact the success of the network or the value of the crypto-asset generally.

(vi) Purchasers would reasonably expect the promoter to undertake efforts to promote its own interests and enhance the value of the network or crypto-asset, such as where:

(a) The promoter has the ability to realize capital appreciation from the value of the crypto-asset. This can be demonstrated, for example, if the promoter retains a stake or interest in the crypto-asset. In these instances, purchasers would reasonably expect the promoter to undertake efforts to promote its own interests and enhance the value of the network or crypto-asset.

(b) The promoter distributes the crypto-asset as compensation to management or the promoter's compensation is tied to the price of the crypto-asset in the secondary market. To the extent these facts are present, the compensated individuals can be expected to take steps to build the value of the crypto-asset.

(c) The promoter owns or controls ownership of intellectual property rights of the network or crypto-asset, directly or indirectly.

(d) The promoter monetizes the value of the crypto-asset, especially where the crypto-asset has limited functionality.

In evaluating whether a crypto-asset previously sold as a security should be reevaluated at the time of later offers or sales, there would be additional considerations as they relate to the "efforts of others", including but not limited to:

(i) Whether or not the efforts of the promoter, including any successor, continue to be important to the value of an investment in the crypto-asset.

(ii) Whether the network on which the crypto-asset is to function operates in such a manner that purchasers would no longer reasonably expect the promoter to carry out essential managerial or entrepreneurial efforts.

(iii) Whether the efforts of the promoter are no longer affecting the enterprise's success.

See on the point, in particular, SEC, *Framework for "Investment Contract" Analysis of Digital Assets*, (April 3, 2019), available at: https://www.sec.gov/corpfin/framework-investment-contract-analysis-digital-assets.

[180] The notion that crypto-assets constitute an "investment of money" was first settled in SEC v. Shavers (SEC v. Trendon T. Shavers, Civil Action No. 4:13- CV-416 (E.D. Tex. filed July 23, 2013)). In that case (the first SEC lawsuit in connection with a fraudulent cryptocurrency investment scheme) the US District Court for the Eastern District of Texas entered a judgment against Trendon T. Shavers and his company Bitcoin Savings and Trust ("**BTCST**") for defrauding investors in a $4.5 million Ponzi scheme involving Bitcoin. Shavers challenged the SEC's jurisdiction on the contention that the BTCST investments were not investment contracts under the *Howey test* because investors paid for the interest in Bitcoins. He argued that Bitcoins are not currency that can be regulated and, therefore, the interests did not involve an "investment of money". The court disagreed and in its August 26, 2014 ruling, held that (i) the BTCST investments were actually investment contracts; (ii) Bitcoin was an investment of money because it could be used as money or currency; (iii) there was a common enterprise in that investors were dependent on Shavers's expertise in Bitcoin markets and his local connections; (iv) that the investors expected profits in the form of weekly interest solely from the efforts of Shavers's Bitcoin arbitrage activity.

were investing in a common enterprise[181] and reasonably expected to earn profits through that enterprise (the SEC stresses that the promotional materials informed prospective purchasers that the DAO was a for-profit entity the objective of which was to fund projects in exchange for a return on investment, and the DAO token holders stood to share in potential profits from those projects); (iii) investors' profits were to be derived from the managerial efforts of others. The SEC's analysis focused on the latter point[182]. The SEC concluded that investors in the DAO, whose expectations were primed by the marketing of the DAO tokens, reasonably expected the founders (as well as the pre-selected curators who were charged with identifying projects to put up for a vote of the DAO token holders) to provide significant managerial efforts after the DAO's launch. While the DAO platform was created and operated on a blockchain, there was no true decentralization in the operation of the DAO (the participants in the DAO ecosystem were not given full control over any investment decision). The DAO tokens were effectively securities and it was relatively easy for the SEC to conclude that[183]. However, it is possible that the SEC would have reached a

---

[181] This issue of whether investments in virtual enterprises satisfy the commonality requirement was squarely addressed in SEC v. SG Ltd (SEC v. SG, Ltd et al., 265 F.3d 42 (1st Circuit 2001)). In that case, the SEC sued a virtual stock exchange for defrauding investors through its cyberspace game. SG Ltd., a Dominican corporation, argued that the virtual shares were part of a legitimate fantasy investment game created for the personal entertainment of each player and therefore there was no "commonality" among the players to implicate the federal securities laws. In holding that the virtual shares in the online game were securities, the First Circuit Court ruled that a showing of "horizontal commonality" satisfies the *Howey test*. Horizontal commonality is shown by the "pooling of assets from multiple investors in such a manner that all share in the "profits and risks" of the enterprise. The court found the horizontal commonality here because SG Ltd ran a Ponzi scheme whereby it depended on a continuous influx of new money from new members to remain in operation, and operated a pyramid scheme whereby it promised to pay current members twenty to thirty percent referral fees, which were to be paid out of the money contributed by the new referrals. This decision has important implications in the context of ICOs because: (i) issuers who are involved in Ponzi or pyramid schemes will automatically be deemed to have satisfied the commonality prong of *the Howey test*; (ii) nearly every ICO to date satisfies the horizontal commonality requirement because the very essence of an ICO is the "pooling of assets" and the sharing in the "profits and risks" of the fundraised project.

[182] The reasonable expectation of profits (or other financial returns) derived from the efforts of others is often prominently used by the SEC and the Courts to determine if unusual financial instruments are subject to federal securities law.

[183] The DAO report implicitly validates the exclusion of crypto-assets with functions of currencies from securities laws by mentioning that both Bitcoin and Ether qualify as "virtual currencies" (on the contrary, some commentators, including former Chairman of the CFTC Gary Gensler, have suggested that Ether – which as of January 2019 was the third-largest virtual currency by market capitalization – may qualify as a "security" because it was issued by a centralized entity before the Ethereum network was fully functional; see N. Popper, *A Former Top Wall Street Regulator Turns to the Blockchain*, New York Times (Apr. 22, 2018), available at: https://www.nytimes.com/2018/04/22/technology/gensler-mit-blockchain.html). The SEC failed to acknowledge DAO tokens' capacity as a virtual currency (because doing so could omit the DAO tokens from the purview of securities laws). In the DAO report, a virtual currency seems to be something altogether different from the DAO tokens (and other security crypto-assets whose primary purpose is raising capital). This is particularly notable because security crypto-assets and virtual currencies have many commonalities. Nearly all security crypto-assets could conceivably meet the SEC's functional test for determining whether an instrument

different conclusion had the platform operated on a truly decentralized basis[184].

In December 2017, the SEC issued an accompanying order regarding Munchee Inc ("**Munchee**")[185]. Munchee was in the process of conducting an ICO of MUN tokens ("**MUN Tokens**"). The MUN tokens were available for purchase worldwide. They were described as utility tokens that would represent the right to use or access Munchee's services. Munchee was seeking $15 million to improve an existing iPhone app centered on restaurant meal reviews and to create an ecosystem in which Munchee and others would buy and sell goods and services using the MUN tokens. The SEC's summary of Munchee's activities focuses largely on the promotional activities of Munchee and associated persons. In particular, Munchee and such persons heavily promoted the potential for the MUN tokens to increase in value. Such promotion included, among other things: (i) indications in the MUN whitepaper that MUN tokens would increase in value as a result of increased participation in the Munchee "ecosystem"; (ii) statements by Munchee and its agents (in the whitepaper, on the Munchee website and elsewhere) emphasizing that Munchee would run its business in ways that would cause MUN tokens to rise in value; (iii) statements by Munchee that it would work to ensure that MUN holders would be able to sell their MUN tokens on secondary

---

qualifies as a virtual currency because a cryptocurrency, by definition, operates as a store of value that is generally freely transferable (and thus a medium of exchange) and supported by a blockchain that records each transaction (such that it is also a unit of account). For example, the DAO tokens were freely transferable and ran on the Ethereum blockchain. Similarly, virtual currencies tend to have at least some of the attributes of securities because of their reliance on blockchain technology. Each blockchain is typically developed by a small and close group of developers. The holders, conversely, tend to be diffuse and numerous, limited ability to act in concert. Thus, like the DAO tokens, virtual currencies tend to exhibit at least some hallmarks of stock ownership which the SEC weighed so heavily against the DAO Tokens.

[184] In June 2018, the SEC's Director of the Division of Corporation Finance, William Hinman, made an important speech (see W. Hinman, *Digital Asset Transactions: When Howey Met Gary (Plastic)*, Remarks at the Yahoo Finance All Markets Summit: Crypto (June 14, 2018), available at: https://www.sec.gov/news/speech/speech-hinman-061418) in which he refined the SEC's analysis of a crypto-asset as an investment contract. First, he framed the question differently by focusing not on the crypto-asset itself, but rather on the circumstances surrounding the crypto-asset and the manner in which it is sold. He conceded that the crypto-asset is not a security all by itself. The crypto-asset *"is simply code"*. Instead, *"the way it is sold – as part of an investment; to non-users; by promoters to develop the enterprise – can be, and, in that context, most often is, a security – because it evidences an investment contract. And regulating these transactions as securities transactions makes sense"*. When there is information asymmetry between promoters or founders and investors, then the protections of the Securities Act – namely, disclosure and liability for material misstatements and omissions – are necessary and appropriate. On the other hand, Hinman noted that *"if the network on which the token or coin is to function is sufficiently decentralized – where purchasers would no longer reasonably expect a person or group to carry out essential managerial or entrepreneurial efforts – the assets may not represent an investment contract. Moreover, when the efforts of the third party are no longer a key factor for determining the enterprise's success, material information asymmetries recede"*.

[185] See *In the Matter of Munchee*, Securities Act Release No. 10445 (Dec. 11, 2017), available at: https://www.sec.gov/litigation/admin/2017/33-10445.pdf.

markets and that Munchee would buy or sell MUN tokens using its retained holdings in order to ensure there was a liquid secondary market in the tokens. The SEC concluded that the MUN tokens were investment contracts, and therefore securities, under *Howey*. The SEC focused on investor expectations of profits to be derived from the efforts of others[186] and noted that: (i) purchasers of MUN tokens had a reasonable expectation of profits from their investment in the Munchee enterprise (the proceeds were intended to be used by Munchee to build an ecosystem that would create demand for MUN tokens and make them more valuable and Munchee highlighted that it would ensure that a secondary market for MUN tokens would be available shortly after completion of the offering and prior to the creation of the ecosystem); (ii) investors' profits were to be derived from the significant entrepreneurial and managerial efforts of others – specifically Munchee and its agents – who were to revise the Munchee app, create the ecosystem that would increase the value of the MUN tokens and support secondary markets. Munchee may ultimately prove not to be the best precedent for two reasons, though: (i) in relation to the investor expectations of profits, it has to be noted that the fact that a purchased asset has the possibility of increasing in monetary value over time does not necessarily indicate that the purchaser's primary motive is the realization of profit; (ii) the mere fact that an issuer of crypto-assets facilitates secondary trading markets for the crypto-asset should not be a deciding factor, because although the existence of an active secondary market for tokens is likely to increase their value by creating improved opportunities for liquidity, there are other valid reasons for secondary markets (efforts of issuers to secure secondary markets for crypto-assets should not end the analysis, in case of absent factors that demonstrate that the purpose of securing a secondary market is to provide purchasers with profit opportunities from an investment in the crypto-assets).

Almost a year after, the SEC took a major step on November 16, 2018 in bringing two enforcement cases[187] against ICO projects that each imposed a substantial penalty of $250,000 and required registration of the issued tokens and the violators to inform their investors of their right

---

[186] For more extended guidance on the reasonable expectation of profits (or other financial returns) derived from the efforts of others see, again, SEC, *Framework for "Investment Contract" Analysis of Digital Assets*, (April 3, 2019), available at: https://www.sec.gov/corpfin/framework-investment-contract-analysis-digital-assets.

[187] They are nearly identical in structure. In a number of sections the language is identical. The introductory paragraphs are exactly the same language, including the same initial footnote. The same is true of the language describing the remedial actions and penalties at the end of each order. In both cases the remedial actions and undertakings by the companies are identical – payment of a $250,000 penalty to the SEC, registration of the token as a class of security, publication of a "claim form" to token purchasers, ongoing Exchange Act reporting for at least one year, and a number of other reporting obligations to the SEC regarding compliance with the order. In short, the SEC has developed or appears to be developing a template for ICO enforcement.

to rescind the investment and get a refund. These settlements are a strong warning that the SEC intends to enforce its registration requirements and at the same time provide some guidance[188] about the types of ICOs that are likely to trigger enforcement. These projects, indeed, were not functional and did not offer a roadmap to decentralization[189]: (i) one was essentially the expansion of a pre-existing business that sold discounted airtime on mobile phones[190]; (ii) the other offered a vague plan to deploy a suite of blockchain enabled products to organize, systemize and bring verification and stability to the cannabis industry[191].

On November 27, 2018 U.S. District Judge Gonzalo Curiel of the Southern District of California, who previously granted the SEC's *ex parte* request for a temporary restraining order and froze the assets involved in Blockvest ICO, denied the SEC's motion for a preliminary injunction because at this stage, without full discovery and disputed issues of material facts, the SEC couldn't show that investors bought into the Blockvest offering with the expectation of making a profit from the efforts as others[192] – part of *Howey Test*. The Court broke down the *Howey Test* into its composite parts to determine whether a crypto-asset issue represents a security offering. It came to a number of conclusions that could have a significant impact on the ICOs market. To pass the *Howey Test*, investors must face a risk of financial loss. If no monetary investment is made in return for the crypto-assets, investors do not face any risk of loss, and those crypto-assets, then, fail the *Howey Test*. That element of the Court's findings is particularly significant for airdrops[193].

---

[188] The legal analysis is exactly the same in both orders. It's pretty much straight the *Howey test*, with a nod to the DAO report and a wave at In re Munchee.

[189] Projects that are further along with a clearer plan for decentralization might be more likely to avoid SEC enforcement.

[190] *In the Matter of Carriereq, Inc., D/B/A Airfox*, Securities Act Release No. 10575 (Nov. 16, 2018), available at: https://www.sec.gov/litigation/admin/2018/33-10575.pdf.

[191] *In the Matter of Paragon Coin, Inc.*, Securities Act Release No. 10573 (Nov. 16, 2018), available at: https://www.sec.gov/litigation/admin/2018/33-10574.pdf.

[192] This does not mean that the SEC could not pursue an action against the defendants. Rather it just means that the SEC didn't meet the high burden required to receive a preliminary injunction of proving (i) a prima facie case of previous violations of federal securities laws, and (ii) a reasonable likelihood that the wrong will be repeated.

[193] In airdrops investors, indeed, are not exposed to a risk of financial loss. The SEC has directly addressed the compliance of airdrops and bounty campaigns with the securities laws in the Tomahawk Order (see *In the Matter of Tomahawk Exploration LLC and David Thompson Laurance, Inc.*, Securities Act Release No. 83839 (Aug. 14, 2018), available at: https://www.sec.gov/litigation/admin/2018/33-10530.pdf). On August 14, 2018, the SEC issued a cease and desist order against Tomahawk Exploration and David Thompson Laurance for their actions in connection with an offering of crypto-assets called Tomahawkcoins. As part of its bounty program, Tomahawk Exploration dedicated 200,000 Tomahawkcoins, and offered third-parties 4,000 Tomahawkcoins for activities such as making requests to list Tomahawkcoins on crypto-assets trading platforms, promoting Tomahawkcoins on blogs and other online forums, and creating professional images, videos or other promotional materials. Ultimately, Tomahawk airdropped more than 80,000 Tomahawkcoins to approximately 40

Secondly, the Court found that the crypto-asset being offered must, in and of itself, be a security. Merely being offered is insufficient for crypto-assets to pass the *Howey Test*. Two further findings of the Court make this case particularly interesting. The first relates to where the crypto-assets are bought. For an issuer to engage in securities transactions, it must be the direct beneficiary of the investment made in return for the crypto-assets. Crypto-assets purchased at a third-party location – on an exchange, for example – are not, in those particular transactions, securities, because the investment was not directly made to the

---

wallet holders as part of its bounty program. In the Tomahawk Order, the SEC found that Tomahawk's bounty program constituted an offer and sale of securities because *"[Tomahawk] provided Tomahawkcoins to investors in exchange for services designed to advance Tomahawk's economic interests and foster a trading market for its securities"*. Despite not receiving payment in exchange for the airdropped Tomahawkcoins, the SEC nonetheless found that the airdrops made in connection with the bounty program constituted the offer and sale of securities: *"a gift of a security is a sale within the meaning of the Securities Act when the donor receives some real benefit (...) Tomahawk received value in exchange for the bounty distributions, in the form of online marketing (...) in the creation of a public trading market for its securities"*. The Tomahawk Order is a new application of the principle that the issuance of free securities for some economic benefit would still constitute a sale of, or an offer to sell, securities. The SEC previously applied this principle in 1999, when it issued at least three No-Action Letters indicating its view that Internet stock giveaways would constitute unlawful sales of securities if not subject to a registration statement or a valid exemption from registration:
(i) In the Vanderkam & Sanders No-Action Letter, SEC No-Action Letter 1999 WL 38281 (Jan. 27, 1999), the SEC opined that *"the issuance of securities in consideration of a person's registration on or visit to an issuer's Internet site would be an event of sale"*. According to the No-Action Letter, such an issuance would violate Section 5 of the Securities Act unless it was the subject of a registration statement or a valid exemption from registration.
(ii) In the Simplystocks.com No-Action Letter, SEC No-Action Letter, 1999 WL 51836 (Feb. 4, 1999), Simplystocks proposed to distribute free stocks randomly to members of a pool of entrants who logged in to Simplystocks' website and provided their name, address, social security number, phone number and email address and chose a login name and password. Visitors would receive one entry into the stock pool for each day they logged in to the Simplystocks website. The SEC was of the opinion that the Simplystocks.com stock giveaway would be an event of sale within the meaning of Section 2(a)(3) of the Securities Act and must be the subject of a registration statement or a valid exemption from registration.
(iii) In the Andrew Jones and James Rutten No-Action Letter, SEC No-Action Letter, 1999 WL 377873 (Jun. 8, 1999), the SEC opined that the issuance of three free shares of common stock to the first one million people who register with the issuer to receive the shares, whether or not through the issuer's website, and the issuance of one additional share (up to a specified maximum) to each shareholder who referred others who also become a shareholder, was an event of sale within Section 2(a)(3) of the Securities Act. The SEC opined that such an issuance would be unlawful under Section 5 of the Securities Act unless registered or exempt from registration.
The SEC claimed, then, in a subsequent press release about different cases (see SEC, *SEC Brings First Actions To Halt Unregistered Online Offerings of So-Called "Free Stock"*, (July 22, 1999), available at: https://www.sec.gov/news/headlines/webstock.htm), *"free stock is really a misnomer in these cases. While cash did not change hands, the companies that issued the stock received valuable benefits. Under these circumstances, the securities laws entitle investors to full and fair disclosure, which they did not receive in these cases"*. The valuable benefits for these companies were *"a fledgling public market for their shares, increasing their business, creating publicity, increasing traffic to their websites, and, in two cases, generating possible interest in projected public offerings"*. The reason the valuable benefits to the company are mentioned is because Section 2(a)(3) of the Securities Act defines a "sale" to *"include every contract of sale or disposition of a security or interest in a security, for value"*.

issuer[194]. That ruling alone may change the ICO paradigm substantially. It is possible, for example, that an ICO issuer may release crypto-assets to an exchange and sell them via the market mechanism the exchange provides, and argue it has not engaged in securities offerings[195]. The Court also found that an investor had to rely on assertions made by the crypto-assets issuer. On February 13, 2019, however, the Court has revisited, in an interesting twist, its earlier decision. As part of the reconsideration, the Court said it was addressing the SEC's alternative theory that the promotional materials presented on Blockvest's website, the whitepaper posted online, and social media accounts concerning the offering constituted an offer of unregistered securities, in accordance to the Securities Act[196] and the *Howey Test*. In particular: (i) Blockvest's website and their whitepaper's invitation to potential investors to provide crypto-assets in return for Blockvest's crypto-assets ("**BLV**") satisfied the first "investment of money" prong; (ii) Blockvest's website promoted a "common enterprise" because Blockvest claimed that the funds raised would be pooled and there would be a profit sharing formula; (iii) as described on Blockvest's website and whitepaper, Blockvest's investors would be "passive" investors and the BLV would generate "passive income".

Another important precedent could be set by a potential enforcement action against Kik Interactive Inc. and the Kin Ecosystem Foundation ("**Kik**") over an alleged securities violation[197], if actually commenced by the SEC [198]. The Ontario, Canada-based social media giant, Kik, indeed, is

---

[194] This finding could be particularly significant for Initial Exchange Offerings.

[195] Even if the issuer held practically all of the crypto-assets on the exchange, it may be able to argue it is not offering securities, but trading crypto-assets (which just happen to be their own) on an exchange, and is not the direct beneficiary of the investments traders make in those crypto-assets. Anyway, Initial Exchange Offerings' nature and treatment are currently very controversial.

[196] The Securities Act defines "offer" to *"include every attempt or offer to dispose of, or solicitation of an offer to buy, a security or interest in a security for value"*. Defendants argued that an offer requires a *"manifestation of intent to be bound"*. That argument, however, is based on a contract law analysis, while, as the Court explained, under securities law the definition of "offer" is broad and there is no requirement that performance must be possible or that the issuer must be able to legally bind a purchaser. Thus, the Court concluded that the contents of Blockvest's website, the whitepaper and social media posts concerning the offering of BLV to the public at large constituted an offer of securities under the Securities Act.

[197] The SEC issued a Wells Notice on November 16, 2018, confirming that the Division of Enforcement made a preliminary determination to recommend that the SEC file an enforcement action for the violations of Sections 5(a) and 5(c) of the Securities Act and offering the recipient the opportunity to make a written or videotaped submission setting forth any reasons of law, policy, or fact why the proposed enforcement action should not be filed.

[198] The enforcement action against Kik – first recommended on November 16, 2018 – is yet to be authorized by the SEC's commissioners. In the United States, if the SEC deems that a securities infraction has occurred, it issues an enforcement action recommendation, as well as a letter to the company under scrutiny (known as a Wells Notice). The proposed action must subsequently be authorized in a vote by the agency's commissioners, and the company in question is given thirty days to issue its response and/or rebuttal in a "Wells Response" letter.

looking into challenging the SEC in court[199] over the expected enforcement action against the offer and sale of the digital currency "Kin" ("**Kin**"), which raised $100 million. In Kik's official Wells Submissions to the SEC[200], Kik argues – anticipating its defense strategy – that:

> (i) *"Through its enforcement efforts, it is the Commission that has stretched the definition of a "security" – and, in particular, the definition of an "investment contract" that the Supreme Court adopted over 70 years ago in SEC v. W.J. Howey Co., 328 U.S. 293, 301 (1946) – beyond its original meaning and intent. In other words, in its attempt to assert regulatory authority over effectively all digital currencies (other than Bitcoin and Ether, whose apparent exemption from scrutiny by the Enforcement Division cannot be reconciled with the Division's current approach), the Commission has strayed well beyond the scope of its statutory authority to regulate the offer and sale of securities. But the Commission's attempt to water down the Howey analysis to expand its regulatory authority will not stand up to meaningful judicial scrutiny. To see this, one need only compare the relatively superficial "investment contract" analysis set forth in the Commission's recent settlement orders in Airfox and Paragon Coin (as well as the Munchee settlement that preceded them) with the much more rigorous analysis that led a federal court to deny the Commission's motion for a preliminary injunction for failure to show that the defendant offered or promised an investment opportunity to token purchasers. See S.E.C. v. Blockvest, LLC, 2018 WL 6181408, at n. 5 (S.D. Cal. Nov. 27, 2018)"*[201].

---

[199] See P. Vigna, D. Michaels, *Are ICO Tokens Securities? Startup Wants a Judge to Decide*, The Wall Street Journal (Jan 27, 2019), available at: https://www.wsj.com/articles/are-ico-tokens-securities-startup-wants-a-judge-to-decide-11548604800.

[200] See SEC's wells notice to Kik Interactive Inc. and the Kin Ecosystem Foundation (Nov. 16, 2018) and their response (Dec. 10, 2018), available at http://kinecosystem.org/wells_response.pdf.

[201] Similar argument at page 16: *"As an initial matter, it is worth emphasizing that the Commission's regulatory authority is not unlimited, but rather is bounded by the statutes that the Commission is charged with enforcing. Ernst & Ernst v. Hochfelder, 425 U.S. 185, 213 (1976). Moreover, the Commission may not unilaterally define, much less expand, the scope of its statutory authority. Business Roundtable v. S.E.C., 905 F.2d 406, 408 (D.C. Cir. 1990). Rather, the statues that define the scope of the Commission's authority are to be interpreted by the courts. To date, the Commission's attempt to regulate cryptocurrencies under the rubric of "investment contracts" has faced only limited judicial scrutiny. There have been a handful of preliminary decisions, all of which involved allegations of fraud, unlike this case. See, e.g., S.E.C. v. PlexCorps, 2017 WL 6398722, at *2 (E.D.N.Y. Dec. 14, 2017); U.S. v. Zaslaviskiy, 2018 WL 4346339, at *1–9 (E.D.N.Y. Sept. 11, 2018); but see Blockvest, 2018 WL 6181408, at *4 (denying preliminary injunction and holding that "[b]ecause they [i.e., the tokens] are not securities, Plaintiff's causes of action fail"). Beyond that, the Commission has issued a number of unilateral statements purporting to define the scope of its authority, and has gotten a handful of small companies to agree to settled cease-and-desist orders that reflect a similar approach." In all of these efforts, the Commission has relied on a superficial application of the Supreme Court's decision in Howey, one that would effectively expand the scope of the Commission's authority in this area beyond*

(ii) *"Kin was designed, marketed, and offered as a currency to be used as a medium of exchange within a new digital economy. This takes it outside the statutory definition of a "security" under the federal securities laws, and gives it a consumptive use[202] that is inconsistent with an investment purpose. Simply put, Kik did not offer or promote Kin as a passive investment opportunity. Doing so would have doomed the project, which could only succeed if Kin purchasers used Kin as a medium of exchange (rather than simply*

---

*its statutory limits. Indeed, in one recent case where the court applied a more rigorous application of the Howey test, the court flatly rejected the Commission's claim that a sale of a cryptocurrency amounted to an "investment contract." See Blockvest, 2018 WL 6181408, at *4"*.

[202] Although no one of the following characteristics of use or consumption is necessarily determinative, the stronger their presence, the less likely the *Howey test* is met:
(i) The distributed ledger network and crypto-asset are fully developed and operational.
(ii) Holders of the crypto-asset are immediately able to use it for its intended functionality on the network, particularly where there are built-in incentives to encourage such use.
(iii) The crypto-assets' creation and structure is designed and implemented to meet the needs of its users, rather than to feed speculation as to its value or development of its network. For example, the crypto-asset can only be used on the network and generally can be held or transferred only in amounts that correspond to a purchaser's expected use.
(iv) Prospects for appreciation in the value of the crypto-asset are limited. For example, the design of the crypto-asset provides that its value will remain constant or even degrade over time, and, therefore, a reasonable purchaser would not be expected to hold the crypto-asset for extended periods as an investment.
(v) With respect to a crypto-asset referred to as a virtual currency, it can immediately be used to make payments in a wide variety of contexts, or acts as a substitute for real (or fiat) currency.
   (vi)(i) This means that it is possible to pay for goods or services with the crypto-asset without first having to convert it to another crypto-asset or real currency.
   (vi)(ii) If it is characterized as a virtual currency, the crypto-asset actually operates as a store of value that can be saved, retrieved, and exchanged for something of value at a later time.
(vi) With respect to a crypto-asset that represents rights to a good or service, it currently can be redeemed within a developed network or platform to acquire or otherwise use those goods or services. Relevant factors may include:
   (a) There is a correlation between the purchase price of the crypto-asset and a market price of the particular good or service for which it may be redeemed or exchanged.
   (b) The crypto-asset is available in increments that correlate with a consumptive intent versus an investment or speculative purpose.
   (c) An intent to consume the crypto-asset may also be more evident if the good or service underlying the crypto-asset can only be acquired, or more efficiently acquired, through the use of the crypto-asset on the network.
(vii) Any economic benefit that may be derived from appreciation in the value of the crypto-asset is incidental to obtaining the right to use it for its intended functionality.
(viii) The crypto-asset is marketed in a manner that emphasizes the functionality of the crypto-asset, and not the potential for the increase in market value of the crypto-asset.
(ix) Potential purchasers have the ability to use the network and use (or have used) the crypto-asset for its intended functionality.
(x) Restrictions on the transferability of the crypto-asset are consistent with the asset's use and not facilitating a speculative market.
(xi) If the promoter facilitates the creation of a secondary market, transfers of the crypto-asset may only be made by and among users of the platform.
See on the point, in particular, SEC, *Framework for "Investment Contract" Analysis of Digital Assets*, (April 3, 2019), available at: https://www.sec.gov/corpfin/framework-investment-contract-analysis-digital-assets.

holding it as a passive investment). Accordingly, Kik marketed Kin, not as an investment opportunity, but rather as a way to participate in a fundamentally new way for consumers to access digital products and services, and for innovative developers, and their users, to be compensated for the value they provide. Consistent with Kik's stated vision, Kin has been adopted, integrated, and used within over 30 digital applications. (...) The terms of the sale itself, moreover, are flatly inconsistent with an "investment contract": in the sale, Kik transferred ownership of the Kin tokens to purchasers, who had full control over their tokens once received, and Kik did not assume any ongoing obligations to Kin purchasers. As such, the offer and sale once delivered of Kin tokens did not involve or create any common enterprise between Kin purchasers and either Kik or the Kin Foundation. In sum, the offer and sale of Kin did not involve the type of passive investment opportunity that the term "investment contract" was intended to cover, and does not meet the definition that the Supreme Court adopted in Howey".

(iii) *"At all times, Kik made clear that, in the Kin ecosystem, Kik messenger would be "just one of thousands of services in the Kin ecosystem". (...) Indeed, in this new digital economy, Kik would serve as a "participant rather than a landlord". (...) This meant that, for the Kin ecosystem to grow, many developers other than Kik would have to join the ecosystem by offering products and services in exchange for Kin".*

(iv) *To implement its vision, Kik planned to sell Kin through (1) a pre-sale to accredited participants under Regulation D and (2) the TDE to the public. In the pre-sale, participants agreed to a Simple Agreement for Future Tokens ("SAFT") where they received the right to receive Kin at a discount, if and when there was a "Network Launch," meaning when Kik sold Kin to the public. (...) In consideration of various factors distinguishing the pre-sale from the TDE, Kik decided to structure the pre-sale as an exempt offering under Regulation D. Kik retained a third-party vendor to conduct diligence to ensure that each of the roughly 50 pre-sale participants were accredited. Kik filed its Form D with the SEC on September 11, 2017. (...) By the time of the TDE, Kik did not need additional cash to sustain its business. It sold Kin to the public, not because it needed the money, but rather to allow for an immediate and broad community centered around Kin, in line with its vision. Broad adoption and contribution by consumers and developers would foster a "virtuous cycle in which the ecosystem grows in both size and quality". (...) Indeed, with the understanding that the project would only succeed if Kin* purchasers actually used the token as a medium of exchange, Kik structured the TDE to encourage broad participation and to discourage speculation. To that end, Kik capped the amount of tokens a participant could purchase, meaning that within the first 24 hours, purchasers could only buy up to approximately $4,400 worth of Kin to "ensure all registered participants had a fair chance to purchase," and participate within the ecosystem. The cap worked to prevent small numbers of large purchasers from monopolizing allocations to the exclusion of others who were interested in using Kin and developing on the platform. And, unlike the vast majority of other token sales at around this time, Kik required no minimum purchase amount, meaning that a participant could pay $1 and receive Kin. (...) In fact, around 50% of participants purchased $1,000 or less worth of Kin – amounts that are simply inconsistent with an investment purpose. Further, and in accordance with its treatment of Kin as a currency, Kik required participants to pass rigorous KYC, AML, and OFAC screening, by submitting personal information, such as government issued photo identification, passport photos, addresses, and a self-portrait to verify their identities".

(v) Courts have long recognized that the definition of a "security" under the Securities Act and the Exchange Act are "virtually identical". See, e.g., Reves v. Ernst & Young, 494 U.S. 56, 61 (1990); see also Great Rivers Co-op. of Southeastern Iowa v. Farmland Indus., Inc., 198 F.3d 685, 698 (8th Cir. 1999). In that regard, the definition of "security" in the Securities Act does not include the term "currency" (15 U.S.C. § 77b(a)(1)), and the Exchange Act expressly excludes "currency" from the definition of a "security." See 15 U.S.C. § 78c(a)(10) ("The term 'security' means (...) but shall not include currency." (emphasis added)). "Currency" is not defined under the federal securities laws, but the term has long been understood to mean a store of value or a "medium of exchange." (See Black's Law Dictionary (an item that circulates "as a medium of exchange")). On that point, cryptocurrencies can be used for peer-to-peer transactions, are convertible to other currencies, including Kin, and have been widely accepted by digital applications and retailers. (See Merriam Webster (cryptocurrency is "any form of currency that only exists digitally, that usually has no central issuing or regulating authority but instead uses a decentralized system to record transactions and manage the issuance of new units")). Further, for purposes of the federal securities laws, "currency" need not be legal tender, or recognized by the United States or any other foreign country. See generally Sea Pines of Va., Inc. v. PLD, Ltd., 399 F. Supp. 708, 711–12 (M.D. Fla. 1975) (promissory note, as a "cash substitute", was "within the exclusion for currency", and therefore not a security). In any event, courts and federal agencies have repeatedly characterized cryptocurrencies as "currencies". Earlier this year a federal court explained that "[v]irtual currencies are generally defined as "digital assets used as a medium of exchange". Commodity Futures Trading Comm'n v. McDonnell, 287 F. Supp. 3d 213, 218 (E.D.N.Y. 2018); see also Commodity Futures Trading Comm'n v. My Big Coin Pay, Inc. et al, 2018 WL 4621727, at *5 (D. Mass. Sept. 26, 2018) (Memorandum of Decision) (quoting In re BFXNA Inc., CFTC Docket 16–19, at 5–6 (June 2, 2016)) ("[V]irtual currencies are (...) properly defined as commodities"). This interpretation is consistent with enforcement actions and guidance issued by the United States Financial Crimes Network ("FinCEN"), the Internal Revenue Service ("IRS"), and OFAC, which describe virtual currencies as "a medium of exchange, a unit of account, and/or a store of value". (...) Kin possesses all the characteristics of a currency like Bitcoin and Ether (which Director Hinman acknowledges are not securities). They are blockchain-based tokens that serve as a medium of exchange".

(vi) *Sales of Kin, whether in the pre-sale, the TDE, or after the TDE, do not constitute "investment contracts" because no common enterprise exists between Kik and/or the Kin Foundation, on the one hand, and Kin purchasers, on the other hand.* As an initial matter, the Staff has taken the remarkable position that Howey test does not require proof of a "common enterprise", which would surely come as a surprise to the Supreme Court and the Circuit Courts of Appeal that have uniformly held that it does. See e.g., United Housing Found., Inc. v. Forman, 421 U.S. 837, 852 (1975) ("The touchstone [of an investment contract] is the presence of an investment in a common venture premised on a reasonable expectation of profit to be derived from the entrepreneurial or managerial efforts of others" (emphasis added)); see also Milnarik v. M-S Commodities, Inc., 457 F.2d 274, 276 (7th Cir.1972) (judicial analyses of the question whether particular investment contracts are "securities" within the statutory definition have repeatedly stressed the significance of finding a common enterprise" (emphasis added)). More recently, the Staff has equivocated on this question. (See Dec. 4, 2018 Letter from B. Mitchell). But in any event, to date, the Staff has never actually identified or described any specific "common enterprise" between owners of Kin and either Kik or the Kin Foundation. This stands in stark contrast with the many cases finding "investment contracts" under the Howey framework, which uniformly involve some kind of identifiable entity or business venture – things like the management of the orange grove in Howey".

(vii) *Moreover, the Commission will be unable to show that purchasers expected to profit from the entrepreneurial or managerial efforts of Kik or the Kin Foundation. In applying Howey, courts center their analysis on what was "offered or promised" to potential purchasers to determine whether the promoter held out an investment opportunity. See Blockvest, 2018 WL 6181408, at *6. Indeed, determining whether there was a reasonable expectation of profits hinges on "an objective inquiry into the character of the instrument or transaction offered based on what the purchasers were "led to expect". See Warfield, 569 F.3d at 1021 (quoting Howey, 328 U.S. at 298–99). For example, there is no expectation of profits where purchasers are primarily led to expect an item for use or consumption, even in the future. Forman, 421 U.S. at 852–53. Nor is there a reasonable expectation of profits merely because the promoter mentions that an item could increase in value or that the purchaser could profit. See Alunni, 445 F. App'x at 292 (no investment contract in purchase of condominiums where promotional materials stated that purchasers would receive immediate income and did not have to manage their units); Revak v. SEC Realty Corp., 18 F.3d 81, 84 (2d Cir. 1994) (no investment contract where condominiums were marketed for "the income to be derived from rentals, and the prospect of capital appreciation"); Hart, 735 F.2d at 1003 (no investment contract for model home purchases where promotional materials touted "the potential for excellent appreciation in value during the holding period"). But even if purchasers reasonably expect profits, such expectation must be based on the "undeniably significant" entrepreneurial or managerial efforts of the promoter. S.E.C. v. Glenn W. Turner Enters., Inc., 474 F.2d 476, 482 (9th Cir. 1973). These efforts must be value generating, which excludes foundational efforts, such as building infrastructure. See, e.g., Terracor, 574 F.2d at 1025. And profits from resale on the secondary market based on market forces similarly falls outside the scope of Howey. Importantly, if the purchaser has complete control over the item or interest purchased, he or she does not expect profits from the efforts of others. See Alunni, 445 F. App'x 288".*

(viii) *In any event, to the extent that any TDE participants expected to profit from their purchases of Kin, the Commission will be unable to show that they expected to profit from the "undeniably significant" entrepreneurial or managerial efforts of either Kik or the Kin Foundation, as required under Howey and its progeny. Glenn W. Turner, 474 F.2d at 482. As an initial matter, courts have held that where a contract involves a sale of a commodity and expected profits arise primarily from resale on the secondary market, the final prong of Howey is not satisfied. See Noa v. Key Futures, Inc., 638 F.2d 77, 79 (9th Cir. 1980) (no expectation of profits from the efforts of others under Howey because, once the commodity was purchased, the profits of the investor depended on market fluctuations, not the managerial efforts of the defendant); see also S.E.C. v. Belmont Reid & Co., Inc., 794 F.2d 1388, 1391 (9th Cir. 1986) (same). As in Noa and Belmont Reid, any fluctuation of Kin's value is a consequence of market forces, as opposed to any entrepreneurial or managerial efforts of Kik or the Kin Foundation, as required under Howey. The Second Circuit's decision in Gary Plastic Packaging Corp. v. Merrill Lynch, Pierce, Fenner & Smith, Inc., 756 F.2d 230, 241 (2d Cir. 1985), does not change this analysis. In Gary Plastic, the Second Circuit found that investors in certificates of deposit (which were established investment vehicles) expected profits from Merrill Lynch's efforts because the bank had promised to create and operate a secondary market for the certificates, and agreed to re-purchase the certificates if interest rates decreased. As such, purchasers "bought an opportunity to participate in the CD Program and its secondary market. And, they are paying for the security of knowing that they may liquidate at a moment's notice free from concern as to loss of income or capital, while waiting for FDIC or FSLIC insurance proceeds". Id. Unlike Merrill Lynch, in Gary Plastic, neither Kik nor the Kin Foundation has guaranteed liquidity for Kin purchasers, nor have they promised to create and operate an exchange or to re-purchase Kin. Indeed, when asked about exchange trading, Kik noted that it "[was] up to the exchanges" (...). Under those facts, there is no expectation of profits from the essential "managerial or entrepreneurial efforts" of either Kik or the Foundation".*

If the SEC pursues its enforcement action against Kik, the case is likely to culminate in a civil court case and can potentially set an important precedent for the question of whether ICO sales are unquestionably to be regulated as securities offerings in the US.

Anyway, crypto-assets resembling securities may not be lawfully sold without SEC registration or an exemption therefrom, such as under Regulation D or Regulation S. Indeed, crypto-assets to be qualified as securities do not necessarily mean that the ICO must be done on a registered basis. An ICO that is a security can be structured so that it qualifies for an applicable exemption from registration. On the contrary, the public offering of crypto-assets that qualify as securities needs a registration statement and a SEC-approved prospectus to comply with US securities laws.

On March 6, 2018, Judge Jack Weinstein of the US District Court for the Eastern of New York ruled[203] that crypto-assets are commodities under the Commodity Exchange Act ("**CEA**")[204] and therefore subject to the Commodity Futures Trading Commission's ("**CFTC**") anti-fraud and anti-manipulation enforcement authority [205]. This was not surprising since the CFTC has openly defined virtual currencies as commodities for federal regulatory purposes as far back as 2015. Indeed, in October 2017, the CFTC indicated that there is no inconsistency between the SEC's analysis that ICO-issued crypto-assets may be securities and the CFTC's determination that crypto-assets may be commodities or derivatives contracts depending on the particular facts and circumstances[206].

More surprising was the unofficial statement from the FinCEN that indicated that it regards developers as well as exchanges of ICO coins or tokens as "money transmitters" for the purposes of the US Bank Secrecy Act[207]. As such, they would be required to register with FinCEN, collect

---

[203] *Commodity Futures Trading Commission v. McDonnell*, No. 1:18-cv-00361-JBW-RLM, slip op. (E.D.N.Y. March 6, 2018).

[204] See K. Tucker, *Federal Judge Opens the Door to CFTC to Regulate Virtual Currency*, New York Law Journal (March 6, 2018), available at: https://www.law.com/newyorklawjournal/2018/03/06/federal-judge-opens-the-door-to-cftc-to-regulate-virtual-currency/.

[205] The CFTC alleged that the defendants violated the CEA by operating a fraudulent scheme involving virtual currency trading and misappropriating investor funds. The primary issue before the court was whether the CFTC had standing to sue the defendants under the CEA. To resolve that issue, the court had to determine whether (1) virtual currency may be regulated by the CFTC as a commodity and (2) the CEA permits the CFTC to exercise jurisdiction over fraud in connection with commodities that do not directly involve futures or derivative contracts. The court answered both questions in the affirmative and held that the CFTC can pursue fraud and manipulation claims in virtual currency spot markets. First, the court found that the term "commodity" encompasses virtual currency "both in economic function and in the language of the statute". According to the court, virtual currencies are "'goods' exchanged in a market for a uniform quality and value." As such, the court reasoned that they "fall well-within" the common definition of commodity as well as the CEA's broad definition of commodity, which includes *"all other goods and articles (...) and all services, rights, and interests (...) in which contracts for future delivery are presently or in the future dealt in"*. Second, the court held that the CEA grants the CFTC enforcement authority over fraud or manipulation in both derivatives markets and underlying spot markets. In so ruling, the court nonetheless recognized a significant distinction regarding the CFTC's regulatory authority over derivatives markets on the one hand and over cash or spot transactions on the other. Unlike the full regulatory authority the CFTC exercises over the derivative markets, the court explained that the CFTC's authority over the spot markets extended only to *"manipulation or fraud"*. For the CFTC's limited spot market authority, the court pointed to the CEA's anti-manipulation and fraud provisions under Section 6(c) and CFTC regulations implementing those provisions that prohibit employing a fraudulent scheme *"in connection with (...) a contract of sale of any commodity in interstate commerce"*.

[206] See CFTC, *A CFTC Primer on Virtual Currencies*, (October 17, 2017), available at: https://www.cftc.gov/sites/default/files/idc/groups/public/documents/file/labcftc_primercurrencies100417.pdf.

[207] See R. Kim, *FinCEN's ICO Letter: Not FinCEN's, Not ICO Focused, and Not Surprising*, Bloomberg (April 6, 2018), available at: https://www.bna.com/fincens-ico-letter-n57982090869/.

information about their customers and take steps to combat money laundering and terrorist financing.

The combined result is that ICOs can potentially fall within at three regulatory buckets and the jurisdiction of at least three federal regulators in the US, namely: the SEC – on the basis that crypto-assets may be securities[208]; the CTFC – on the basis that crypto-assets may be commodities; and FinCEN and the Bank Secrecy Act – on the basis that crypto-assets may be money.

1.2 *The Simple Agreement for Future Tokens.* On October 2, 2017, Protocol Labs and Cooley LLP released a whitepaper ("**Whitepaper**") entitled *"The SAFT Project: Toward a Compliant Token Sale Framework"*[209], proposing an attractive path toward a new framework that supposedly is consistent with US securities laws[210] – called the Simple Agreement for Future Tokens

---

[208] In September 29, 2018 a group of U.S. lawmakers, *"concerned about the use of enforcement actions alone to clarify policy"*, asked the SEC to:
(i) clarify how it is approaching crypto-assets sales, saying that current uncertainty surrounding the treatment of offers and sales of crypto-assets is hindering innovation in the United States and will ultimately drive business elsewhere;
(ii) clarify when crypto-assets sales should be classified as investment contracts, whether a token sold as a security can later become a non-security;
(iii) say what tools are available for the SEC to offer more concrete guidance to innovators SEC chairman Jay Clayton to clarify when ICOs are considered securities sales.
The aim to protect the US economy from over-regulation and ensure the country's leading role in the crypto sector culminated in late December 2018 in the "Token Taxonomy Act" by US Congressmen Warren Davidson and Darren Soto. The proposed law defines a "digital token" and clarifies that securities laws would not apply to crypto-assets once they become a fully functioning network.
Although it is a reasonable assumption that the strict SEC enforcement policies are the major driver for token issuers leaving the US market (see D.A. Zetzsche, R.P. Buckley, D.W. Arner, L. Fôhr, *The ICO Gold Rush: It's a scam, It's a bubble, It's a super challenge for regulators*, European Banking Institute Working Paper Series 2018 – NO. 18 (2018)), it is our view that the SEC approach to ICOs is sensible. Its strict application of established case law to ICOs might be unpopular amongst issuers, but it is logical and provides a high level of investor protection. Lowering the regulatory standards for token sales could lead to a "race to the bottom", with potentially severe consequences for the stability of the financial markets. Actually, the SEC faces significant pressure to promote entrepreneurship in a context in which it must weigh competing policy goals – protecting investors while promoting capital raising. Soon after he initially condemned ICOs as frauds, SEC Chairman Clayton suggested that rules governing private funding by entrepreneurs are too burdensome (See D. Michaels, *SEC Chairman Wants to Let More Main Street Investors in on Private Deals*, The Wall Street Journal (Oct. 7, 2018), available at: https://www.wsj.com/articles/sec-chairman-wants-to-let-more-main-street-investors-in-on-private-deals-1535648208). The SEC is considering whether to liberalize such rules, in part so that retail investors can potentially invest at an early stage in the next Facebook or Google.
[209] See J. B. Benet, M. Santori, J. Clayburgh, *The SAFT Project: Toward a Compliant Sale Framework*, (October 2, 2017), available at: http://www.saftproject.com/static/SAFT-Project-Whitepaper.pdf.
[210] The Whitepaper acknowledged that the framework has limitations, and invited a conversation within the blockchain and legal community. In accordance to that invitation, together with the publication of the Whitepaper, they launched the SAFT Project – a forum for discussion and development of the SAFT framework – available at: www.saftproject.com.

("**SAFT**")[211] – for engaging in ICOs. The goal of the SAFT is to obtain certain advantages related to securities, money services, and tax laws for ICOs that would otherwise involve "pre-functional utility tokens"[212].

The SAFT is an investment contract and demands compliance with the securities laws. It is, indeed, nothing else that a window-dressed Regulation D. Therefore, the harsh reality is that the SAFT introduces regulatory limitations that are contrary to the spirit of ICOs: the offering of free-trading instruments open to all investors. Securities offered in a Regulation D offering are, indeed, illiquid, restricted, and not freely tradeable until exempt or registered in a subsequent registration statement (which requires full public disclosure of all material information). Only accredited investors can participate in a SAFT offering.

A SAFT contemplates an initial sale of a SAFT by founders to accredited investors, who are obligated to immediately fund the project. These founders use, then, the funds to develop a functional network, with crypto-assets with real intrinsic usage, and then deliver those crypto-assets to the investors once functional[213]. The investors may then resell the crypto-assets, presumably for a profit, and so may the founders.

By and large, existing laws do not appear to allow SAFTs, or their later-issued crypto-assets with real intrinsic usage, to escape regulation as securities or compliance with the securities laws. Artificially bifurcating the overall investment scheme into multiple events does not change the underlying investment purpose[214]. The rights to purchase crypto-assets derived from any SAFT offering are derivative securities, subject to the same limitations that apply to the SAFT itself.

The Whitepaper seemingly advances an approach that[215]:

---

[211] The Whitepaper basically proposes a modification of the existing SAFE framework – a convertible note alternative in securities-based crowdfunding – for ICOs, in effect repackaging the SAFE funding mechanism to define crypto-assets as utilities rather than securities.

[212] As discussed, a "utility token" is a token purchased not for investment purposes but primarily to use or consume a good or service for which the token can be exchanged. A "pre-functional utility token", instead, is a token that lacks utility when it is sold, but will become useful (that is, exchangeable for some good or service) at some later date, perhaps after the construction of a platform or products on which the tokens will be used. A "functional utility token," by contrast, is a utility token that is useful when it is delivered to purchasers.

[213] The basic goal of the SAFT vis-à-vis securities laws is to allow companies to raise money through a token offering for the development of a platform or service that is not yet fully functional, but without offering "pre-functional utility tokens" (which are arguably more likely than "functional utility tokens" to qualify as "securities").

[214] Also, the premise on which the SAFT concept relies – that the timing of a token creator's efforts makes a difference in assessing the "efforts of others" element of the Howey test – lacks meaningful support in the case law.

[215] As highlighted by the Cardozo Blockchain Project 's research report #1 (Nov. 21, 2017), *Not so fast—risks related to the use of a "saft" for token sales* made by Cardozo Law School in New York,

(i) obscures the test of how crypto-assets are assessed under US securities law, in contravention of underlying principles and established precedent, which are highly dependent on the relevant facts and circumstances[216];

(ii) increases the risk that crypto-assets underlying a SAFT are deemed securities[217], because of the emphasis of both the crypto-asset's profit-generating potential and the vague notions of "functionality" as a wall against securities laws implications;

(iii) could result in institutional and sophisticated investors playing an unnecessarily prominent role in the development of the next generation of global technology platforms and potentially could exacerbate speculation.

It has to be noted, in addition, that the SAFT is not a one-size-fits-all solution. If, for example, the network / platform is already functional or the company already has the financial resources to complete the development of the network / capital without, the SAFT does not improve the company's regulatory position. In those cases, numerous arguments in defense of a public sale of crypto-assets exist regardless of whether the company used a SAFT. Furthermore, the SAFT is not useful to crypto-assets that are themselves securities.

Courts and the SEC[218] have not evaluated whether the SAFT framework in fact achieves its intended goal of avoiding regulation under the securities laws. Moreover, in February 2018, the Wall Street Journal reported that the SEC had issued subpoenas and information requests to a number of token issuers, including issuers who have relied upon the SAFT framework.[219] Some commentators, however, have argued that William Hinman's[220] speech[221] may have important implications for the viability of the SAFT. After the speech, one of the SAFT's developers argued that Hinman's emphasis on a network's "decentralization" is similar to the concept of "functional" utility tokens on which the Whitepaper relied, because Hinman had explained that a network is "decentralized" when purchasers no longer expect a third party to carry out essential managerial efforts to support its value[222]. Notably, the

---

available at: https://cardozo.yu.edu/sites/default/files/Cardozo%20Blockchain%20Project%20-%20Not%20So%20Fast%20-%20SAFT%20Response_final.pdf.

[216] The *Howey test*, indeed, is not a black-and-white metric and it is a highly variable facts and circumstances test.
[217] Subjecting the issuer to significant legal or economic risks.
[218] And other non-US financial market authorities.
[219] See J. Eaglesham and P. Vigna, *Cryptocurrency Firms Targeted in SEC Probe*, The Wall Street Journal (Feb. 28, 2018), available at: https://www.wsj.com/articles/sec-launches-cryptocurrency-probe-1519856266.
[220] SEC's Director of the Division of Corporation Finance.
[221] See note 156.
[222] See M. Santori (@msantoriESQ), June 14, 2018, 10:55 am, tweet, https://twitter.com/msantoriESQ/status/1007320533397069825.

text of Hinman's speech contains a footnote indicating that because the *Howey test* depends upon the facts and circumstances of individual offerings, "nothing in" the speech was "meant to opine on the legality or appropriateness of a SAFT"[223]. Accordingly, while Hinman's views are certainly relevant in assessing the viability of the SAFT, any firm legal conclusions about that framework remain premature.

Lastly, despite its actual global use[224], the SAFT framework could be not useful, or it could increase the risk that the underlying crypto-assets are deemed securities, with regard to crypto finance transactions subject to jurisdictions different from the US[225].

1.3 *A corporate crypto conduct code for ICOs*. As noted, decisions and regulations made by the SEC tend to have global knock-on effects[226], as the financial regulators of the most important jurisdictions often imitate US regulations. This effect is stronger in relation to ICOs. Hence, it is highly recommended that ICOs, regardless of the jurisdiction of incorporation of the entity generating or offering the crypto-assets, disclose a condensed version of the SEC form to potential investors, even if (and especially when) not required to comply with SEC or local securities regulations. The disclosure should cover details such as the nature of the business, properties, contributors or founders, budgets, plans for distribution and running of the ICO, and governance details (bylaws, disclosure to auditors, etc.). The issuers should also state clearly that no-one of the key people has experienced disqualifying events, such as being convicted of, or subject to court or administrative sanctions for security, financial and white-collar frauds and crimes.

Typically, companies seeking to raise money are subject to securities laws. In the US, the Securities Act requires all offers and sales of security financial instruments to be registered unless an exemption from registration is available. If no such exemption exists, private companies planning to offer stock to the public must first comply with the IPO requirements set forth by the SEC. In 2015, the SEC adopted Regulation Crowdfunding, an exemption from registration for certain crowdfunding transactions. Crowdfunding focuses on the size and number of investors who back a project, allowing for the use of small amounts of capital from a large number

---

[223] See W. Hinman, *Digital Asset Transactions: When Howey Met Gary (Plastic)*, Remarks at the Yahoo Finance All Markets Summit: Crypto (June 14, 2018), available at: https://www.sec.gov/news/speech/speech-hinman-061418.
[224] The SAFT became a *de facto* standard worldwide.
[225] The SAFT framework has been developed focusing on the US laws only.
[226] SEC jurisdiction actually goes far beyond US borders, impacting investment opportunities purveyed from anywhere at any time. US federal securities laws are oddly idiosyncratic and drafted as laws of inclusion, rather than exclusion. In other words, the US federal securities laws boldly apply to everyone in the world, with exceptions being available to the extent the person or organization in question does not actually transact in the US or with US persons or companies.

of individuals to finance a new business venture. In order to fall under this exemption, a company issuing securities must have a maximum offering amount of $1 million and cap individual contributions based on his/her net worth or annual income. This regulatory structure allows for small businesses and startups to raise funds for their new innovations, while still protecting investors from unethical or illegal practices.

For private companies looking to register an IPO, the SEC requires: (i) a description of the company's business, properties, and competition; (ii) a description of the risks of investing in the company; (iii) a discussion and analysis of the company's financial results and financial condition as seen through the eyes of management; (iv) the identity of the company's officers and directors and their compensation; (v) a description of material transactions between the company and its officers, directors, and significant shareholders; (vi) a description of material legal proceedings involving the company and its officers and directors; (vii) a description of the company's material contracts; (viii) a description of the securities being offered; (ix) the plan for distributing the securities; (x) the intended use of the proceeds of the offering; (xi) important facts about its business operations, financial condition, results of operations, risk factors, and management; (xii) audited financial statements; (xiii) copies of material contracts.

For crowdfunding falling under the Regulation Crowdfunding, the SEC requires: (i) information about officers, directors, and owners of 20 percent or more of the issuer; (ii) a description of the issuer's business and the use of proceeds from the offering; (iii) the price to the public of the securities or the method for determining the price; (iv) the target offering amount and the deadline to reach the target offering amount; (v) whether the issuer will accept investments in excess of the target offering amount; (vi) certain related-party transactions; (vii) a discussion of the issuer's financial condition and financial statements.

A reasonable balance that provides investors with necessary disclosure while not placing excessive burdens on smaller ICO issuers seeking to innovate could be something in the middle. Therefore, a good whitepaper should be very clear and structured as follow: (i) a description of the entity's business, properties, and competition; (ii) a description of the corporate structure (e.g. separation between ICO issuing entity and OpCo? Foundation or corporation?) and the reasons behind the adoption of the jurisdiction(s); (iii) a description of the risks of investing in the project; (iv) the identity of the entity's key people and management; (v) the statement that no-one of the key people has experienced disqualifying events; (vi) a description of legal proceedings involving the entity and its key people; (vii) a description of the crypto-assets being offered; (viii) a description of the insider trading policy; (ix) the plan for distributing the crypto-assets; (x) the intended use and handling of the proceeds of the offering and the purchaser's return on investment.

At the same time ICO issuers should avoid complex (and sometimes shady) corporate structures, as they should avoid the jurisdiction shopping. We underline that ICO issuers must comply with the laws of each jurisdiction within which the crypto-assets could be considered to be offered or sold, or in which a regulated activity may be deemed to be carried out, in addition to the laws of the jurisdiction in which the entity issuing or generating the crypto-assets is incorporated or established. Therefore, except in case of effective grounds, visiting the Swiss city of Zug to set up a foundation, create a Gibraltar corporation to benefit from attracting local rules and adopt the jurisdiction of Cayman Islands and other smaller nations who are trying to attract the best companies while promising amazing tax benefits or whatever they can come up with, not only is a nonsolution that makes all the project opaque and adds an additional layer of uncertainty, but probably is also going to be viewed as sketchy by investors.

Currently, the regulatory environment is uncertain internationally, with regulators still assessing how to regulate ICOs. Some of the highlighted points likely conflict with the promise of decentralization and anonymity in blockchain, and will require discretional judgement on a case-by-case basis. Nevertheless, there are good reasons why similar measures have arisen in the wider corporate world over time – to ensure a sustainable ecosystem with resources directed at better quality projects, to ensure that bad actors are (to the extent possible) contained, and to ensure that legal and professional risks are mitigated by a better balance between the interests of all stakeholders. Hence, we believe that adopting in the meantime as form of self-regulation the approach above when ICO issuers are not clearly required to comply with securities regulations (for example in case of non-speculative crypto-assets with real intrinsic usage) could help to mitigate commercial and legal risks for both crypto-assets issuers and purchasers. For the wider industry, it is vital to put pressure on ICO issuers to adopt these disclosure standards and code of conduct, and ensure bad players and fraudulent practices are publicly identified end exposed (ideally before they create any harm). Unfortunately, the blockchain industry and its gatekeepers have largely failed to police against bad actors (without the intervention of regulators). The fundamental idea underpinning blockchain technology – replacing a trusted third party with a consensus based on cryptographic proof – has not yet fully come to fruition in real world applications. Disparity in information and technological sophistication make it difficult to achieve true decentralization. These factors also contribute to a high possibility of fraud and other bad acts on the part of promoters and operators of platforms. Lastly, ICO issuers should implement new model of crypto-assets holder engagement under which companies will engage in a year-long discussion with their crypto-assets holders on how to create long-term value, and embrace not only a path to financial performance, but also a positive (real) contribution to society[227].

1.4 *Initial Exchange Offerings*. IEOs basically are ICOs launched through the IEO platform (dubbed "launchpad") of a crypto-assets exchange[228]. IEOs are based on agreements between project developers and crypto-assets exchanges for initial placement of the crypto-assets on the exchange[229]. Crypto-assets exchanges serve as underwriters, review the projects and offer crypto-assets to vetted customers[230]. IEOs bring on the table: (i) easy access to a large potential purchaser base; (ii) help with crypto-assets distribution; (iii) a marketing boost from being promoted on the exchange's social media; (iv) an immediate listing on the crypto-assets exchange post-IEO[231]. From the perspective of a purchaser, instead of sending Ether, Bitcoin or other crypto-assets to a smart contract governing the ICO, each IEO participant has to create an account with the crypto-assets exchange and send Ether, Bitcoin or other crypto-assets to this account. When the IEO starts, the participant can purchase the launched crypto-asset directly from the exchange. IEOs have potentially some advantages, including: (i) preventing a "gas war" between sale participants, assuming the crypto-assets exchange is not decentralized[232]; (ii) eliminating scam and dubious projects from raising funds[233]. IEOs has not yet caught the attention of regulators and financial market authorities. Potentially, some of the characteristics of IEOs could lead them to fall squarely within the category of an investment contract (and therefore within the securities perimeter)[234]. By and large, existing laws do

---

[227] Academic research shows that more ethical companies have better financial performance in the long run. In the corporate world a call for a new definition of basic corporate responsibility is receiving growing attention. See, for example, L. Fink, *2019 Letter to Ceos – Purpose & Profits*, available at: https://www.blackrock.com/corporate/investor-relations/larry-fink-ceo-letter.

[228] Crypto-assets are "minted" solely by the project developers before the IEO and sent to the crypto-assets exchanges.

[229] The crypto-assets exchange essentially becomes the counterparty in the entire crypto-asset launching process, enabling the projects to fundraise directly on the platform, in a much more direct, centralized, hands-on manner.

[230] Crypto-assets exchanges perform the analysis of projects prior to the IEO on their launchpad through audits, technical analysis, and the potential of the crypto-asset in addition to managing the sale directly on their platform throughout the entire process.

[231] This can potentially be an issue as pre-IEO purchasers might start selling their crypto-assets (as seen with various Binance Launchpad projects).

[232] So far there have been no IEOs conducted on decentralized crypto-assets exchanges.

[233] As the crypto-assets sale is conducted on a crypto-assets exchange platform, every project that seeks to launch an IEO should be carefully screened. Recently, Bittrex announced that it had canceled its IEO for the RAID project a few hours before the start of the sale. The reason for canceling RAID's plan to raise $6 million was a terminated partnership between RAID and the e-gaming data analytics company OP.GG. According to Bittrex, the partnership between the two companies was a vital part of the project, and when the crypto-assets exchange became aware of the event, it decided to cancel the sale as they believed it was not in the interest of Bittrex's customers. See A. Shome, *Bittrex International Cancels RAID's IEO*, Finance Magnates (Mar. 15, 2019), available at: https://www.financemagnates.com/cryptocurrency/news/bittrex-international-cancels-raids-ieo/.

[234] Also, crypto-assets exchanges appear to be acting as broker-dealers.

not appear to allow IEOs, or the issued crypto-assets, to escape regulation as securities or compliance with the securities laws.

Chapter 4
SECURITY TOKEN OFFERINGS

1.1 Security crypto-assets • 1.2 Securities regulatory environments: 1.2.1 Australia; 1.2.2 Brazil; 1.2.3 Canada; 1.2.4 China; 1.2.5. European Union and EAA: 1.2.5.1 Austria; 1.2.5.2 France; 1.2.5.3 Germany; 1.2.5.4 Ireland; 1.2.5.5 Italy; 1.2.5.6 Luxemburg; 1.2.5.7 Netherlands; 1.2.5.8 Norway; 1.2.5.9 United Kingdom; *1.2.6 Hong Kong; 1.2.7 India; 1.2.8 Israel; 1.2.9 Japan; 1.2.10 Nigeria; 1.2.11 Russia; 1.2.12 Saudi Arabia; 1.2.13 Singapore; 1.2.14 South Africa; 1.2.15 South Korea; 1.2.16 Switzerland; 1.2.17 United Arab Emirates:* 1.2.17.1 Dubai International Financial Centre; *1.2.18 United States:* 1.2.18.1 Rule 506 of Regulation D in detail; 1.2.18.2 Regulation S in detail; 1.2.18.2.1 Resales into the United States; 1.2.18.3 Rule 144A in detail; 1.2.18.3.1 Restricted securities.

1.1 *Security crypto-assets*. Security crypto-assets are digitized conventional securities[235]. Security, in a financial context, is a certificate or other financial instrument that has monetary value. It can be traded through a medium between exchanges or peer-to-peer. Securities are classified as either equity (e.g. stocks) or debt securities (e.g. bonds and debentures). In simpler terms, security crypto-assets are crypto-assets that pay dividends, share profits, pay interest or invest in other crypto-assets or assets to generate profits for the crypto-assets holders. This takes care of the liquidity issues.

A crypto-asset that, for example, passes the *Howey Test* is deemed as a security crypto-asset. These usually derive their value from an external, tradable asset. Because the crypto-assets are deemed security, they are unquestionable subject to securities regulations. If all the regulations were properly met, then these crypto-assets have immensely powerful use-cases[236], because:

> (i) Compliance is programmed into the crypto-asset. Security crypto-assets are made out of many smart contracts. A smart contract is a simple program designed to execute once a specified criterion is automatically satisfied. Smart contracts also determine how the crypto-asset can be purchased, traded and sold in a compliant fashion, and since they are blockchain based, the transactions are immutable, traceable, and fully transparent[237].

---

[235] For a more in-depth analysis of how securities can be offered and traded using blockchain, see R. Ryan, M. Donohue, *Securities on Blockchain*, Business Law 73, 85 (Winter 2017–2018).

[236] Analysts and executives in the industry see security tokens as a development that could have a significant impact on the mainstream securities and financial markets. See R. Browne, *Apple and Tesla shares on the blockchain could be the next big thing in crypto*, CNBC (Jan. 8, 2019), available at: https://www.cnbc.com/2019/01/07/bitcoin-security-token-and-sto-explained.html.

[237] Security crypto-assets may make compliance so frictionless that regulators at some point could require securities to be tokenized. A precedent for technology adoption is already here. As far back as

(ii) Security crypto-assets tend to enjoy high levels of liquidity (liquidity is what makes "token finance" different from traditional private securities), as they are eligible for trading on the global scene, allowing for anyone around the world to access them (on the contrary private company stocks are highly illiquid)[238]. Reasons why liquidity is important for investors:

(a) optionality: investors invest in Startup A, but then see a better deal in Startup B and want to sell their equity in Startup A in order to buy that better deal in Startup B without changing their allocation to early stage equity;

(b) macro story: investors may want to change their macro allocations and reduce exposure to early stage equity regardless of whether changing allocation is the right move, having the option to do so is clearly desirable.

(iii) They are a decisive feature-rich replacement for traditional securities[239]. Security crypto-assets essentially eliminate most of the burdens of traditional private securities[240]. Within the

---

1996, the SEC required electronic filing of financial statements through EDGAR, and later adopted XML technology. At that time there were only 36 million users on the Internet (0.9% of the world population), so the SEC was ahead of the curve in this respect.

[238] While the crypto-assets with real intrinsic usage (i.e. utility tokens) space currently shows greater liquidity in comparison to more traditional asset classes because they are sold on unregulated markets to unsophisticated investors (in most cases this means cutting corners), in relation to security crypto-assets liquidity becomes available by transforming the illiquid asset (the private company stock) in a more easily tradable asset (in a context of full compliance with the current securities regulations).

[239] All the contractual features such as liquidation preferences, ratchets, and drag-along rights could be baked directly into the security crypto-assets allowing to easily run scenario analysis to calculate payoffs under different assumptions.

[240] Many years ago, the securities markets went digital and now there are not many investors holding physical certificates. However, true benefits of digitization will only reach the securities industry when its layers of settlement processes are finally streamlined, so that securities issuers and investors can again interact directly, which is something that could be achieved by blockchain technology. With blockchain, buyers of shares and corporations will have clear ownership record, lenders holding security interests in pledged stock expect to be able to foreclose after a triggering event, distribution of dividends and payments should clearer as well. Knowing who owns which shares is a fundamental corporate governance requirement. Blockchain technology should make it easy to know at a specific moment the number of shares that a shareholder owns and who exactly are those shareholders. Cap tables could be reconciled in real time by code. Nowadays corporations – especially publicly trades corporations – rely on intermediaries to know this information (i.e. when using omnibus accounts, central depositories, etc.). The Dole Food Company Inc class action is only an example of why accurate stock ownership is not achieved in markets today. In this case, there were more than 36 million shares in the class, but claimants submitted facially valid claims for more than 49 million shares, 33% more Dole common stock than actually existed. Clearly, no single ledger kept track – in real time – of stock ownership. When an investor buys a share of common stock in a publicly traded corporation, the investor typically does not hold that share directly. Generally, from the corporation's perspective, a

traditional securities markets, deal execution is, for the most part, annihilated due to the number of intermediaries involved. Trading is practically not possible. Traditional securities are managed by ways of a combo of excel spreadsheets, paper certificates, lawyers, custodians, accountants, and transfer retailers which cost a lot of time and money[241], not mentioning the probability of human error. However, because security crypto-assets are digitized, much of these processes become unnecessary[242], making the security crypto-assets more accurate and efficient.

(iv) They are trustless. All operations related to a security crypto-asset (issuance, trading, purchasing, selling, and so on) are listed on the blockchain, which is viewed as a "trustless" procedure since blockchains are immutable and public in nature. There is no need for trust between parties when performing a transaction via security crypto-assets. Mathematics takes care of that.

In practice, selling security crypto-assets is comparable to ICOs, though the process is instead termed a Security Token Offering. Much like an ICO, STOs issue crypto-assets to investors. However, similarities usually end there. In an ICO, investors are purchasing crypto-assets to benefit from the possibility of crypto-assets appreciation or to unlock the ecosystem's utility. By comparison, STO investors are investing with the expectation of receiving

---

company called Cede & Co. (a nominee of the Depositary Trust Company) is the "record owner" of all the stock, all the time. Investor's broker keeps an entry in its database showing you as the stock's beneficial owner, and DTC keeps an entry in its database of the investor broker's ownership.

[241] Dell's 2013 go-private merger is another type of case blockchain technology could potentially help to prevent. T. Rowe Price lost standing to seek appraisal even though it had vocally opposed and repeatedly tried to vote against the merger. In order to vote its Dell shares, T. Rowe Price had to send its vote through intermediaries. A service provider – third party – later provided an updated record related to the merger. This updated record triggered T. Rowe Price's automated voting system, which was set to vote in favor of any management-recommended merger, like the Dell merger was. Despite T. Rowe Price's intention to oppose to the Dell merger, it ultimately voted in favor losing standing to sue for appraisal. T. Rowe Price ended up paying $194 million to compensate its clients for actions for loss of appraisal rights derived from this proxy voting mistake.

[242] In order to make these processes unnecessary, however, it is currently often needed to utilize advanced corporate structures. Imagine you own a Limited Liability Company incorporated in the Netherlands (i.e. a Besloten Vennootschap – B.V.). You currently are allowed to offer shares of the B.V. to investors (in accordance, for instance, to one of the EU prospectus exemptions), but these shares are transferable only via notarial deed. Tokenizing shares of a B.V., therefore, would not make the security crypto-asset so valuable in this case, because it would still be needed the notarial deed to formalize the transfer. The solution is the involvement in the corporate structure of a Stichting Administratiekantoor – STAK, a special structure (basically a foundation) that, backing the B.V., allows to split economic and governance rights of the shares. After the transfer of all the shares of the B.V. to the STAK, indeed, the STAK allows the creation of two types of certificates – one with governance rights and another with economic rights – that can then be tokenized. The involvement of the STAK in the corporate structure has, in particular, three advantages: (i) economic ownership certificates are tradable without notarial deed; (ii) economic ownership certificates can also include rights to profits and dividends; (iii) the split of economic rights from governance rights leaves the control of the company to the issuer while sharing the economic rights.

future cash flows, dividends, or voting rights directly tied to the security. Security crypto-assets are backed by assets, profits, or cash flows, and thus have an intrinsic value from the moment they are issued unlike utility crypto-assets, where the value is largely theoretical until an application is developed. Additionally, STOs are fully compliant with regulatory frameworks, allowing investors from all over the world to participate without violating respective securities laws. Another key aspect of STOs is that they allow companies to create whitelists and blacklists, a factor that easier to comply with know-your-customer ("**KYC**") and anti-money-laundering ("**AML**") reporting requirements. By operating more transparently, STOs can effectively negate some of the bigger issues facing utility token offerings — a lack of corporate accountability, the possibility of fraud, and no recourse in the event of a company failure.

1.2 *Securities regulatory environments*. Security crypto-assets are securities by definition, so they are subject to securities regulations[243]. Below a quick analysis of the current regulatory securities environment for some of the most important jurisdictions, with specific focus on the private placements and prospectus exemptions frameworks. Due to more relaxed statutory requirements, private placements have become globally the most popular capital raising tools for companies seeking injection of capital. Compared to offers to the public, private placements provide an alternative avenue to raise capital from a limited number of investors in a quicker and less expensive way. In addition, private placements enable a company to specifically target investors possessing the relevant knowledge and experience in the business sectors in which the company operates, so that the management of the company may benefit from the assistance offered by these investors. Last but not least, a company raising capital through a private placement, can also preserve its private company status and avoid the onerous disclosure obligations imposed on a company raising capital through public offering.

1.2.1   *Australia*. The issuance[244] and trading of debt and equity securities, derivatives, securitization and other financial products is primarily governed by chapters 6D and 7 of the Corporations Act 2001 of Australia

---

[243] As subject to securities regulations are speculative crypto-assets without real intrinsic usage (generally deemed securities by regulators and financial market authorities worldwide).

[244] An Australian entity is not required to obtain any general government authorizations or consents prior to issuing securities in Australia. In most cases, the only authorizations and consents required are those prescribed by the issuer's constitutional documents or governing statute. Foreign companies are also not subject to any direct government controls in issuing securities in Australia. However, the issuance of other types of financial products, and the trading of both securities and other financial products, may require the issuer or trader to hold an Australian financial services license ("**AFSL**") from ASIC under Chapter 7 of the Corporations Act (or be exempt from the requirement to do so). A person who undertakes the business of providing financial product advice (e.g., recommending the purchase of securities) requires a license (Sections 766A(1)(b), 766B and 911A of the Corporations Act).

("**Corporations Act**"), as well as by the common law and principles of equity.

As a general matter, a person must not offer or invite applications for the issue, sale or purchase of securities[245] in Australia[246] unless a prospectus or other disclosure document that complies with the form and content requirements of the Corporations Act has been registered with the Australian Securities and Investment Commission ("**ASIC**"). A similar requirement in relation to the registration with ASIC of a product disclosure statement ("**PDS**") is set out in part 7.9 of the Corporations Act in relation to offers for the issue, and (in certain cases) the sale or purchase, of other financial products[247].

The Corporations Act has two separate streams for regulating offerings/private placements depending on whether the products are classified as:

(i) Securities, for which a prospectus is required for an offering, unless a private placement exemption applies;
(ii) Financial products, other than securities, for which a PDS is required unless a private placement exemption applies.

Instead of regulating "offers to the public" or "public offerings", the Corporations Act focuses on each particular offer of products to each investor in Australia to determine if a product disclosure statement is required for that offer, or if that particular offer is within a private placement exemption.

Exemptions are provided from the disclosure documents requirements of the Corporations Act for offers to certain classes of investors including:

---

[245] Securities are defined as: (i) debentures, stocks or bonds issued or proposed to be issued by a government; (ii) shares in, or debentures of, a body; or (iii) interests in a managed investment scheme; or (iv) units of such shares. Securities are not: (i) derivatives as defined in Chapter 7, other than an option to acquire by way of transfer a security covered by paragraph (a), (b), (c) or (d); or (ii) excluded securities.

[246] Including an offer or invitation that is received by a person in Australia.

[247] Under the Corporations Act, the term "financial product" is defined in general terms, and there are specific inclusions and exclusions. Broadly a financial product is any facility through which a person makes a financial investment, manages financial risk or makes non-cash payments, even if the facility is used for some other purpose. The specific inclusions illustrate the wide scope of the concept, and include equity and debt securities, interests in managed investment schemes (i.e., unit trusts and other collective investments), derivatives, foreign exchange contracts, most insurance contracts, most superannuation (retirement savings) products, most deposit-taking facilities provided by Australian banks and other authorized deposit-taking institutions ("**ADIs**"), and government debenture and bond issues. The specific exclusions are generally products that are more suitably regulated under some other regime (such as credit facilities and payment systems).

(i) Offers to sophisticated investors. An offer where one of the following applies:

(a) the minimum amount payable for the shares on acceptance of the offer is at least A$500,000;
(b) the amount payable by the investor for the shares when aggregated with the amount previously paid by the investor for other shares in the same class is at least A$500,000;
(c) a qualified accountant certifies that the investor has either net assets of at least A$2,5 million, or gross income for each of the previous two financial years of at least A$250,000 per year;
(d) the offer is made to a company or trust controlled by a person who meets any of the above requirements;
(e) the offer is made through a financial services licensee who has given certain certifications as to the sophistication of the investors.

(ii) Offers to professional investors. An offer to "professional investors" within the meaning of the Corporations Act[248].

(iii) Rights issues or entitlement offers to existing shareholders. Provided that certain conditions are met, a listed company can make a pro rata offer under a rights issue or entitlement offer to its existing shareholders without the need to prepare a full prospectus.

(iv) Rights issues are ordinarily made under a short-form offering document and issuers are required to issue a notice essentially confirming that the issuer has complied with its continuous disclosure and financial reporting obligations under the Corporations Act.

(v) Share purchase plan offers. Provided that certain conditions are met, a listed company can make an offer to existing shareholders to acquire up to A$15,000 of shares each under a share purchase plan. The offer is made under a short-form offer document setting out the key terms of the offer.

---

[248] Australian Financial Services License holders; bodies regulated by the Australian Prudential Regulation Authority; trustee of a superannuation fund net assets of at least A$10 million; a person controlling at least A$10 million; an entity listed on Asia Pacific Exchange, ASX, Chi-X Australia, National Stock Exchange of Australia, SIM Venture Securities Exchange; an Investment Company that has raised its investment moneys via an offer to the public; a foreign entity that, if established or incorporated in Australia, would be covered by one of the preceding paragraphs.

(vi) Small-scale offerings. Personal offers[249] that do not result in securities being issued to more than 20 investors, to raise no more than A$2 million in any 12-month period.

(vii) Offers to senior managers. An offer to senior managers[250] of the company or of a related body corporate or to a family member or a body corporate controlled by the senior manager or such relative. Senior managers are persons (other than directors and secretaries of a corporation) who make or participate in making decisions that affect either the whole or a substantial part of the business of a corporation or have the capacity to affect significantly the corporation's financial standing.

(viii) Bonus issues and dividend reinvestment plans. An offer of fully paid shares to existing shareholders under a dividend reinvestment plan or a bonus share plan. A "personal offer" is one that can only be made to a person whom the offeror is aware is likely to be interested in the offer, having regard to previous contact, a professional or other connection or statements or actions by the person indicating that they are interested in offers of that kind and it may only be accepted by that person.

(ix) Employee incentive plan offers. An offer to employees under an employee incentive plan.

(x) Offers for nil consideration: the offer is for the issue or transfer of securities (excluding options) for no consideration.

(xi) Offers of options for no consideration: the offer is for options over securities or options over unissued securities, where no consideration is to be paid for the issue or transfer of options and no consideration is to be provided for the underlying securities on the exercise of the options. Similarly, an option to subscribe for an unissued share does not require a disclosure document at the time of the offer.

Most of these exemptions can be aggregated, for example, to allow an offer of shares to sophisticated and professional investors and to certain members of senior management as part of a single capital raising.

---

[249] Offers must be personal, which means there must be some connection with a person who is likely to be interested in the offer.
[250] Central to the exemption is the definition of senior manager. This definition is amended by legislative instrument so that it includes any person who is concerned in, or takes part in, the management of the company (regardless of designation and whether or not the person is a director or secretary of the company).

There are separate, but broadly similar, categories of exemptions for offering units in managed investment schemes.

The combination of these exceptions makes the legal regime in Australia more favorable to equity capital raising activity compared to many overseas jurisdictions and facilitates offers to be conducted relatively quickly and, in the case of secondary offerings (i.e. placements, rights issues, entitlement offers), often without a formal prospectus or PDS.

1.2.2 **Brazil**. The offering and trading of securities[251] are regulated by the National Monetary Council ("**CMN**") and the Brazilian Securities and Exchange Commission ("**CVM**"), through five main statutes:

>(i) Law 6385, of December 7, 1976, as amended ("**Securities Market Law**"), which rules the securities market and creates the CVM;
>(ii) Law 6404, of December 15, 1976, as amended ("**Corporations Law**") that regulates publicly held companies;
>(iii) Law 4728, of July 14, 1965, as amended ("**Capital Markets Law**") that created the CMN and established guidelines for the development of the securities market;
>(iv) Regulation No. 400/2003, enacted by the CVM, as amended ("**Regulation 400**"), which regulates securities offerings and their registration; and
>(v) Regulation No. 476/2009, enacted by the CVM, as amended ("**Regulation 476**") that regulates public offerings of securities with restricted selling efforts.

Broadly speaking:

>(i) the Securities Market Law attributed regulatory function to the CVM and therefore powers to regulate the matter set forth in such law and in the Corporations Law;

---

[251] The concept of securities under the Capital Markets Law is composed of a list of instruments that expressly classify as securities under Brazilian law:
(i) shares, debentures and subscription bonus;
(ii) coupons, rights, subscription receipts and certificates of unfolding of coupons, rights and subscription receipts;
(iii) certificates of deposit of securities;
(iv) debenture notes;
(v) quotas of investment funds in securities or investment clubs in any assets;
(vi) commercial notes;
(vii) futures, options and other derivative contracts, which underlying assets are securities;
(viii) other derivative contracts, regardless of the underlying assets; and
(ix) when publicly offered, any other securities or collective investment contracts that generate share, partnership or remuneration rights, including those resulting from the provision of services, whose income comes from the efforts of the entrepreneur or third parties.

(ii) the CVM has the authority to issue administrative rules concerning matters of the securities market and its participants.

No specific rules define a private placement, although the Capital Markets Law and Regulation 400 define public offerings by reference to a list of factors that suggest a public offering of securities. Over time, the CVM has provided guidance, on a case-by-case basis, on the kinds of offerings that fall outside registration and prospectus requirements. Specifically, a private placement is characterized by the absence of general solicitation, as defined by applicable regulations, and previously identified offerees who are employees, shareholders or other affiliates of the issuer. As a practical matter, issuers and other parties will submit any offering that may trigger registration requirements to the CVM for a confirmation that the proposed transaction does not constitute a public offering.

Regulation 400 provides that the following public offer distributions shall be automatically exempted from registration:

(i) those regarding the sale of shares of government-controlled entities;
(ii) a single and indivisible lot of securities;
(iii) securities issued by small businesses companies, as defined under Brazilian law.

Regulation 400 provides also the possibility of an exemption from registration and prospectus requirements available for offerings aimed at qualified investors. The only guidance provided by Regulation 400 is that qualified investors must represent to the offeror that they are knowledgeable and experienced investors, have had access to information regarding the issuer that they deem sufficient for their investment decision and are aware of the exemption from registration requirements.

Please note that offerings made to a limited number and type of investors, and not to the general public, are also regulated by Regulation 476. Under the terms of Regulation 476, only professional investors may be approached. Professional investors are the following:

(i) financial institutions;
(ii) insurance companies;
(iii) private welfare opened or closed capital organizations;
(iv) individuals or entities that hold financial investments in an amount exceeding 10 million reais, provided that such investor declares his or her condition as professional investor;
(v) investment funds;

(vi) investment clubs, provided that their manager is authorized to execute such services by the CVM;
(vii) portfolio administrators and securities consultants who are authorized by the CVM, in relation to their own resources; and
(viii) foreign investors.

Moreover, up to 75 professional investors may be approached in the selling efforts, and no more than 50 professional investors may purchase securities in such offering. However, offeror's shareholders exercising their priority or preference rights and foreign investors shall not be considered for the purpose of determining the maximum number of investors to be approached or that may acquire securities in the offering.

No information requirements apply to a private placement of securities under CVM regulations. The CVM, however, suggests that the information to be provided to investors for their investment decision should correspond to what is usually provided in a prospectus. Offerors and issuers may consider providing a disclosure document to prospective investors, if only to document the representations made at the time of the investment decision. Any offeror in a private placement will be liable for material misstatements or omissions under a general theory of liability for fraud.

Generally, securities acquired in a private placement may only be transferred in private transactions; however, if the same class of securities is traded on a stock exchange or other qualified market, any holder may sell its securities on the stock exchange or other market immediately. Public offerings distributed with restricted selling efforts also have certain trading restrictions. Securities acquired in such public offerings may not be transferred during a 90-day period counted as from the date of their initial sale. Pursuant to Regulation 476, such lock-up rule does not apply to public offerings of shares, warrants and depositary receipts.

In addition, securities acquired by professional investors in a public offering distributed with restricted selling efforts can only be traded among qualified investors, which are:

(i) professional investors;
(ii) individuals or entities that hold financial investments in an amount exceeding 1 million reais, provided that such investors declare their condition as a qualified investor;
(iii) individuals who have been approved on technical qualification examinations or have certifications approved by the CVM as requirements for the registration of autonomous investment

agents, portfolio managers, analysts and consultants of securities, in relation to their own securities; and

(iv) investment clubs, provided that at least one of the quotaholders manages the fund and is considered a qualified investor.

Such restriction will be exempt in case the issuer is registered as an issuer of public securities or, in relation to shares, warrants, convertible or exchangeable debentures or deposit certificates, there has been a previous public offering of securities of the same type and class registered with the CVM or 18 months have passed from the date of the listing of securities of the same type and class with the stock exchange.

1.2.3 *Canada*. Generally speaking, Canadian securities law focuses on three principal areas, namely, registration of securities advisers and dealers, issuers and securities, and enforcement, with each of the 10 Canadian provinces and three territories regulating itself by way of its local securities law statute (e.g., the Securities Act (Ontario) ("**OSA**")) falling largely under the purview of a securities regulator in each such province or territory (the Regulators).

The securities law statutes ("**Statutes**") for each of the 10 Canadian provinces and three territories are as follows:

(i) Ontario: Securities Act, RSO 1990, c S.5;
(ii) British Columbia: Securities Act, RSBC 1996, c 418;
(iii) Alberta: Securities Act, RSA 2000, c S-4;
(iv) Saskatchewan: Securities Act, 1988, The, SS 1988-89, c S-42.2;
(v) Manitoba: Securities Act, CCSM c S50;
(vi) Quebec: Securities Act, CQLR c V-1.1;
(vii) New Brunswick: Securities Act, SNB 2004, c S-5.5;
(viii) Nova Scotia: Securities Act, RSNS 1989, c 418;
(ix) PEI: Securities Act, RSPEI 1988, c S-3.1;
(x) Newfoundland: Securities Act, RSNL 1990, c S-13;
(xi) Yukon: Securities Act, SY 2007, c 16;
(xii) Northwest Territories: Securities Act, SNWT 2008, c 10;
(xiii) Nunavut: Securities Act, SNu 2008, c 12.

In an effort to harmonize their regimes across Canada, the Canadian provinces and territories have formed the Canadian Securities Administrators ("**CSA**"), which facilitates the promulgation of national instruments ("**NIs**"), multilateral instruments ("**MIs**") and their related companion policies ("**CPs**"). The NIs, MIs and CPs are incorporated into the Statutes in the form of regulations, which form many of the main operative regulatory provisions governing securities offerings throughout Canada.

Key NIs and MIs include NI 31-103 Registration Requirements, Exemptions and Ongoing Registrant Obligations; NI 41-101 General Prospectus Requirements; NI 45-106 Prospectus Exemptions; NI 51-102 Continuous Disclosure Obligations; NI 55-102 System for Electronic Disclosure by Insiders ("**SEDI**"); NI 55-104 Insider Reporting Requirements and Exemptions; Criminal Code of Canada; MI 61-101 Protection of Minority Security Holders in Special Transactions; NI 62-103 The Early Warning System and Related Take-Over Bid and Insider Reporting Issues; and NI 62-104 Take-Over Bids and Issuer Bids.

The above-listed statutes, NIs and MIs form a constituent part of the basic regulatory framework for securities regulation in Canada. Compliance with this framework is achieved by the regulators through the review and enforcement of their requirements, including dealer registration, adviser registration, continuous disclosure obligations (quarterly and annual financial filings), corporate governance implementation, proxy solicitation regulation, director independence, audit committee independence, minority shareholder protection, the sale of securities by way of a prospectus or by way of a prospectus exemptions, takeover bid regulation, and the early warning reporting and SEDI insider reporting regime.

Canadian securities laws generally require the filing of a prospectus to qualify any distribution of securities[252]. No person or company may trade in a security where the trade constitutes a distribution unless a prospectus has been filed or the trade is made in reliance upon a prospectus exemption. Securities originally distributed under a prospectus exemption are generally subject to resale restrictions that require the issuer to have been a reporting issuer (i.e., a public company) for a specified period of time and, in some cases, that the securities be held for a specified period of time.

The principal rule governing the private placement of securities, both debt and equity, in Ontario and the remainder of Canada is National Instrument 45-106 Prospectus Exemptions (NI 45-106) and/or Part XVII of the OSA. Commonly relied-upon prospectus exemptions within NI 45-106 and/or Part XVII of the OSA for an entity financing a business in Canada include the following exemptions:

---

[252] The definition of securities in Canada includes, among other things, an investment contract. The leading case in Canada for determining whether an investment contract exists is Pacific Coast Coin Exchange v. Ontario (Securities Commission) (Pacific Coast Coin Exchange v. Ontario (Securities Commission), [1978] 2 SCR 112) where the Supreme Court of Canada identified the four central attributes of an investment contract, namely: (i) an investment of money; (ii) in a common enterprise; (iii) with the expectation of profit; and (iv) which profit is to be derived in significant measure from the efforts of others. If an instrument satisfies the *Pacific Coin test*, the instrument will be considered an investment contract and, therefore, a security under Canadian securities laws.

(i) the "accredited investor" exemption, which allows certain qualified investors, including institutional investors and persons or companies that meet income or asset tests and, in certain circumstances, who have completed a prescribed risk acknowledgement form, to acquire securities. Accredited investor means:

(a) except in Ontario, a Canadian financial institution, or a Schedule III bank;
(b) except in Ontario, the Business Development Bank of Canada incorporated under the Business Development Bank of Canada Act;
(c) except in Ontario, a subsidiary of any person referred to in paragraphs (a) or (b), if the person owns all of the voting securities of the subsidiary, except the voting securities required by law to be owned by directors of that subsidiary;
(d) except in Ontario, a person registered under the securities legislation of a jurisdiction of Canada as an adviser or dealer;
(e) an individual registered under the securities legislation of a jurisdiction of Canada as a representative of a person referred to in paragraph (d);
(e.1) an individual formerly registered under the securities legislation of a jurisdiction of Canada, other than an individual formerly registered solely as a representative of a limited market dealer under one or both of the OSA or the Securities Act (Newfoundland and Labrador);
(f) except in Ontario, the Government of Canada or a jurisdiction of Canada, or any crown corporation, agency or wholly owned entity of the Government of Canada or a jurisdiction of Canada;
(g) except in Ontario, a municipality, public board or commission in Canada and a metropolitan community, school board, the Comité de gestion de la taxe scolaire de l'île de Montréal or an intermunicipal management board in Québec;
(h) except in Ontario, any national, federal, state, provincial, territorial or municipal government of or in any foreign jurisdiction, or any agency of that government;
(i) except in Ontario, a pension fund that is regulated by the Office of the Superintendent of Financial Institutions (Canada), a pension commission or similar regulatory authority of a jurisdiction of Canada;

(j) an individual[253] who, either alone or with a spouse, beneficially owns financial assets having an aggregate

---

[253] Subsection 3.5 of the Companion Policy to National Instrument 45-106 Prospectus and Registration Exemptions provides clarification as to how individuals determine whether they meet the income or net asset requirements of an accredited investor.
3.5 Accredited investor
(1) Individual qualification – financial tests
An individual is an accredited investor" for the purposes of NI 45-106 if the individual satisfies one of four tests set out in the "accredited investor" definition in section 1.1 of NI 45-106:
      (i) the C$1,000,000 financial asset test in paragraph (j)
      (ii) the C$5,000,000 financial asset test in paragraph (j.1)
      (iii) the net income test in paragraph (k)
      (iv) the net asset test in paragraph (l)
Three branches of the definition (in paragraphs (j), (k) and (l)) are designed to treat spouses as a single investing unit, so that either spouse qualifies as an accredited investor if the combined financial assets of both spouses exceed C$1,000,000, the combined net income of both spouses exceeds C$300,000, or the combined net assets of both spouses exceeds C$5,000,000.
The fourth branch, the C$5,000,000 financial asset test, does not treat spouses as a single investing unit. If an individual meets the C$5,000,000 financial asset test, they also meet the test to be a "permitted client" under NI 31-103. Permitted clients are entitled to waive the "know your client" and suitability obligations of registered dealers and advisers under NI 31-103. Under subsection 2.3(7) of NI 45-106, an issuer distributing securities under the accredited investor exemption to an individual who meets the C$5,000,000 financial asset test in paragraph (j.1) under the definition of accredited investor is not required to obtain a signed risk acknowledgement in Form 45-106F9 Form for Individual Accredited Investors from that individual.
For the purposes of the financial asset tests in paragraphs (j) and (j.1), "financial assets" are defined in NI 45-106 to mean cash, securities, or a contract of insurance, a deposit or an evidence of a deposit that is not a security for the purposes of securities legislation. These financial assets are generally liquid or relatively easy to liquidate. The value of a purchaser's personal residence is not included in a calculation of financial assets.
By comparison, the net asset test under paragraph (l) means all of the purchaser's total assets minus all of the purchaser's total liabilities. Accordingly, for the purposes of the net asset test, the calculation of total assets would include the value of a purchaser's personal residence and the calculation of total liabilities would include the amount of any liability (such as a mortgage) in respect of the purchaser's personal residence.
If the combined net income of both spouses does not exceed C$300,000, but the net income of one of the spouses exceeds C$200,000, only the spouse whose net income exceeds C$200,000 qualifies as an accredited investor.
(2) Bright-line standards – individuals
The monetary thresholds in the accredited investor definition are intended to create "brightline" standards. Investors who do not satisfy these monetary thresholds do not qualify as accredited investors under the applicable paragraph.
(3) Beneficial ownership of financial assets
Paragraphs (j) and (j.1) of the accredited investor definition refer to the beneficial ownership of financial assets. As a general matter, it should not be difficult to determine whether financial assets are beneficially owned by an individual, an individual's spouse, or both, in any particular instance. However, in the case where financial assets are held in a trust or in another type of investment vehicle for the benefit of an individual there may be questions as to whether the individual beneficially owns the financial assets. The following factors are indicative of beneficial ownership of financial assets:
(a) physical or constructive possession of evidence of ownership of the financial asset;
(b) entitlement to receipt of any income generated by the financial asset;
(c) risk of loss of the value of the financial asset; and
(d) the ability to dispose of the financial asset or otherwise deal with it as the individual sees fit.
For example, securities held in a self-directed RRSP, for the sole benefit of an individual, are beneficially owned by that individual. In general, financial assets in a spousal RRSP would also be

realizable value that, before taxes but net of any related liabilities, exceeds C$1,000,000;

(j.1) an individual who beneficially owns financial assets having an aggregate realizable value that, before taxes but net of any related liabilities, exceeds C$5,000,000;

(k) an individual whose net income before taxes exceeded C$200,000 in each of the 2 most recent calendar years or whose net income before taxes combined with that of a

---

included for the purposes of the C$1,000,000 financial asset test in paragraph (j) because it takes into account financial assets owned beneficially by a spouse. However, financial assets in a spousal RRSP would not be included for purposes of the C$5,000,000 financial asset test in paragraph (j.1).

Financial assets held in a group RRSP under which the individual does not have the ability to acquire the financial assets and deal with them directly would not meet the beneficial ownership requirements in either paragraph (j) or paragraph (j.1).

(4) Calculation of an individual purchaser's net assets

To calculate a purchaser's net assets under the net asset test in paragraph (l) of the accredited investor definition, subtract the purchaser's total liabilities from the purchaser's total assets. The value attributed to assets should reasonably reflect their estimated fair value. Income tax should be considered a liability if the obligation to pay it is outstanding at the time of the distribution of the security.

(4.1) Risk acknowledgement from individual investors

Persons relying on the accredited investor exemption in section 2.3 of NI 45-106 and section 73.3 of the Securities Act (Ontario) to distribute securities to individual accredited investors described in paragraphs (j), (k) and (l) of the "accredited investor" definition must obtain a completed and signed risk acknowledgement from that individual accredited investor.

"Individual" is defined in the securities legislation of certain jurisdictions to mean a natural person. The definition specifically excludes partnerships, unincorporated associations, unincorporated syndicates, unincorporated organizations and trusts. It also specifically excludes a natural person acting in the capacity of trustee, executor, administrator or personal or other legal representative.

(5) Financial statements

The minimum net asset threshold of C$5,000,000 specified in paragraph (m) of the accredited investor definition must, in the case of a non-individual entity, be shown on the entity's "most recently prepared financial statements". The financial statements must be prepared in accordance with applicable generally accepted accounting principles.

(6) Time for assessing qualification

The financial tests prescribed in the accredited investor definition are to be applied only at the time of the distribution of the security. The person is not required to monitor the purchaser's continuing qualification as an accredited investor after the distribution of the security is completed.

(7) Recognition or designation as an accredited investor

Paragraph (v) of the "accredited investor" definition in NI 45-106 contemplates that a person may apply to be recognized or designated as an accredited investor by the securities regulatory authorities or, except in Ontario and Québec, the regulators. The securities regulatory authorities or regulators have not adopted any specific criteria for granting accredited investor recognition or designation to applicants, as the securities regulatory authorities or regulators believe that the accredited investor definition generally covers all types of persons that do not require the protection of the prospectus requirement. Accordingly, the securities regulatory authorities or regulators expect that applications for accredited investor recognition or designation will be utilized on a very limited basis. If a securities regulatory authority or regulator considers it appropriate in the circumstances, it may grant accredited investor recognition or designation to a person on terms and conditions, including a requirement that the person apply annually for renewal of accredited investor recognition or designation.

(8) Verifying accredited investor status

Persons relying on the accredited investor exemption are responsible for determining whether a purchaser meets the definition of accredited investor.

spouse exceeded C$300,000 in each of the 2 most recent calendar years and who, in either case, reasonably expects to exceed that net income level in the current calendar year;
(l) an individual who, either alone or with a spouse, has net assets of at least C$5,000,000;
(m) a person, other than an individual or investment fund, that has net assets of at least C$5,000,000, as shown on its most recently prepared financial statements;
(n) an investment fund that distributes or has distributed its securities only to:
> a person that is or was an accredited investor at the time of the distribution;
> a person that acquires or acquired securities in the circumstances referred to in sections 2.10 [Minimum amount investment], or 2.19 [Additional investment in investment funds]; or
> a person described in paragraph (i) or (ii) that acquires or acquired securities under section 2.18 [Investment fund reinvestment];
(o) an investment fund that distributes or has distributed securities under a prospectus in a jurisdiction of Canada for which the regulator or, in Québec, the securities regulatory authority, has issued a receipt;
(p) a trust company or trust corporation registered or authorized to carry on business under the Trust and Loan Companies Act (Canada) or under comparable legislation in a jurisdiction of Canada or a foreign jurisdiction, acting on behalf of a fully managed account managed by the trust company or trust corporation, as the case may be;
(q) a person acting on behalf of a fully managed account managed by that person, if that person is registered or authorized to carry on business as an adviser or the equivalent under the securities legislation of a jurisdiction of Canada or a foreign jurisdiction;
(r) a registered charity under the Income Tax Act (Canada) that, in regard to the trade, has obtained advice from an eligibility adviser or an adviser registered under the securities legislation of the jurisdiction of the registered charity to give advice on the securities being traded;
(s) an entity organized in a foreign jurisdiction that is analogous to any of the entities referred to in paragraphs (a) to (d) or paragraph (i) in form and function;
(t) a person in respect of which all of the owners of interests, direct, indirect or beneficial, except the voting securities required by law to be owned by directors, are persons that are accredited investors;

(u) an investment fund that is advised by a person registered as an adviser or a person that is exempt from registration as an adviser;

(v) a person that is recognized or designated by the securities regulatory authority or, except in Ontario and Québec, the regulator as an accredited investor;

(w) a trust established by an accredited investor for the benefit of the accredited investor's family members of which a majority of the trustees are accredited investors and all of the beneficiaries are the accredited investor's spouse, a former spouse of the accredited investor or a parent, grandparent, brother, sister, child or grandchild of that accredited investor, of that accredited investor's spouse or of that accredited investor's former spouse.

(ii) the "minimum investment amount" exemption permits a person (though not an individual) to acquire securities on a prospectus-exempt basis where each purchaser invests no less than C$150,000 paid in cash; and

(iii) the "private issuer" exemption, which permits an issuer to issue securities to not more than 50 beneficial security holders (excluding holders of non-convertible debt) from a prescribed list of persons, including directors, officers and employees of the issuer, but the issuer must have restrictions on share transfers in either the issuer's originating documents or shareholders' agreement.

NI 45-106 contains other prospectus exemptions, including an exemption for friends, family and close business associates of persons related to the issuer and, for the employees, executive officers, directors and consultants of the issuer.

To rely on certain prospectus exemptions (although not the "accredited investor", "minimum investment amount" or "private issuer" exemptions), an issuer is required to deliver a disclosure document to prospective investors (i.e., an offering memorandum). That disclosure document is required to contain certain information about the business, operations, affairs and financial results of the issuer in a prescribed form.

The principal rule related to restrictions to the transferability of securities in a private placement, both debt and equity, in Ontario and the remainder of Canada is National Instrument 45-102 Resale of Securities (NI 45-102). Generally speaking, NI 45-102 states that purchasers of privately placed securities are prohibited from freely trading the securities (that is, selling the securities without providing a prospectus to subsequent purchasers) except either: in reliance upon a further prospectus exemption; or if the issuer of the securities is or becomes a "reporting issuer" in any Canadian jurisdiction, a four-month and one day restricted period has elapsed, and the certificate representing the securities carries a prescribed legend. Generally speaking, the four-month and a day restricted period runs from the date of the closing of private placement, or for non-public issuers, the later of the date of the closing of the private placement and the date on which the issuer becomes a "reporting issuer" under the securities legislation of any jurisdiction of Canada.

1.2.4   *China*. The legislation that regulates the offering and trading of securities[254] includes several fundamental laws, most importantly the Company Law of the PRC and the judicial interpretations of that law made by the Supreme Court of the PRC (together, the "**Company Law**"), and the Securities Law of the PRC ("**Securities Law**")[255], followed by a fiddly series of rules promulgated by central government (including the State Council of China ("**State Council**") and its delegated departments).

Private placements of securities in China are regulated depending on who is actually doing the private placement. Historically, private placements of securities in China are sorted into three main categories, and each category is regulated by different agencies with their own rules and regulations:

> (i) Private placement of securities by publicly listed companies: regulated by the China Securities Regulatory Commission ("**CSRC**")[256].
> (ii) Private placement of securities by private equity funds and venture capital funds (the money raised is intended to be used for investing in other securities): historically regulated by a hodgepodge of regulators, including the National Development and Reform Commission ("**NDRC**"), the CSRC and various local regulators.
> (iii) Private placement of equity securities by non-publicly listed companies: this is a regulatory gray area and no definitive regulation has been set for such capital raising activity.

---

[254] Compared to most western economies, China's securities market is very young, having been created in the 1980s under the policy of *Gaige Kaifang*.
[255] *Zhonghua Renmin Gongheguo Zhenquan Fa* [Securities Law of the People's Republic of China] (promulgated on 29 December 1998 and effective from 1 July 1999, amended in 2004 and 2005).
[256] The CSRC is a ministry rank unit directly under the leadership of the State Council charged with implementing centralized and unified regulation of China's securities market. It therefore has jurisdiction and powers over securities offerings in China.

Recent changes appear to portend a shift towards a more uniform way of regulating capital raising by private placements of securities in China. On May 8, 2014, the State Council released its Several Opinions of the State Council on Further Promoting the Healthy Development of the Capital Market ("**2014 State Council Opinions**"), promulgating the requirements laid down at the 18th National Congress of the Communist Party of China ("**CPC**") and the Second and Third Plenum Sessions of the 18th Central Committee of the CPC.

The 2014 State Council Opinions state:

> *"private placement system shall be established and improved. It is important to formulate a set of criteria on qualified investors, specify the investor suitability requirements on the private placement of various products and the information disclosure requirements on private placement to the same type of investors, and standardize placement activities. No administrative examination and approval shall be instituted for private placement. Instead, issuers of all types are allowed to issue, on the basis of compliance, stocks, bonds, funds and other products to an accumulated number of investors that does not exceed the number specified by laws".*

Although the 2014 State Council Opinions are only a declarative document and not actual regulation, the State Council Opinions and a series of recent laws in China are fundamentally changing the regulatory framework for private placements in China.

Historically, there is no uniform definition of what is a private placement of securities in China. More importantly, there is no regulation that allows for and regulates private placements of equity securities by private companies that need operational capital. Therefore, whether a private company can, and under what circumstances will it be allowed to, raise capital via a private placement of its securities has always been a legal gray area.

A rough concept of what is and is not a private placement of securities does exist in the Securities Law by negative inference. The Securities Law defines a "public offering" as issuing securities to "more than 200 specific individuals"[257]. However, it is important to note that the Securities Law

---

[257] Article 10 of the Securities Law: "*A public issuance of securities shall satisfy the requirements of the relevant laws and administrative regulations and shall be reported to the securities regulatory authority under the State Council or a department upon authorization by the State Council for examination and approval according to law. Without any examination and approval according to law, no entity or individual may make a public issuance of any securities. It shall be deemed as a public issuance upon the occurrence of any of the following circumstances:*

generally does not apply to companies or funds that are not publicly listed in China, so even this general "200 specific individual" standard may or may not apply to such other entities.

To make matters more confusing, private placements of securities in China are regulated by different regulators, including the CSRC, the NDRC and multiple layers of local governments.

We recommend the following approaches to mitigate risks relating to offering of securities in China:

(i) marketing, offering, or selling any interests to no more than 200 Chinese specified potential investors;
(ii) making communications and holding any in-person meetings only with specified potential investors;
(iii) communications and in-person meetings should take place on a one-to-one basis in private places without utilizing any of the general advertising, general solicitation, or other disguised public dissemination methods prohibited by the Securities Law;
(iv) marketing activities should generally be restricted to a limited number of prospective clients that are believed to be sophisticated institutional investors or high net worth individuals. Unsolicited communications with prospective Chinese investors should be avoided to the extent practicable;
(v) any overview materials or offering documents sent to the previously identified Chinese investors should be sent to their personal addresses or emails, and should indicate that the materials may not be copied or distributed to persons other than the party to whom they are addressed;
(vi) in case any Chinese investors have any affiliates or trustees outside China, addressing the offering and sale documents to their overseas affiliates or trustees would be recommended to the extent applicable;
(vii) investment documentation should be governed by laws of a jurisdiction other than China and should provide for a non-Chinese forum for resolving disputes; and
(viii) subscription funds should be received by the fund sponsor in an account outside China, and the execution of the investment documentation and completion of the transaction should take place outside China.

(i) Making a public issuance of securities to non-specified objects;
(ii) Making a public issuance of securities to accumulatively more than 200 specified objects;
(iii) Making a public issuance as prescribed by any law or administrative regulation. For any securities that are not issued in a public manner, the means of advertising, public inducement or public issuance in any disguised form may not be adopted thereto".

The Securities Investment Funds Law (effective June 1, 2013), as a central government promulgated statute, for the first time formalized a single regulatory regime for private fund-raising activities of investment funds within China. It also resolved the "turf wars" between the various regulators by declaring that the CSRC shall be the one and only regulator of private placement activities in the investment funds area. The CSRC in turn promulgated the Interim Regulations on the Supervision and Administration of Private Investment Funds ("**CSRC Regulations**") in August 2014. The CSRC Regulations introduced registration and filing requirements, a "qualified investor" standard, and the definition and prohibition of general solicitation. Even though the Securities Investment Funds Law applies only to fund raising activities by entities that raise funds for reinvestment of such funds into another company's securities (i.e., investment funds), its promulgation introduced many concepts that are already being used in private placement activities outside the investment funds industry.

The CSRC Regulations lay out the requirements for what constitutes a qualified investor who can participate in a private placement and invest in an investment fund. Such "qualified investor" must:

> (i) invest at least CNY1 million (US$162,359) as a capital commitment in the fund; and
> (ii) as an institutional investor, must have net assets of at least CNY10 million (US$1,623,590); or
> (iii) as an individual investor, must own financial assets (including bank deposits, stocks, bonds and other financial assets, but excluding real property) of at least CNY3 million (US$487,077), or have annual income during the preceding three years of at least CNY500,000 (US$81,179).

The CSRC Regulations further list certain institutions to be qualified investors with no asset requirements, including social/public interest-related funds such as pension funds, annuity funds, charity funds, other investment plans already registered with the Asset Management Association of China ("**AMAC**"), or fund managers and their employees who co-invest in the relevant funds under their management, etc.

A fund manager in China is required to prepare a detailed questionnaire for each potential investor to assess whether the investor meets the requirements of a qualified investor. However, the methodologies and standards of verifying a qualified investor (i.e., to what extent should the fund manager conduct diligence) remain unclear under the CSRC Regulations.

The CSRC Regulations also prohibit promoting the investment fund to non-specific investors through general solicitation or general advertising for a legal private placement. General solicitation is defined to include promoting the fund to the public by means of newspapers, radio, television, Internet and other public media networks, or via seminars, colloquiums, posters, etc. In addition, any form of principal-protected commitments or minimum returns guarantee are strictly prohibited in the marketing materials used to solicit prospective investors.

In addition to rules surrounding public offering, Chinese laws regulate Chinese outbound investments. Chinese laws and regulations have not provided the specific procedures for Chinese individual investors to make their investments in any non-financial entities incorporated outside China.

Outbound investments in non-financial enterprises outside China by Chinese corporate investors normally require prior approvals from, and/or filing with, several competent governmental authorities in China. Typically, an outbound transaction could require the involvement of the NDRC, the Ministry of Commerce ("**MOFCOM**"), and State Administration of Foreign Exchange ("**SAFE**"), or their local counterparts. If State-owned enterprises ("**SOEs**") are involved, the approval of the State-owned Assets Supervision and Administration Commission ("**SASAC**") may also be required.

> (i) NDRC Approval/Filing. If the proposed investment does not involve any "sensitive countries or regions" ("*countries and regions that have not yet established diplomatic relations with China; countries and regions where wars and civil strife occur; countries and regions where investment made by enterprises shall be restricted according to the international treaties and protocols concluded or acceded by China; and other sensitive countries and regions*") or "sensitive industries" ("*research, production, maintenance and repair of weapons and equipment; development and utilization of cross-border water resources; news media; and industries for which outbound investments by enterprises shall be restricted according to Chinese laws, regulations and related regulatory policies*"), a Chinese corporate investor should file a record-filing application with the NDRC or its provincial branch depending on the total investment amount[258]. It takes seven

---

[258] [Prohibited category] Outbound investments that jeopardize (or may jeopardize) national interests and security are prohibited. These include: (a) outbound investments in relation to unauthorized export of Chinese military core technology and products; (b) outbound investments utilizing technologies, crafts, and products which are banned for export; (c) outbound investments in the gambling and pornography industries; (d) outbound investments prohibited by the international

business days for the applicant to obtain a notification letter from the NDRC or the provincial branch after the filing is accepted. The relevant NDRC filing must be completed before either (a) the parties enter into a definitive agreement or (b) the signed definitive agreement takes effect, if the NDRC filing is stated as a closing condition.

(ii) MOFCOM Filing. The MOFCOM regulatory framework for outbound investments is also mainly a record filing system. It takes three business days for the applicant to obtain an Outbound Investment Certificate from the MOFCOM or the provincial counterparts after the MOFCOM accepts the filing application. Specific approval is required only in exceptional cases, such as the establishment of overseas companies in sensitive countries/regions or sensitive industries. The purpose of any review undertaken by the MOFCOM is mainly to determine if the establishment of overseas entities is carried out in compliance with applicable procedures for outbound investments. The application documents required by the NDRC and the MOFCOM are basically the same. After both (NDRC and MOFCOM) record filings have been accomplished, the investor must contact the SAFE qualified banks for foreign exchange registration and fund remittance.

The regulatory framework for outbound investments provides that SAFE-qualified banks in China deal directly with the foreign exchange registration of outbound investment transactions and process subsequent matters, such as opening capital accounts and remitting outbound funds, while the SAFE indirectly supervises the foreign exchange registration of outbound investments. However, since November 2016, when the Chinese

---

treaties China concluded or acceded to, and (e) other outbound investments that jeopardize or may jeopardize national interest or national security.

[Restricted category] Outbound investments which are inconsistent with foreign policies regarding peaceful development, mutually beneficial strategies and macro-control are restricted. These include: (a) outbound investments in any sensitive country and region without diplomatic relations with China, experiencing war or strife, or where investment by enterprise is restricted by international treaties, or agreements China concluded or acceded to; (b) outbound investments in the real estate, hotel, cinema, entertainment and sport club industries; (c) formation of equity investment funds or investment platforms without specific industrial projects; (d) outbound investments that utilize obsolete manufacturing equipment which cannot satisfy the technology standard of the destination country; or (e) outbound investments in violation of the destination country's environment, energy efficiency and security standards. Verification of relevant authorities is required for outbound investments falling under categories (a) to (c). Outbound investments under category (a) above are toward sensitive countries and regions, while outbound investments under categories (b) and (c) are toward sensitive industries, all of which are subject to verification. Outbound investments under categories (d) and (e) are not subject to verification but will be closely supervised by authorities.

rules for capital control became stricter for transactions with overseas fund transfers in excess of US$5 million, any foreign exchange registration and remittance has required permission from the SAFE before it can be dealt with by qualified banks. In addition, the local SAFE authority now interviews the relevant Chinese investors to assess the authenticity and compliance of the outbound investment target. In summary, the SAFE has moved to center stage from its previous indirect supervision function since the capital control measures were intensified.

Besides the aforementioned generally applicable regulatory framework, there are specific regulatory aspects that apply to SOEs and listed companies, respectively, both of which are the main players in the outbound investment market.

(iii) SASAC Approval/Filing. Under the SASAC Rules, a central SOE, or any of its subsidiaries which intends to purchase or merge with an overseas listed company, or to otherwise make any major overseas investments, must report the intended transaction to the SASAC for filing or approval, whichever the case may be, and the process must be completed before starting the record filing or approval process with the NDRC. At the beginning of 2017, the SASAC released a list of industry categories in which SOEs are not allowed to invest. In addition, SOEs must not invest in businesses outside their sector of business activity.

(iv) CSRC and Stock Exchanges Approval. CSRC approval is required only for an overseas investment by a Chinese-listed company if the outbound investment constitutes a so-called "material asset restructuring" of the listed company. Cash transactions that do not constitute a material asset restructuring of listed companies account for the majority of outbound investment for Chinese-listed companies.

However, pursuant to the relevant rules of the Shanghai and Shenzhen Stock Exchanges, if a listed company purchases assets which fulfill certain criteria requiring a disclosure of the transaction, either a board meeting or a shareholders' meeting (subject to the company's articles of association) must be held to review and approve the intended transaction. Pursuant to approval, an announcement must be released in a timely manner that briefly describes the basic conditions of the transaction with information on the deal structure, the counterparty, the target, the main terms of the transaction agreement, the purpose of the acquisition and the impact on the company. Listed companies generally do not need to suspend trading or accept exchange inquiries.

1.2.5 **European Union and EAA**. In the European Union the financial markets[259] are regulated on the EU level. Since the 1990s, the EU (and its predecessor, the European Community) has enacted a huge array of Directives and Regulations setting out the rules of initial public disclosure, intermediaries' regulation and market conduct rules, to name but a few. Regulation (EU) 2017/1129 ("**Prospectus Regulation**")[260] published on June 30, 2017 and entered into force on 20 July, 2017 will be applicable to EU member countries starting from July 21, 2019. The Prospectus Regulation[261] seeks to level the playing field by removing the existing differences between the rules applicable in different member states[262].

The pivotal term of EU financial markets regulation is "transferable[263] securities"[264]. For example, Prospectus Regulation applies to offers of

---

[259] The term "capital markets" is not defined under EU law. However, the European Commission applies a broad interpretation which includes all contexts where buying and selling interests in securities meet. Generally, anyway, one main difference between capital markets and other parts of the financial markets (for example money markets or commodities markets), or markets other than financial markets, is the ongoing relationship between the issuer and the investor – based on the traded instrument.

[260] The Prospectus Regulation provides, inter alia, that:
(i) member states could, as from 21 July 2018, exempt offers of securities to the public with a total consideration in the European Union of between €1 million and €8 million (calculated over a 12-month period) from the requirement to publish a prospectus; in this respect, France decided to exempt offers of securities below the threshold of €8 million from the publication of a prospectus;
(ii) a "universal registration document" detailing the issuer's business and financial position may be filed with a competent authority every year. This document may then be incorporated by reference into the prospectus. This mechanism would enable issuers to have their prospectuses approved more quickly by a competent authority; and
(iii) the prospectus summary is to be shortened to a maximum length of seven A4 pages. A set format will be required, based on the key information document ("**KID**") for packaged retail and insurance-based investment products, with four main sections specifying the following: (a) introductory warning language; (b) key information about the issuer; (c) key information about the securities; and (d) key information about the offer of securities to the public and admission to trading.

[261] The Prospectus Regulation will replace the existing Prospectus Directive (EU Directive 2003/71/EC) and all related level 2 measures.

[262] In many cases most of the following exemptions are already aligned with the applicable laws of the UE members. In other an alignment will be needed.

[263] In order to be negotiable, a security needs to be transferable. This means that there cannot be any obstacles that make the transfer impossible and there cannot be any dependency on the fulfilment of certain formal criteria, such as notarial certification. The units do not require a physical embodiment, such as a certificate, to be transferable.

[264] The formalistic "black letter law" approach of EU regulation – i.e. the statutory requirements are set out in the regulation in a lot of details – is a major deviation from the "substance over form" approach taken by the US Supreme Court. This black-letter approach usually (but not always) provides a high level of legal certainty for the markets. The "substance over form" approach taken by the US Supreme Court, would be in conflict with the desired harmonization in the EU because courts in

securities to the public[265]. Directive 2014/65/EU on Markets in Financial Instruments ("**MiFiD II**") revolves around "financial instruments", which pursuant to Section C of Annex I includes "transferable securities"[266]. Regulation (EU) 596/2014 on Market Abuse ("**MAR**") also applies to "financial instruments"[267] as defined under MiFiD II.

An offer to the public is defined widely as being a communication to any person which presents sufficient information on the transferable securities to be offered, and the terms on which they are to be offered, to enable an investor to decide to buy or subscribe for the securities in question.

Key exemptions from the prospectus requirement include where:

> (i) an offer is made to fewer than 150 people per EU member state (no matter if they are qualified[268] or not);

---

different EU member states could come up with different approaches, resulting in regulatory patchwork.
[265] See Art. 1(1) of Regulation (EU) 2017/1129.
[266] Art. 4(1)(44) MiFiD II also lists shares, bonds and respective derivatives as examples of transferable securities. Importantly, no definition of securities as such is provided. Furthermore, to our knowledge there has not been a single decision of the Court of Justice of the European Union ("**CJEU**") regarding the definition of securities in general.
[267] See Art. 2(1) and Art. 3(1)(1) MAR.
[268] For this purpose, Qualified Investors are:
  (i) Legal entities authorized to act on the capital market, including – credit institutions, investment companies, other supervised financial entities, trust funds and their managers, insurance companies, pension funds and their managing companies, and other corporations which were incorporated for investment on the capital market.
  (ii) Governmental institutions, central banks, international financial entities.
  (iii) Corporations complying with two of the three conditions, listed below:
    (a) More than 250 employees;
    (b) The balance is over €43 million;
    (c) Turnover or scope of activities are over €50 million.
  (iv) Certain individuals – subject to mutual agreement, the EU member state can permit an individual, who is not a resident of the country and who applies to be recognized as a Qualified Investor, to be recognized as such if he complies with two of the following conditions:
    (a) Carries out significant transactions on the securities market at the average rate of at least 10 transactions in a quarter, during the last 4 quarters;
    (b) His investment portfolio is over €0,5 million;
    (c) He is employed or has been employed in the financial sector for at least one year, in a professional capacity requiring understanding of investment in securities.
The European Directive – Markets and Financial Instruments ("**MiFID**") 2004/39/EC – obligates providers of financial services, in the EU member states, to classify their clients according to three categories: professional clients, eligible counterparties and retail clients; and to ensure that the financial instruments offered to each client correspond with that client's ability to understand it and the risks it carries. The last group of investors is supposed to enjoy the broadest protection, while making investments. According to the aforesaid directive the "retail client" is any client who is not professional. The definition of professional clients includes the following:

(ii) the minimum consideration payable by any person is at least €100,000;

(iii) the securities are denominated in amounts of at least €100,000;

(iv) the total consideration in the EU is less than €1,000,000, calculated over a period of 12 months (EU state members, anyway, have the possibility to exempt offers of securities to the public greater than €1,000,000, but not exceeding €8,000,000 from the obligation to publish a prospectus);

(v) the securities are offered in connection with a takeover offer provided a document is available containing information which is regarded as equivalent to that of a prospectus;

(vi) shares already admitted to trading are offered to existing or former employees or directors, if certain information is made available.

1.2.5.1 *Austria*. The key laws applicable to securities offerings in Austria are:

(i) the Capital Markets Act ("**KMG**");
(ii) the Stock Exchange Act ("**BörseG**"); and
(iii) the Securities Supervision Act 2007 ("**WAG 2007**").

The KMG implements Directive 2003/71/EC ("**Prospectus Directive**")[269], as amended, and is the primary source governing the offering of

---

(i) Legal entities authorized to act on the capital market, including – credit institutions, investment companies, other supervised financial entities, trust funds and their managers, insurance companies, pension funds and their managing companies.
(ii) Corporations that comply with two of the three conditions, detailed below:
   (a) Own funds that worth €2 million;
   (b) Have a balance above €20 million;
   (c) Have a turnover or scope of activities over €40 million.
(iii) Governmental institutions, central banks, international financial entities.
(iv) Other corporations, incorporated for the purpose of investment in financial instruments or for securitization of assets or other financial transactions.
(v) Certain individuals – the EU member state can permit an individual, who is not a resident of the country and who applies to be recognized as a Qualified Investor, to be recognized as such if he complies with two of the following conditions:
   (a) Carries out significant transactions on the securities market at the average rate of at least 10 transactions in a quarter, during the last 4 quarters;
   (b) His investment portfolio is over €0.5 million;
   (c) He is employed or has been employed in the financial sector for at least one year, in a professional capacity requiring understanding of investment in securities.

[269] The Prospectus Directive and all related level 2 measures will be replaced by the Prospectus Regulation (Regulation (EU) 2017/1129) on July 21, 2019. The Prospectus Regulation will provide a common legal basis for securities offerings in the European Union and its rules will be binding and directly applicable in all EU member states. The Prospectus Regulation aims to: (i) make it easier and cheaper for smaller companies to access capital; (ii) introduce simplification and flexibility for all types of issuers, in particular for secondary issuances and frequent issuers which are already known to

securities[270] and investments[271] in Austria, including in particular the prospectus obligation (publication of an approved prospectus for public offers of securities or investments) as well as exemptions from the prospectus obligation.

The BörseG constitutes the primary framework for the admission of securities to a regulated market in Austria, as well as for ongoing obligations of issuers of listed equity and debt instruments. In addition to the provisions of the KMG, BörseG and the WAG 2007, parts of other relevant laws and regulations, have to be considered, including the Austrian Stock Corporation Act ("**AktG**"), as well as the Austrian Takeover Code in relation to takeover bids for listed companies.

The KMG, BörseG and WAG 2007 are primarily administered and enforced by the Austrian Financial Market Authority ("**FMA**"). If a listing of securities is sought, the prospectus, along with other documents, has to be filed with Wiener Börse AG (Vienna Stock Exchange – "**VSE**"), which operates the only two regulated markets in Austria: the Official Market and the Second Regulated Market. In addition, any prospectus for an offer of securities in Austria has to be submitted to Oesterreichische Kontrollbank AG ("**OeKB**").

According to section 2 of the KMG, the general rule is that the public offering of securities or investments is only permitted if a prospectus has been published, at the latest one banking day prior to the launch of the offer.

Private placements may be exempt from the obligation to publish a prospectus. Pursuant to section 3 (1)(14) KMG, an offer addressed to fewer than 150 natural or legal persons per European Economic Area member state not being qualified investors is considered as a prospectus exempt "private placement". In addition, there are several other prospectus exemptions excluding certain types of offers from the obligation to publish a prospectus. Pursuant to section 3 (1)(11) KMG,

---

capital markets; (iii) improve prospectuses for investors by introducing a retail investor-friendly summary of key information, catering for the specific information and protection needs of investors. The new prospectus regime will ensure that appropriate rules cover the full life-cycle of companies from startup until maturity as frequent issuers on regulated markets.

[270] With respect to securities, the KMG implements the transferable securities concept in accordance with the MiFID II. This mainly includes equities and equity-type securities, as well as non-equity securities such as debt securities and other securitized debt securities.

[271] In accordance with section 1 (1)(3) KMG, investments are uncertificated property rights (rights to claims, membership rights or rights in rem) for the direct or indirect investment of several investors who carry the risk, either alone or jointly with the issuer, and that investors do not administer themselves. The term investment includes uncertificated profit participation rights, limited partnerships and silent participations. Prospectuses for investments do not follow the scheme of the Prospectus Regulation, but those according to the annexes provided in the KMG.

the publication of a prospectus is not required if the securities are offered exclusively to qualified investors, which includes credit institutions, investment firms, insurance companies, investment funds, pension funds, the government, certain small and medium-sized enterprises and also certain natural persons applying for a classification as qualified investors. Other relevant prospectus exemptions include security offerings addressed to investors subject to a minimum investment amount of €100,000 per investor as well as offerings of securities with a minimum denomination of €100,000, offerings in a total amount of less than €250,000 during a period of 12 months[272], and certain offerings by preferred issuers or security offerings to employees.

To rely upon one or more prospectus exemptions, no specific formalities must be followed. However, anyone having the intention of offering securities for the first time is obliged to notify the New Issue Calendar, which provides an insight into the extent and manner of the expected capital market utilization. The New Issue Calendar is maintained by OeKB for statistical purposes. The issuer must refer to a specific exemption from the obligation to publish a prospectus and expressly indicate the facts pertaining to this exemption.

Private placement memoranda or promotional material on the offering that are circulated to potential investors usually include appropriate disclaimers stating that investors are exclusively targeted on a private placement basis and that the document is not an approved securities prospectus. Nevertheless, information provided shall not be inaccurate or misleading and shall not deviate from other information provided to potential investors in order to avoid civil law liability.

Austrian law does not impose any mandatory requirements for information to be made available to potential investors in a private placement as long as no listing of securities on a regulated market in Austria (i.e., on the Official Market or Second Regulated Market of the VSE) takes place. In the absence of a mandatory requirement, potential investors will, nevertheless, require certain information about the issuer and the offered securities to decide on an investment in the securities. Such information is commonly provided in a voluntarily supplied information memorandum providing information and certain standard disclaimers. If the offeror provides potential investors with such

---

[272] If there is an investment as per the KMG, the issuer's other legal obligations also depend on the issuance volume. For issuance volumes from €250,000 to €2 million, the provisions of the Alternative Financing Act ("**AltFG**") apply, but not the requirements of the KMG with regard to a prospectus. In this case, the issuer must prepare an information sheet in accordance with the AltFG. For issuance volumes from €2 million to €5 million, the issuer may draw up a simplified prospectus according to Scheme F of the KMG. For issuance volumes from €5 million onwards, a KMG brochure according to Scheme C is required.

information, the information should in any case be understandable, accurate, true and not misleading in order to avoid any claims by potential investors resulting from *culpa in contrahendo*. Further, care should be taken that no material information is missing from the information memorandum and that potential investors are treated equally.

There are no statutory restrictions on the transferability of debt or equity securities acquired in a private placement. Such securities can be transferred pursuant to the rules on transferability of the relevant security. If the securities shall be listed on a regulated market in Austria, a prospectus exemption provided for in the BörseG has to be relied upon. As soon as the securities are admitted to the regulated market they can be traded in accordance with applicable laws and regulations. If no listing is sought, any transfer restrictions provided for in the issuer's articles of association (registered shares) have to be assessed. As a resale of securities acquired under the private placement exemption by way of a public offering may trigger a prospectus obligation pursuant to the KMG, unless a prospectus exemption can be relied upon, respective selling and transfer restrictions and corresponding investor representations for re-sales of such securities are typically included in the information or private placement memorandum.

1.2.5.2 **France**. The main rules applicable to securities offerings are contained in:

> (i) Directive 2003/71/EC on the prospectus to be published when securities are offered to the public or admitted to trading ("**Prospectus Directive**");
> (ii) Regulation (EC) 809/2004 implementing the Prospectus Directive as regards prospectuses and dissemination of advertisements ("**Prospectus Regulation**")[273];
> (iii) The French Monetary and Financial Code ("**MFC**") (in particular articles L411-1 *et seq*);
> (iv) The Autorite Des Marchés Financiers ("**AMF**") general regulations and related instructions and recommendations;
> (v) Regulations issued by NYSE Euronext (in particular Euronext Market Rules Books I and II)[274].

---

[273] The Prospectus Directive and all related level 2 measures will be replaced by the Prospectus Regulation (Regulation (EU) 2017/1129) on July 21, 2019. The Prospectus Regulation will provide a common legal basis for securities offerings in the European Union and its rules will be binding and directly applicable in all EU member states. The Prospectus Regulation aims to: (i) make it easier and cheaper for smaller companies to access capital; (ii) introduce simplification and flexibility for all types of issuers, in particular for secondary issuances and frequent issuers which are already known to capital markets; (iii) improve prospectuses for investors by introducing a retail investor-friendly summary of key information, catering for the specific information and protection needs of investors. The new prospectus regime will ensure that appropriate rules cover the full life-cycle of companies from startup until maturity as frequent issuers on regulated markets.

Security Token Offerings

In France, every issuer that makes a public offering of equity or debt securities must file a prospectus with the AMF[275]. In compliance with the Prospectus Directive's definition of "offers of securities to the public", in France a public offering is[276]:

(i) a communication to persons in any form and by any means, presenting sufficient information on the terms of the offer and the securities to be offered, so as to enable an investor to decide to purchase or subscribe to these securities; or
(ii) the placing of securities through financial intermediaries.

A private placement is not considered as an offer to the public and therefore no prospectus is required. Private placement encompasses offers:

(i) Made exclusively to providers of portfolio management services on a discretionary basis ("*personnes fournissant le service d'investissement de gestion de portefeuille pour compte de tiers*").
(ii) Made exclusively to qualified investors ("*investisseurs qualifiés*") acting for their own account. A qualified investor is a person or a legal entity with the expertise and the facilities required to understand the risks inherent in transactions relating to securities[277].
(iii) Made exclusively to restricted circle of investors ("*cercle restreint d'investisseurs*") acting for their own account. The

---

[274] Many other EU Directives and Regulations related to capital market transactions (e.g., the Money Market Fund Regulation, the Benchmark Regulation, the Packaged Retail and Insurance-based Investment Products ("**PRIIPs**") Regulation, the Market Abuse Directive and the Market Abuse Regulation, the Alternative Investment Fund Managers Directive ("**AIFMD**"), and others) have been implemented under French law, in addition to the Markets in Financial Instruments Directive ("**MiFID**"), which came into effect on January 3, 2018, and the Regulation on over-the-counter ("**OTC**") derivatives, central counterparties and trade repositories.
[275] Article L.412-1 of the MFC.
[276] Article L.411-1 of the MFC.
[277] The definition of qualified investors includes large companies; *i.e.*, legal entities which, according to their last annual or consolidated accounts, meet two of the following criteria: (i) an average of more than 250 employees during the financial year; (ii) a total balance sheet exceeding €43 million; and (iii) an annual net turnover exceeding €50 million.
Qualified investors also include small and medium-sized companies that expressly choose qualified investor status. Small and medium- sized companies are defined as those which, according to their last annual or consolidated accounts, meet at least two of the following criteria: an average of less than 250 employees during the financial year, a total balance sheet not exceeding €43 million and an annual net turnover not exceeding €50 million.
Under the New Prospectus Directive, certain individuals may also be considered qualified investors, if they elect to be so treated, and if they meet at least two of the following criteria: (i) the investor has carried out transactions of a significant size on securities markets at an average frequency of at least 10 per quarter over the previous four quarters; (ii) the size of the investor's securities portfolio exceeds €500,000; and (iii) the investor works or has worked for at least one year in the financial sector in a professional position that requires knowledge of securities investment.

number of investors to whom the offer is made was originally to be lower than 150 persons.

(iv) Within the European Economic Area whose total consideration is lesser than €8 million[278] over a 12-month period do not qualify as public offering.

(v) Addressed to investors who acquired for a total consideration of at least €100,000 or offers of securities with a nominal value of at least €100,000.

The issuance and sale of foreign securities in France is regulated by Decree No. 2003-196 of March 7, 2003 ("**Foreign Investment Decree**"). Pursuant to the Foreign Investment Decree, the private placement of foreign shares and bonds in France requires no prior authorization from the French authorities. However, such a placement may still be restricted under the MFC.

1.2.5.3 **Germany**. Securities[279] offerings and trading in Germany are governed by several relevant statutes, rules and regulations, in particular:

(i) the Act on the Strengthening of Investor Protection and Improved Functioning of the Capital Markets;
(ii) the Act on the Strengthening of German Financial Supervision;
(iii) the Bond Act ("**SchVG**");
(iv) Commission Delegated Regulation (EU) No. 382/2014 of March 7, 2014 supplementing Directive 2003/71/EC of the European Parliament and of the Council with regard to regulatory technical standards for publication of supplements to the prospectus;

---

[278] Originally, it was €5 million. The Prospectus Regulation provides, inter alia, that member states could, as from July 21, 2018, exempt offers of securities to the public with a total consideration in the European Union of between €1 million and €8 million (calculated over a 12-month period) from the requirement to publish a prospectus; in this respect, France decided to exempt offers of securities below the threshold of €8 million from the publication of a prospectus.

[279] In accordance with section 2 of the WpPG:
(i) securities means transferable securities which can be traded on a market, in particular
   (a) shares and other securities equivalent to shares or units in limited companies (Kapitalgesellschaften) or other legal entities, and certificates representing shares;
   (b) debt securities, in particular bonds and certificates representing securities other than those mentioned in (a);
   (c) any other securities giving the right to acquire or sell such securities or to receive a cash amount determined by reference to transferable securities, currencies, interest rates or payments, commodities or other indices or measures;
with the exception of money market instruments having a maturity of less than 12 months;
(ii) equity securities means shares and other transferable securities equivalent to shares in companies, as well as any other type of transferable securities giving the right to acquire any of the aforementioned securities as a consequence of their being converted or the rights conferred by them being exercised, provided that securities of the latter type are issued by the issuer of the underlying shares or by an entity belonging to the group of the said issuer;
(iii) non-equity securities means all securities that are not equity securities.

(v) the Delegated Regulation (EU) No. 1392/2014 of April 15, 2014 supplementing Directive 2003/71/EC of the European Parliament and Council with regard to regulatory standards for publication of supplements to the prospectus;
(vi) Commission Regulation (EU) No. 596/2014 of April 16, 2014 on market abuse;
(vii) Commission Regulation (EU) No. 600/2014) of May 15, 2014 on markets in financial instruments and amending Regulation (EU) 648/2012;
(viii) Commission Regulation (EU) No. 909/2014 of July 23, 2014 on securities settlement and the Central Securities Depositories;
(ix) Commission Regulation (EU) No. 1286/2014 of November 26, 2014 on key information documents for packaged retail and insurance-based investment products ("**PRIIPs**");
(x) Commission Delegated Regulation (EU) 2015/761 of December 17, 2014 supplementing Directive 2004/109/EC of the European Parliament and of the Council with regard to certain regulatory technical standards on major holdings ("**Regulation 2015/761/EU**");
(xi) Commission Delegated Regulation (EU) of November 30, 2015 supplementing Directive 2003/71/EC of the European Parliament and of the Council with regard to regulatory technical standards for approval and publication of the prospectus and dissemination of advertisements and amending Commission Regulation (EC) No. 809/2004 has been adopted;
(xii) the Proposal for a Regulation of the European Parliament and of the Council of November 30, 2015 on the prospectus to be published when securities are offered to the public or admitted to trading;
(xiii) Commission Implementation Regulation (EU) 2016/347 of March 10, 2016 laying down implementing technical standards with regard to the precise format of insider lists and for updating insider lists in accordance with Regulation (EU) No. 596/2014;
(xiv) Commission Delegated Regulation (EU) 2017/653 of March 8, 2017 supplementing Regulation (EU) No 1286/2014 on key information documents for PRIIPs by laying down regulatory technical standards with regard to the presentation, content, review and revision of key information documents and the conditions for fulfilling the requirement to provide such documents;
(xv) the First Act Amending Financial Market Regulations of June 30, 2016 ("**FiMaNoG**");
(xvi) the German Securities Trading Reporting and Insider List Regulation ("**WpAIV**");
(xvii) the Exchange Rules of the Frankfurt Stock Exchange;
(xviii) the Financial Stability Act ("**FinStabG**");

(xix) the General Terms and Conditions (Open Market) of Deutsche Börse AG for the Regulated Unofficial Market on the FWB Frankfurter Wertpapierbörse;
(xx) the German Banking Act ("**KWG**");
(xxi) the Investment in Assets Act ("**VermAnlG**");
(xxii) the Investment Services Rules of Conduct and Organization Regulation;
(xxiii) the Ordinance for the Ascertainment of the Prohibition of Manipulation Practices ("**MaKonV**");
(xxiv) the Ordinance concerning the Admission of Securities to Official Listing on a Stock Exchange ("**BörsZulV**");
(xxv) the Safe Custody Act ("**DepotG**");
(xxvi) the Securities Prospectus Act ("**WpPG**");
(xxvii) the Securities Trading Act ("**WpHG**");
(xxviii) the Stock Corporation Act ("**AktG**");
(xxix) the Stock Exchange Act ("**BörsG**");
(xxx) the Act Implementing the Transparency Directive Amending Directive ("**TRL-ÄndRL-UmsG**");
(xxxi) the Trading Regulations for the Regulated Unofficial Market on the Frankfurt Stock Exchange; and
(xxxii) the Act Adapting Legislation in the Financial Market Area ("**KAGB-*Anpassungsgesetz***").

In addition, various EU directives have been implemented[280] in the aforementioned German rules and regulations, particularly including:

(i) Directive 2001/34/EC of May 28, 2001 on the admission of securities to official stock exchange listing and on information to be published on those securities;
(ii) Directive 2004/39/EC of April 21, 2004 on markets in financial instruments (amending Council Directives 85/611/EEC and 93/6 EEC and Directive 2000/12/EC and repealing Council Directive 93/22/EEC ("**MiFID**"));
(iii) Directive 2004/109/EC of December 15, 2004 on the harmonization of transparency requirements in relation to information about issuers whose securities are admitted to

---

[280] The Prospectus Directive (Directive 2003/71/EC) and all related level 2 measures will be replaced by the Prospectus Regulation (Regulation (EU) 2017/1129) on July 21, 2019. The Prospectus Regulation will provide a common legal basis for securities offerings in the European Union and its rules will be binding and directly applicable in all EU member states. The Prospectus Regulation aims to: (i) make it easier and cheaper for smaller companies to access capital; (ii) introduce simplification and flexibility for all types of issuers, in particular for secondary issuances and frequent issuers which are already known to capital markets; (iii) improve prospectuses for investors by introducing a retail investor-friendly summary of key information, catering for the specific information and protection needs of investors. The new prospectus regime will ensure that appropriate rules cover the full life-cycle of companies from startup until maturity as frequent issuers on regulated markets.

trading on a regulated market and amending Directive 2001/34/EC;

(iv) Directive 2010/73/EU of November 24, 2010 amending Directive 2003/71/EC of November 4, 2003 on the prospectus to be published when securities are offered to the public or admitted to trading;

(v) Directive 2011/61/EC of June 8, 2011 on Alternative Investment Fund Managers, and amending Directives 2003/41/EC and 2009/65/EC ("**AIFMD**");

(vi) Directive 2014/95/EU of October 22, 2014 amending Directive 2013/34/EU as regards disclosure of non-financial and diversity information by certain large undertakings and groups;

(vii) Directive 2014/49 EU on Deposit Guarantee Schemes;

(viii) Directive 2014/57/EU of April 16, 2014 on criminal sanctions for market abuse ("**CSMAD**"); and

(ix) Directive 2014/64/EU of May 15, 2014.

The result is that more than 85 per cent of the German rules and regulations on securities are directly applicable EU regulations.

As a basic description, an offer to the public is an offer directed at the general public, which means an offer that targets an unlimited number of potential investors. In contrast, a private placement of securities (debt and equity) requires, for example, a personal relationship between the issuer and the actual investor prior to the offer. Hence, Germany has broad exemptions from disclosure requirements for sales to sophisticated investors or to market professionals. An offer is not deemed to be an offer to the public (and therefore no prospectus is required) if it is made only to certain categories of investors. The key exemptions (some of which may be combined) in this regard are in accordance with section 3, clause 2 of the WpPG and include offers:

(i) solely addressed to qualified investors (defined as professional investors in line with the definition under MiFID);

(ii) addressed to fewer than 150 individuals or legal entities (other than qualified investors) per EU/EEA state. In this case, the offering notice may only be accessible to a maximum of 149 persons. This means that either a maximum of 149 persons are specifically addressed, or that technical measures are in place to prevent more than 149 persons from being able to read the offering notice. However, this exemption rule cannot be utilized by arbitrarily breaking down the offer into multiple parts and addressing each of these to fewer than 150 persons. Such parts of an offer would together be considered as one offer, which would trigger the prospectus requirement;

> (iii) addressed to investors only who acquire securities for at least €100,000 per investor with respect to each separate offering of securities;
> (iv) where the minimum denomination per unit amounts to at least €100,000; or
> (v) where the total consideration for all offered securities in the EEA is less than €8,000,000 over a period of 12 months (the limit of €8,000,000 applies to the offer concerned and not, for example, to the aggregate of all of an issuer's offerings)[281].

Pursuant to section 1, clause 2 WpPG there is no prospectus requirement where securities are issued by institutions licensed under the KWG for deposit taking or by issuers, the shares of which are already listed on a regulated market and the overall subscription price for all shares offered does not exceed €5 million.

Further, under section 4, clause 2 of the WpPG, an issuer is not required to publish a prospectus for admission to trading if the securities being issued are exempt, in particular:

> (i) shares representing, over a 12-month period, less than 10 per cent of the number of shares of the same class already admitted to trading on the same regulated market;
> (ii) shares being offered in exchange for shares of the same class already admitted in the same regulated market, provided that the issuance does not require a capital increase;
> (iii) shares being offered in connection with a takeover offer or spin-off, provided that a document is available containing information that is equivalent to that of a prospectus; and
> (iv) shares already admitted to trading that are offered to existing or former employees or directors, provided that certain information is supplied.

In case of a private placement of securities, there are no specific statutory requirements for any information to be provided to potential investors. However, if the issuer is providing potential investors with information, such private placement documents might be expected to contain, in an understandable manner, all information necessary to enable investors to make an informed assessment of the issuer's assets and liabilities, financial situation, profits, losses and future prospects and the rights attached to the securities. In relation to minimum requirements, Commission Regulation (EC) No. 809/2004 as amended

---

[281] Investors are protected by transparency requirements in the form of a securities information sheet for offers between €100,000 and €8 million; a prospectus is only required for offers greater than €8 million.

and section 5 of the WpPG can therefore be used in an analogous manner. Further, if an issuer does not make use of an exemption under section 3, clause 2 of the WpPG and prepares an informational document, such a document will be regarded as a prospectus and the WpPG and other rules will apply.

There are no statutory provisions that apply especially to the transferability of securities (debt and equity) acquired by investors through a private placement. If the exceptions stated in WpPG apply and the securities are admitted to trading on the stock exchange, the related securities can be traded on the stock exchange in accordance with the applicable laws and regulations of such stock exchange. Where such securities are not admitted to trading, it should be noted that in the issuer company's articles of association the transferability of securities may also be defined, and such articles may restrict the transferability of such securities.

1.2.5.4 *Ireland*. The principal statutes and regulations governing securities offerings in Ireland are incorporated in the Companies Acts 2014[282] ("**Companies Act**") and related secondary legislation. These include the following suite of EU-derived securities laws[283]:

> (i) Investment Funds, Companies and Miscellaneous Provisions Act 2005 ("**2005 Act**");
> (ii) Investment Funds, Companies and Miscellaneous Provisions Act 2006;

---

[282] The Companies Act 2014 commenced into law on 1 June 2015 and replaced all existing Irish companies' statutes in what was largely a consolidation, simplification and codification exercise. Among other things, the Companies Act 2014 created a new type of private company limited by shares called a designated activity company ("**DAC**") and changed the form of the existing private company limited by shares ("**LTD**"). The LTD is a more streamlined, simplified form of an existing private company limited by shares. The key difference between an LTD and a DAC is that an LTD shall neither:
(i) apply to have securities (or interests in them) admitted to trading or to be listed; nor
(ii) have securities (or interests in them) admitted to trading or listed.
This applies on any market, whether regulated or not, in Ireland or elsewhere (an LTD must also not have an objects clause).
However, a DAC is not subject to restrictions as regards the listing of its securities. Other than the ability to issue listed debt securities, there is little difference in the company law applicable to DACs and that currently applicable to existing private limited companies.

[283] The Prospectus Directive and all related level 2 measures will be replaced by the Prospectus Regulation (Regulation (EU) 2017/1129) on July 21, 2019. The Prospectus Regulation will provide a common legal basis for securities offerings in the European Union and its rules will be binding and directly applicable in all EU member states. The Prospectus Regulation aims to: (i) make it easier and cheaper for smaller companies to access capital; (ii) introduce simplification and flexibility for all types of issuers, in particular for secondary issuances and frequent issuers which are already known to capital markets; (iii) improve prospectuses for investors by introducing a retail investor-friendly summary of key information, catering for the specific information and protection needs of investors. The new prospectus regime will ensure that appropriate rules cover the full life-cycle of companies from startup until maturity as frequent issuers on regulated markets.

(iii) Prospectus (Directive 2003/71/EC) Regulations 2005 ("**Prospectus Directive Regulations**");
(iv) Market Abuse (Directive 2003/6/EC) Regulations 2005 ("**Irish Market Abuse Regulations**");
(v) European Communities (Admissions to Listing and Miscellaneous Provisions) Regulations 2007 (which transposes the Consolidated and Admissions and Reporting Directive ("**CARD**");
(vi) Transparency (Directive 2004/109/EC) Regulations 2007.

As in other EU member states and EEA countries, directly applicable EU regulations including the Prospectus Regulation 809/2004 ("**EU Prospectus Regulation**") and EU Market Abuse Regulation (EC) 2273/2003 ("**EU Market Abuse Regulation**") are law in Ireland. The Central Bank of Ireland ("**Central Bank**") is responsible for the regulation and supervision of regulated markets in Ireland. The Central Bank has also been designated as the competent authority for the purposes of the Prospectus Directive, the Market Abuse Directive and the Transparency Regulations. The Irish Stock Exchange has been designated as the competent authority for the purposes of CARD.

The Central Bank sets out procedural and administrative requirements and guidance in the following subordinate rules:

(i) the Prospectus Rules;
(ii) the Transparency Rules; and
(iii) the Market Abuse Rules.

The regulated market in Ireland is the Main Securities Market of the Irish Stock Exchange. The Irish Stock Exchange additionally operates two non-regulated markets that are multilateral trading facilities under MiFID, the Enterprise Securities Market ("**ESM**") and the Global Exchange Market.

The Irish Stock Exchange publishes and administers the following as the competent authority in the areas of listing and admission to trading:

(i) the Listing Rules; and
(ii) the Admission to Trading Rules.

The recommendations of the European Securities and Markets Authority (and before 1 January 2011, the Committee of European Securities Regulators) are applied in Ireland. While they do not have legal effect, they will guide regulators and the courts on the interpretation of the law. In order to avail of the exemption from the obligation to publish a prospectus, a private placing must be made to fewer than 150 natural or legal persons, other than qualified investors.

There are also exemptions for offers of securities with large minimum consideration levels (at least €100,000 per investor) or large denominations per unit (at least €100,000) or a small total consideration for the offer (less than €100,000)[284].

The Minister for Finance signed the Prospectus Regulation 2018 on August 3, 2018. The prospectus regime will not apply to securities included in an offer where the total consideration for the offer in the EU is less than €1,000,000 (until July 21, 2018, that threshold was €5,000,000). To benefit from this exemption, the total consideration for the offer must be aggregated with the consideration for all previous offers of securities of the same type in that issuer within the previous 12 months, and that aggregate consideration must be less than €1,000,000. The Prospectus Regulation allows EU member states to impose other disclosure requirements in respect of offers below €1,000,000. Ireland, however, has not sought to impose any such additional disclosure requirements on issuers. Until 21 July 2018, one of the exemptions from the obligation to publish a prospectus on an offer of securities to the public was in respect of an offer of securities with a total consideration in the EU of less than €100,000, calculated over a period of 12 months. Each Member State was given discretion to increase that threshold to not more than €8,000,000. Ireland has increased that threshold to €5,000,000. As a result, in Ireland, an offer of securities to the public with a total consideration in the EU of less than €5,000,000 (calculated over a 12-month period) will be exempt from the obligation to publish a prospectus. The other exemptions from the obligation to publish a prospect on an offer of securities to the public are unchanged, and can be used in conjunction with this amended exemption. The net effect of both of the above amendments means that the exemption threshold in Ireland remains at €5,000,000 (calculated over a 12-month period).

There are no generally applicable statutory restrictions on the transferability of securities in a private placement.

1.2.5.5 *Italy*. The principal statutes and regulations governing securities offerings in Italy (in addition to the various EU directives[285]) consist of:

---

[284] Section 68 (and Section 981, in relation to DACs) of the Companies Act.
[285] The Prospectus Directive and all related level 2 measures will be replaced by the Prospectus Regulation (Regulation (EU) 2017/1129) on July 21, 2019. The Prospectus Regulation will provide a common legal basis for securities offerings in the European Union and its rules will be binding and directly applicable in all EU member states. The Prospectus Regulation aims to: (i) make it easier and cheaper for smaller companies to access capital; (ii) introduce simplification and flexibility for all types of issuers, in particular for secondary issuances and frequent issuers which are already known to capital markets; (iii) improve prospectuses for investors by introducing a retail investor-friendly summary of key information, catering for the specific information and protection needs of investors.

(i) Italian Consolidated Financial Act ("**Italian Consolidated Financial Act**")[286], which governs all legislation applicable to companies' and intermediaries' public offerings, tender offers and listed companies operating in both the regulated and unregulated equity capital markets[287];

(ii) Italian Consolidated Banking Act ("**Italian Consolidated Banking Act**")[288], which governs the rules applicable to banks and financial intermediaries. It also sets out some provisions regarding the issue of securities;

(iii) Consob[289] resolutions 11971/1999 ("**Resolution 11971/1999**") and 16191/2007 ("**Resolution 16191/2007**"), which implements the Italian Consolidated Financial Act provisions concerning issuers and intermediaries;

(iv) Borsa Italiana SpA regulations for the functioning of its markets[290], such as the Rules of the Markets organized and

---

The new prospectus regime will ensure that appropriate rules cover the full life-cycle of companies from startup until maturity as frequent issuers on regulated markets.

[286] Legislative Decree 58/1998.

[287] According to section 1, paragraph 1, letter "u" of the Italian Consolidated Financial Act a "financial product" is not only a "financial instrument" (a definition that includes the category of transferable securities) but also "any other financial investment". In order for a product or a contractual scheme to be considered a "financial investment", such product or scheme shall have, according to Consob's consolidated interpretation on the matter, the following features: (i) require the payment of a sum of money by the investor; (ii) entail an expectation of return; and (iii) entail a risk directly associated with the payment of the sum of money.

[288] Legislative Decree 385/1993.

[289] Italian Securities and Exchange Commission (*Commissione Nazionale per le Società e la Borsa* – Consob).

[290] There are two regulated markets in Italy:

(i) The Screen-based Stock Exchange (Mercato Telematico Azionario) ("**MTA**") is the main Italian equity market and the electronic stock exchange in which shares, convertible bonds, stock options and warrants are negotiated. It is subject to strict requirements that meet the highest international standards and guarantee the capacity to attract institutional investors and private individuals. The MTA has three segments:

    (a) MTA, which is the ordinary market;

    (b) MTA STAR, which is dedicated to small and mid-cap companies that undertake to meet standards of excellence in terms of transparency, communication, liquidity and corporate governance;

    (c) MTA International, which is dedicated to shares of foreign issuers already traded on other EU regulated market.

(ii) The Electronic Investment Vehicles Market (Mercato Telematico Degli Investment Vehicles) ("**MIV**") was created with the aim of offering funds, liquidity and visibility to investment vehicles with a clear strategic vision. It is the market for the trading of shares of investment and real estate investment companies. The MIV has four segments:

    (a) closed-ended fund segment, where the shares and securities of closed-ended funds and real estate funds are traded;

    (b) investment companies segment, where the shares of investment companies are traded;

    (c) professional segment, which is accessible only to professional investors, and where special investment vehicles (such as structured investment vehicles ("**SIVs**") and special purpose acquisition companies ("**SPACs**")) are traded. This segment includes the securities of companies whose investment policy is particularly complex, such as multi-strategy vehicles;

    (d) real estate investment companies segment ("**REIC**").

managed by Borsa Italiana SpA, and Rules concerning AIM Italia, which are also implemented by instructions.

Key exemptions from the prospectus requirement include offerings:

(i) Addressing fewer than 150 persons, other than the qualified investors pursuant to paragraph (ii) below;

(ii) Addressing qualified investors[291], these being understood to be the parties specified under Article 26, paragraph 1, letter d) of the regulation incorporating the implementation rules of the Italian Consolidated Financial Act on intermediaries, adopted by Consob with the Resolution 16191/2007 as subsequently amended. Investment firms and the banks notify their classification, on request, to the issuer, without prejudice to data protection legislation in force. Investment firms and the banks authorized to continue to consider current professional customers as such, in accordance with Article 71, paragraph 6 of Directive 2004/39/EC are authorized to treat such customers as qualified investors;

(iii) Concerning financial products included in an offer for which the total price, calculated within the European Union, is less than €8,000,000[292]. To this end, several offers concerning the same

---

Unregulated markets sit under the Multilateral Trading Facility and are also managed by Borsa Italiana SpA. The unregulated markets are:
    (a) Alternative Capital Market (Mercato Alternativo del Capitale) ("**AIM Italia**"), which is dedicated to small and medium companies with high growth potential.
    (b) Trading After Hours ("**TAH**"), which is dedicated to trading after hours and is open to both retail and professional investors. A selection of the most liquid shares traded on the MTA (including the MTA International) is admitted to trading on the TAH.

[291] The following are considered qualified investors:
(i) National governments and regional authorities, central banks, international and supranational institutions and similar international organizations;
(ii) Persons authorized or regulated to operate on financial markets, both Italian and foreign;
(iii) Large companies which can fulfil at least two of the following requirements:
    > aggregate value of the balance sheet of at least €20 million;
    > net turnover of at least €40 million;
    > own funds of at least €2 million;
(iv) Institutional investors whose main activity is investing in financial instruments, including securitization companies;
(v) Entities that expressly request to an intermediary to be classified as professional customers, provided that specific procedures and at least two of the following requirements are met:
    > execution of significant transactions on the market in question, averaging ten transactions each quarter in the previous four quarters;
    > the value of the customer's financial instrument portfolio is higher than €500,000 including cash deposits;
    > the customer works, or has worked, in the financial sector for at least one year in a professional capacity which presumes awareness of the transactions and services envisaged.

[292] With the resolution 20686/2018 CONSOB, by virtue of the powers granted to it by article 100, paragraph 1, letter c), of the Italian Consolidated Financial Act, amended, with effect from 20 November 2018, article 34ter, paragraph 1, letter c) of the Resolution 11971/1999, increasing the

product, made by the same issuer or offeror in a twelve-month period shall be considered together;
(iv) Involving financial products other than those indicated in paragraphs (vi) and (vii) with a total consideration of at least €100,000 per investor for each separate offer;
(v) involving financial products other than those indicated in paragraphs (vi) and (vii) whose denomination per unit is not less than €100,000;
(vi) involving open-end collective investment undertakings whose minimum subscription amounts equate to at least €100,000;
(vii) involving financial products issued by insurance companies.

The transferability of securities acquired in a private placing is not subject to regulatory restrictions. In case of unlisted securities, their transferability may be conditioned or restricted by *ad hoc* provisions in the by-laws of the issuing company (i.e., a pre-emptive right to the benefit of the existing shareholders) or through provisions of the eventual shareholders' agreements.

1.2.5.6 **Luxemburg**. The legal framework governing the offering of securities[293] results from a blend of national laws and European directives requirements. The offering of securities is primarily governed by the Act of July 10, 2005 on prospectuses for securities ("**Prospectus Law**"), which implements Directive 2003/71/EC of the European Parliament ("**Prospectus Directive**")[294] and of the Council of 4 November 2003 on

---

exemption threshold from 5 to 8 million euro for all offers to the public of financial products made by issuers. Furthermore, with the same resolution, CONSOB extended the obligation to prepare the report of the issuer's management body on the proposal of a capital increase (as per article 72 paragraph 1-bis of the Resolution 11971/1999) also to equity securities issuance carried out through a public offering for an amount of less than 8,000,000 euros exempt from the prospectus obligation pursuant to art 34-ter, paragraph 1, letter c), of the Resolution 11971/1999.

[293] The Law of 30 May 2018 on markets in financial instruments defines transferable securities as those classes of securities that are negotiable on the capital market, with the exception of instruments of payment, such as: (i) shares in companies and other securities equivalent to shares in companies, partnerships or other entities, and depositary receipts in respect of shares; (ii) bonds or other forms of securitized debt, including depositary receipts in respect of such securities; (iii) any other securities giving the right to acquire or sell any such transferable securities or giving rise to a cash settlement determined by reference to transferable securities, currencies, interest rates or yields, commodities or other indices or measures.

[294] The Prospectus Directive and all related level 2 measures will be replaced by the Prospectus Regulation (Regulation (EU) 2017/1129) on July 21, 2019. The Prospectus Regulation will provide a common legal basis for securities offerings in the European Union and its rules will be binding and directly applicable in all EU member states. The Prospectus Regulation aims to: (i) make it easier and cheaper for smaller companies to access capital; (ii) introduce simplification and flexibility for all types of issuers, in particular for secondary issuances and frequent issuers which are already known to capital markets; (iii) improve prospectuses for investors by introducing a retail investor-friendly summary of key information, catering for the specific information and protection needs of investors. The new prospectus regime will ensure that appropriate rules cover the full life-cycle of companies from startup until maturity as frequent issuers on regulated markets.

the prospectus to be published when securities are offered to the public or admitted to trading, and amending Directive 2001/34/EC. The Prospectus Law was further amended on July 3, 2012 ("**2012 Law**") implementing Directive 2010/73/EU and by the Act of December 21, 2012, with the view to take into consideration the EU Regulation 1095/2010 establishing the European Supervisory Authority ("**ESA**"). The Prospectus Law was also recently amended in order to allow more flexibility where the securities of a third country issuer are no longer allowed to trading on the regulated market in its home member state but instead are admitted to trading in one or more other member states by Act of May 10, 2016 implementing Directive 2013/50/EU. The 2012 Law, beyond the strict implementation of the Directive 2010/73/EU, further amended the Prospectus Law in respect of public offerings and the admission to trading on a regulated market of securities that are not subject to Community harmonization under the Prospectus Directive.

The public offering of securities representing units issued by undertakings for collective investment other than the closed-end type are subject to the sole provisions of the Act on Undertaking of Collective Investments dated December 17, 2010.

According to the Prospectus LAW, no offer of transferable securities may be made to the public in Luxembourg without the prior publication of a prospectus approved by the Commission de Surveillance du Secteur Financier ("**CSSF**")[295] or a competent foreign authority. Generally, a prospectus or a simplified prospectus must contain all the information that enables prospective investors to make an informed assessment of the contemplated investment.

Certain types of offers are exempt from the obligation to publish a prospectus, and consequently the obligation to notify the CSSF or the Luxemburg Stock Exchange ("**LSE**"). These are as follows:

(i) Offers of securities addressed solely to qualified investors;
(ii) Offers of securities addressed to fewer than 150 natural or legal persons other than qualified investors, per EU member state;
(iii) Offers of securities addressed to investors who acquire securities for a total consideration of at least €100,000 per investor, for each separate offer;

---

[295] Submissions of approvals must be filed in PDF format via email to prospectus.approval@cssf.lu. Other filings will need to be made to prospectus.filing@cssf.lu, whereas final terms must be filed via the platform available on https://finalterms.apps.cssf.lu/. Finally, queries about the Prospectus Act should be made to prospectus.help@cssf.lu.

> (iv) Offers of securities whose denomination per unit amounts to at least €100,000; and
> (v) Offers of securities with a total consideration in all member states of the European Union of less than €1,000,000, which limit must be calculated over a period of 12 months[296].

Qualified investors are defined by article 2 of the Prospectus Law in a consistent manner with the definition of professional investors for purpose of the MIFID Directive 2004/39/EC of 21 April 2004 ("**MIFID Directive**"). Qualified investors are those listed under category I of Annex II of the MIFID Directive, including those persons or entities who are deemed as professional investors on request, in compliance with Annex II of the MIFID Directive, or who are recognized as an eligible counterparty pursuant to article 24 of this directive, unless they have opted to be treated as non-professionals.

In addition, the offering of certain types of securities are exempt from the obligation to publish a prospectus. These types of securities are the following:

> (i) Shares issued in substitution for shares of the same class already issued, if the issuing of such new shares does not involve any increase in the issued capital;
> (ii) Securities offered in connection with a takeover by means of an exchange offer, provided that a document is available containing information that is regarded by the CSSF as being equivalent to that of the prospectus, taking into account the requirements of the EU legislation on exchange offers;
> (iii) Securities offered, allotted or to be allotted in connection with a merger, provided that a document is available containing information that is regarded by the regulatory authority as being equivalent to that of the prospectus, taking into account the requirements of the EU legislation on mergers;
> (iv) Shares offered, allotted or to be allotted free of charge to existing shareholders, and dividends paid out in the form of shares of the same class as the shares in respect of which such dividends are paid, provided that a document is made available containing information on the number and nature of the shares and the reasons for and details of the offer;
> (v) Securities offered, allotted or to be allotted to existing or former directors or employees by their employer whose securities are already admitted to trading on a regulated market or by an affiliated undertaking, provided that a document is made

---

[296] In accordance with the Prospectus Regulation (Regulation (EU) 2017/1129), EU member states are allowed to increase that threshold up to €8,000,000.

available containing information on the number and nature of the securities and the reasons for and details of the offer;

(vi) Dividends paid out to existing shareholders in the form of shares of the same class as the shares in respect of which such dividends are paid, provided that a document is made available containing information on the number and nature of the shares and the reasons for and details of the offer; this obligation applies also to a company established outside the European Union whose securities are admitted to trading either on a regulated market or on a third-country market. In the latter case, the exemption applies provided that adequate information, including the document referred thereto, is available at least in a language customary in the sphere of international finance and provided that the European Commission has adopted an equivalence decision regarding the third-country market concerned; and

(vii) Securities offered, allotted or to be allotted to existing or former directors or employees by their employer or by an affiliated undertaking provided that the company has its head office or registered office in the European Union and provided that a document is made available containing information on the number and nature of the securities and the reasons for and details of the offer.

There are no specific regulations or legal provisions governing private placement of securities. General principles of law must, however, apply. This involves investors being treated equally and fairly and having access to the same information when subscribing to the securities. Article 17 of the Prospectus Law sets out that when no prospectus is required, material information provided by an issuer or an offeror and addressed to qualified investors or special categories of investors, including information disclosed in the context of meetings relating to offers of securities, must be disclosed to all qualified investors or special categories of investors to whom the offer is exclusively addressed. It is also advisable that the persons who carry out a private placement in Luxembourg inform potential investors that any prospectus relating to the offering of securities has not been submitted to the clearance procedures of the CSSF. They should also take the necessary measures to avoid the placement qualifying as a public offering and require the necessary undertaking from investors that they act for their own account and do not intend to resell the securities under the terms of a public offering. Finally, they should provide accurate and complete information in respect of the placed securities in order to enable the investors to make an informed assessment of the securities.

There are no particular restrictions on the transferability of securities acquired in a private placement, except that any resale to the public of such securities must be made in accordance with the rules on public offerings.

1.2.5.7 **Netherlands**. Most of the rules and regulations governing the Dutch securities originate from the European Union legislation – for example, Directive 2003/71/EC on the prospectus to be published when securities are offered to the public or admitted to trading ("**Prospectus Directive**")[297], Regulation (EC) 809/2004 implementing Directive 2003/71/EC as regards prospectuses and dissemination of advertisements ("**Prospectus Regulation**"), Directive 2004/39/EC on markets in financial instruments ("**MiFID**") and so on. Such EU legislation has been implemented into Dutch law or, in the case of regulations, is directly applicable in the Netherlands. The Financial Supervision Act (*Wet financieel toezicht*) ("**Wft**") is the main body of law governing the Dutch equity markets/exchanges. The Wft mainly contains regulatory law, such as periodic and ongoing obligations and incidental disclosure obligations for listed companies and insider trading prohibition. Additional rules and regulations applicable to listed companies can be found in a variety of other laws, governmental decrees and regulations. Certain legislation is only applicable to listed companies that have their registered seat in the Netherlands, such as the Dutch Corporate Governance Code (which applies on a comply or explain basis to Netherlands incorporated companies listed in the Netherlands or abroad). Certain other rules (such as market rules applicable in a public takeover bid) apply only to companies listed in the Netherlands, irrespective of their jurisdiction of incorporation.

Separately, Euronext has certain specific rules and regulations in place for companies listed on one of their markets. Euronext Rule Book I contains harmonized rules, applicable to all companies listed on any of the Euronext markets (that is, Amsterdam, Brussels, Paris, Lisbon or London). Euronext also has a non-harmonized rule book for each separate market it operates. The non-harmonized rule book for a particular market only applies to the companies listed on that particular market (that is, the rule book for Euronext Amsterdam is only applicable to companies listed on Euronext Amsterdam).

---

[297] The Prospectus Directive and all related level 2 measures will be replaced by the Prospectus Regulation (Regulation (EU) 2017/1129) on July 21, 2019. The Prospectus Regulation will provide a common legal basis for securities offerings in the European Union and its rules will be binding and directly applicable in all EU member states. The Prospectus Regulation aims to: (i) make it easier and cheaper for smaller companies to access capital; (ii) introduce simplification and flexibility for all types of issuers, in particular for secondary issuances and frequent issuers which are already known to capital markets; (iii) improve prospectuses for investors by introducing a retail investor-friendly summary of key information, catering for the specific information and protection needs of investors. The new prospectus regime will ensure that appropriate rules cover the full life-cycle of companies from startup until maturity as frequent issuers on regulated markets.

The Dutch capital markets are supervised by the Dutch Authority for the Financial Markets ("**AFM**").

The obligation to publish a prospectus is triggered when securities are offered to the public or admitted to trading on a regulated market situated or operating within an EEA member state.

In principle, no prospectus needs to be approved by a competent authority and made available to the public if one or more of the exceptions set forth in articles 5:3 and 5:4 of the Wft apply or if one or more of the exemptions sets forth in the Exemption Regulation Financial Supervision Act (Vrijstellingsregeling Wft) ("**exemption regulation Wft**") apply. Pursuant to these articles and this regulation it is not necessary to obtain the approval of a prospectus from a competent authority and make it available to the public in case of:

> (i) An offer of securities addressed to fewer than 150 natural or legal persons (it is not relevant how many persons actually purchase the securities offered, relevant is the number of persons to whom the offer is made).
> (ii) An offer of securities that can only be acquired for a total consideration of at least €100,000 per investor, for each separate offer.
> (iii) An offer of securities whose denomination per unit amounts to at least €100,000.
> (iv) An offer of securities with a total consideration of less than €100,000.
> (v) Shares or certificates of shares representing, over a period of 12 months, less than 10 per cent of the number of shares or certificates of shares of the same class already admitted to trading on the same regulated market located or functioning in the Netherlands.
> (vi) Securities offered in connection with a takeover by means of an exchange offer, provided that a document is available containing information which is regarded as being equivalent to that of the prospectus.
> (vii) Securities offered by an association or institution (*vereniging of instelling*) without the intention of making a profit and with the intention of obtaining funds to realize its non-commercial aims.
> (viii) The total value of the securities offered is less than €5,000,000[298], calculated over a period of 12 months and

---

[298] The [new] Prospectus Regulation (Regulation (EU) 2017/1129) provides for the option of allowing member states, at their discretion, to exempt offers in the EEA of up to €8 million over a period of 12 months. The Dutch legislator has made use of this member state option, setting the maximum amount at €5 million (up from €2.5 million), meaning that offers of securities to the public with a total consideration in the EEA of less than €5 million over the last 12 months does not require the

provided the offer is in compliance with sub clause 3 and sub clause 4 of article 53 of the exemption regulation Wft. For offerors to make use of this exception, the offeror must notify the AFM of the offering prior to its commencement and simultaneously provide the AFM with (i) certain information regarding the issuer, the offeror and the offering, and (ii) an information document in the form prescribed by law[299]. In addition, if the offer is not solely made to qualified investors, additional standard exemption disclosure language is required to be included in documents regarding the offering for offerors to make use of this exception.

1.2.5.8 **Norway**. The primary statutes and regulations governing securities offerings in Norway are the Norwegian Securities Trading Act of 2007 ("**STA**") and the Norwegian Securities Trading Regulations of 2007 ("**STR**") which implement, *inter alia*, the EU Prospectus Directive (2003/71/EC) (as amended)[300]. The STA and the STR set out when a prospectus is required, exemptions from the prospectus requirements as well as the content and disclosure requirements for prospectuses.

The regulatory authority primarily responsible for the administration of these rules is the Financial Supervisory Authority of Norway ("**NFSA**"). The NFSA also issues certain guidelines and statements related to the prospectus rules.

Securities offerings in companies listed on a regulated market or a multilateral trading facility will also be regulated by the rules adopted by the relevant marketplace. Three marketplaces are licensed to offer trading in shares in Norway: the Oslo Stock Exchange, Oslo Axess (a regulated market operated by the Oslo Stock Exchange) and Merkur Market (a multilateral trading facility operated by the Oslo Stock Exchange). The applicable rules are found in the Continuing Obligations

---

publication of a prospectus under Dutch law. For the purposes of calculating the maximum amount, the offerings of the issuer and its affiliates shall be aggregated.

[299] Exemption Regulation Financial Supervision Act, Article 53(4). The requirement to provide the information document does not apply to offerors which are subject to the PRIIPs regulation and managers of investment firms which are required to provide a prospectus to investors on the basis of the Financial Supervision Act, Article 4:37l(1).

[300] The Prospectus Directive and all related level 2 measures will be replaced by the Prospectus Regulation (Regulation (EU) 2017/1129) on July 21, 2019. The Prospectus Regulation will provide a common legal basis for securities offerings in the European Union and its rules will be binding and directly applicable in all EU member states. The Prospectus Regulation aims to: (i) make it easier and cheaper for smaller companies to access capital; (ii) introduce simplification and flexibility for all types of issuers, in particular for secondary issuances and frequent issuers which are already known to capital markets; (iii) improve prospectuses for investors by introducing a retail investor-friendly summary of key information, catering for the specific information and protection needs of investors. The new prospectus regime will ensure that appropriate rules cover the full life-cycle of companies from startup until maturity as frequent issuers on regulated markets.

for Stock Exchange Listed Companies, which apply to companies with shares listed on the Oslo Stock Exchange or Oslo Axess and the Continuing Obligations of companies admitted to trading on the Merkur Market (which applies to companies with shares listed on the Merkur Market).

The requirement to publish a prospectus relates to the offering of transferable securities[301].

Private placements are very common in the Norwegian market as they allow for capital raisings in a timely and cost-efficient manner. This applies both to listed and unlisted companies.

When completing a private placement, the issuer and its advisers must observe the principle of good business conduct and applicable prospectus rules. Except for that, there are no particular statutory securities law provisions regulating private placements. The most relevant prospectus exemptions used in private placements in the Norwegian market are:

> (i) offers made to fewer than 150 non-professional investors;
> (ii) offers of securities with large minimum consideration levels (at least €100,000 per investor) or large denominations per unit (at least €100,000) or a small total consideration for the offer (less than €100,000);
> (iii) offers of securities with a total consideration of less than €1,000,000, which limit must be calculated over a period of 12 months.

In the event that the securities issued in the private placement are to be admitted to trading on a regulated market, the private placement will trigger an obligation to publish a prospectus regardless of whether the above exemptions are applicable if the capital increase pertaining to the private placement amounts to at least 10 per cent of the number of shares already listed in the same class of shares, calculated over a 12-month period (see section 7-5(1) of the STA). Such listing prospectus must be published before the first day of listing of the new shares.

There are no specific procedures that must be implemented to make a valid private placement[302].

---

[301] The STA does not differentiate between offerings of debt securities and equity securities, nor between primary offerings and secondary offerings.

[302] It should be noted that for companies with shares listed on the Oslo Stock Exchange or Oslo Axess, the Oslo Stock Exchange will monitor compliance with the securities law principle of equal treatment of shareholders, which follows from section 5-14 of the STA and the Continuing Obligations for Stock

Private placements in the Norwegian market are often subject to an exemption to publish an offering prospectus[303]. As long as there is no obligation to publish a prospectus there are no formal requirements for specific information to be made available to potential investors. However, section 3-9 of the STA includes a general provision on good business conduct in securities transactions which set out that: conduct of business rules shall be observed in approaches addressed to the general public or to individuals which contain an offer or encouragement to make an offer to purchase, sell or subscribe to financial instruments or which are otherwise intended to promote trade in financial instruments. The requirement of good business conduct must be seen together with customary market practice. If the information provided to potential investors is in line with customary market practice, then the provision will most likely be satisfied with respect to this point. Usually, potential investors in a private placement will receive a company or investor presentation or similar describing the company, the market, risk factors, key financials and transaction details.

Generally, there are no transfer restrictions on shares in Norwegian companies unless these specifically follow from a particular agreement among shareholders or the company's articles of association. For private limited liability companies, the Norwegian Private Limited Liability Act provides that the board of directors must consent to any share transfers unless otherwise follows from the articles of association; however, any refusal to consent must have reasonable cause.

There are no specific statutory restrictions that apply to the transferability of securities acquired in a private placement. Participants in private placements may in some cases enter into lock-up agreements with the seller or issuer or managers.

1.2.5.9 **United Kingdom**[304]. The Financial Services and Markets Act 2000 ("**FSMA**") as amended and supplemented by the Financial Services Act

---

Exchange Listed Companies and is similar to the equal treatment principle set out in the Norwegian company law.

[303] If a public offering of transferable securities exceeds an amount of €1 million over a 12-month period, and no relevant exemptions apply, a prospectus must be prepared prior to commencement of the offering. The STA differentiates between national prospectuses and European Economic Area ("**EEA**") prospectuses. National prospectuses must be prepared for offerings in the amount of between €1 million and €5 million, while EEA prospectuses must be prepared for offerings of at least €5 million. If the prospectus is prepared in connection with a listing on a regulated market, the issuers must always prepare an EEA prospectus. The main differences between national prospectuses and EEA prospectuses are the content requirements and approval or publication process. National prospectuses have significantly less comprehensive content requirements than EEA prospectuses.

[304] At the time of writing, the UK is due to leave the EU on March 29, 2019. While there have been various predictions of what might happen upon exit, there have been rather few concrete steps that enable predictions to be made with any accuracy. On March 29, 2017, the UK gave notice under

2012 ("**FSA 2012**"), together with its subordinate legislation, the Listing Rules ("**LR**") of the United Kingdom Listing Authority ("**UKLA**") and the UKLA Prospectus Rules ("**PR**"), which implement the Prospectus Directive ("**PD**")[305] as amended in the UK, constitute the primary regime governing

---

Article 50 of the Treaty on the European Union of its intention to exit the EU, setting the exit date as March 29, 2019 and starting a process of negotiations with the EU regarding the terms of the exit and the framework of the future trading relationship between the remaining EU member states ("**EU27**") and the UK. In December 2017, agreement in principle was reached between the EU27 and the UK on the first phase of negotiations for the withdrawal of the UK, which was sufficient to allow the negotiations to move on to the second phase concerning the framework for a future trade agreement between the UK and the EU27 and a transition period to cover the time between the UK's exit and the time when the new trading arrangements are actually in place. On March 19, 2018, the UK and the EU announced that their negotiating teams had reached agreement on a transition period, which provides that, although the UK will formally exit the EU on March 29, 2019, it will continue to apply EU law in such a way that it produces in the UK the same legal effects as those it produces within the EU (subject as otherwise provided in the agreement). By the same token, the EU member states will continue to treat the UK as a member state during the transition period (subject as otherwise provided in the agreement). This transition period is scheduled to last until 31 December 2020. However, this agreement on a transition period is to form part of the overall agreement on the terms of the UK's withdrawal ("**Withdrawal Agreement**"), including such issues as the Irish border. As such, the transition period will only come into effect if the entire Withdrawal Agreement is agreed and implemented. On June 26, 2018, the EU (Withdrawal) Act 2018 ("**EUWA**") received Royal Assent. Its purpose is, with effect from the day the UK exits the EU, (i) to repeal the European Communities Act 1972 ("**ECA**"), which incorporates EU law into the UK domestic legal order and (ii) to convert the acquis – the body of European legislation – into UK law at the moment of repeal of the ECA so that, to the greatest practical extent, the same rules and laws will apply in the UK on the day after exit as on the day before. Following enactment of the EUWA, the UK government published a number of papers describing how the UK intends to approach amending financial services legislation to deal with the issues thrown up by the Brexit process. There are two principal themes to this approach: (i) transition period (planning to proceed on the basis that the transition period agreed will be in place between 29 March 2019 and 31 December 2020); (ii) No deal (planning to proceed on the basis that the UK and the EU fail to reach an agreement on the terms of the UK's withdrawal from the EU with the result that no transition period comes into effect when the UK exits the EU on 29 March 2019). Assuming the terms of the Withdrawal Agreement are eventually finalized between the UK and the EU27, the UK government proposes to give legal effect in the UK to the Withdrawal Agreement by primary legislation currently known as the Withdrawal Agreement and Implementation Bill. The text of this Bill has not yet been published but, among other things, it will require some amendment of the EUWA to provide for the continuing implementation of EU law in the UK during the transition period. If the UK and the EU27 fail to reach an agreement on the terms of the UK's withdrawal from the EU, with the result that the transition period does not come into effect, then it is likely that the UK will exit the EU on March 29, 2019 and simply become a "third country" as far as EU legislation is concerned. To prepare for this eventuality, the UK government intends to use powers in the EUWA to ensure that the UK continues to have a functioning financial services regulatory regime. In a no-deal scenario, the UK government envisages that the responsibilities of EU bodies could be reassigned efficiently and effectively to UK authorities. The UK government also recognizes it would be appropriate to introduce what it calls a Temporary Permissions Regime, which would: (i) allow firms within the European Economic Area that have lost their passporting rights on the UK's exit from the EU to continue operating in the UK for a time-limited period after the UK has left the EU; and (ii) provide those firms wishing to maintain their UK business permanently with sufficient time to apply for full authorization from UK regulators.

[305] The Prospectus Directive and all related level 2 measures will be replaced by the Prospectus Regulation (Regulation (EU) 2017/1129) on July 21, 2019. The Prospectus Regulation will provide a common legal basis for securities offerings in the European Union and its rules will be binding and directly applicable in all EU member states. The Prospectus Regulation aims to: (i) make it easier and

offers of listed securities[306]. Listed securities are securities that have been admitted to the Official List of the UKLA. The PR also apply to unlisted securities offered to the public. In the UK, the process of listing is separate from, albeit parallel to, gaining admission to trading.

The regulatory authorities in the UK are: (i) the Financial Services Authority ("**FSA**")[307], the UKLA[308], the London Stock Exchange ("**LSE**")[309].

An approved prospectus is required:

> (i) before transferable securities (i.e. shares and debt securities which are negotiable on the public market) are offered to the public in the UK[310];
> (ii) before an application is made for transferable securities to be admitted to trading on a UK regulated market[311].

An offer to the public is defined widely as being a communication to any person which presents sufficient information on the transferable securities to be offered, and the terms on which they are to be offered, to enable an investor to decide to buy or subscribe for the securities in question.

---

cheaper for smaller companies to access capital; (ii) introduce simplification and flexibility for all types of issuers, in particular for secondary issuances and frequent issuers which are already known to capital markets; (iii) improve prospectuses for investors by introducing a retail investor-friendly summary of key information, catering for the specific information and protection needs of investors. The new prospectus regime will ensure that appropriate rules cover the full life-cycle of companies from startup until maturity as frequent issuers on regulated markets.

[306] The Financial Services and Markets Act 2000 (Regulated Activities) Order 2001 defines securities as including: (i) shares; (ii) bonds, debentures, certificates of deposit, and other instruments creating or acknowledging indebtedness; (iii) warrants and other instruments giving entitlements to investments in shares, bonds, debentures, certificates of deposit, and other instruments creating or acknowledging indebtedness; (iv) certificates representing certain securities (that is, certificates or other instruments that confer contractual or property rights in respect of certain types of securities held by another person and the transfer of which may be effected without the consent of that other person); (v) units in a CIS; (vi) rights under a stakeholder or personal pension scheme; and (vii) greenhouse gas and other emission allowances.

The definition of transferable securities under FSMA cross-refers to MiFID II which in turn defines transferable securities as *"those classes of securities which are negotiable on the capital market, with the exception of instruments of payment"*.

[307] The FSA derives its statutory powers from FSMA and is responsible for regulating the UK financial services sector. In particular, the FSA seeks to maintain market confidence, promote public awareness, protect consumers and reduce financial crime.

[308] The UKLA is the name given to the FSA when acting in its capacity as the competent authority for the purposes of maintaining the FSA's "Official List".

[309] Not strictly a "regulatory authority", London Stock Exchange plc is a publicly traded company which runs London's principal markets.

[310] Section 85(1) FSMA.

[311] Section 85(2) FSMA.

FSMA and the PR contain provisions that may exempt private placements from triggering the public offer prospectus requirement. No prospectus is needed when:

> (i) offers are made to or directed at qualified investors only;
> (ii) offer is made to or directed at fewer than 150 persons, other than qualified investors, per EEA State;
> (iii) the minimum consideration which may be paid by any person for transferable securities acquired by him pursuant to the offer is at least €100,000 (or an equivalent amount);
> (iv) the transferable securities being offered are denominated in amounts of at least €100,000 (or equivalent amounts);
> (v) the total consideration for the transferable securities being offered in the EEA states cannot exceed €8,000,000[312] (or an equivalent amount).

If the securities being placed are not being admitted to trading on a regulated market (or, if they are, if they and other securities of the same class admitted in the previous 12 months represent less than 10 per cent of the number of such securities already admitted to trading on the same market), no requirement for a prospectus under the "admission to trading" rule will arise either.

There are no special procedures that must be followed to implement a valid private placement.

For an exempt private placement, there are no official requirements for providing information to potential investors if there is no additional proposal to admit the securities to listing or trading. Irrespective of whether a prospectus is produced, in practice investors will require information on the issuer and securities in order to decide whether to invest in the securities.

No restrictions apply to the transferability of listed securities acquired in a private placement. However, in the case of unlisted securities in a private limited company, it is usual for placees of shares to enter into lock-up agreements in which they undertake not to dispose of their shares within a certain period (usually six months) of their allotment. This is to avoid the placement being regarded as a public offer of shares

---

[312] The [new] Prospectus Regulation (Regulation (EU) 2017/1129) provides for the option of allowing member states, at their discretion, to exempt offers in the EEA of up to €8 million over a period of 12 months. The UK legislator has made use of this member state option, setting the maximum amount at €8 million. Note, however, that this exemption only applies to the offer trigger for a prospectus. A prospectus will still be required for the admission to trading of the securities unless there is an applicable exemption.

Crypto-assets global corporate finance transactions

in a private company in contravention of section 755 of the Companies Act 2006.

1.2.6   **Hong Kong**. While it is part of the People's Republic of China, Hong Kong maintains its own domestic legal system by virtue of its status as a special administrative region. Chinese laws do not apply in Hong Kong, save as expressly listed in Annex III of the Basic Law. In general, any prospectus, notice, circular, brochure, advertisement, or other document which offers or invites offers to subscribe for or purchase any shares in or debentures of a company in Hong Kong (including a company incorporated outside Hong Kong, and whether or not it has established a place of business in Hong Kong) is required to comply with the content and registration requirements of the Hong Kong Companies Ordinance ("**CO**"). In parallel with the prospectus requirements under the CO, the Securities and Futures Ordinance ("**SFO**") also stipulates that issuing and possessing for the purposes of issue, whether in Hong Kong or elsewhere, an advertisement, invitation or document which contains invitations or offers to acquire shares of a company to the public are prohibited unless it has been authorized by the Securities and Futures Commission of Hong Kong ("**SFC**")[313].

Securities (as defined in Schedule 1 of the SFO) include shares, stocks, debentures, loan stocks, funds, bonds or notes of, or issued by, a body, whether incorporated or unincorporated, or a government or municipal government authority, rights, options or interests, or interests in any collective investment scheme[314].

---

[313] Under the SFO, regulated activities that must be carried out with a license are:
Type 1: dealing in securities;
Type 2: dealing in futures contracts;
Type 3: leveraged foreign exchange trading;
Type 4: advising on securities;
Type 5: advising on futures contracts;
Type 6: advising on corporate finance;
Type 7: providing automated trading services;
Type 8: securities margin financing;
Type 9: asset management;
Type 10: providing credit rating services;
Type 11: dealing in over-the-counter (OTC) derivative products or advising on OTC derivative products;
Type 12: providing client clearing services for OTC derivative transactions.
It is relatively easy to establish whether or not a person is appropriately licensed as the SFC maintains a public register of licensed persons, available at https://www.sfc.hk/web/EN/regulatory-functions/intermediaries/licensing/register-of-licensees-and-registered-institutions.html.
[314] Collective investment schemes (as defined in Schedule 1 of the SFO) are composed of four elements: (i) they involve arrangements in respect of any property; (ii) participants do not have day-to-day control over the management of the property; (iii) the property is managed as a whole by or on behalf of the person operating the arrangements, the contributions of the participants and the profits or income from which payments are made to them are pooled, or both; (iv) and the purpose or effect of acquiring the right and interest in the property is to enable participants to participate in or receive profits, income or other returns arising or likely to arise from the acquisition of the property.

Currently, there are 12 types of offers of shares and debentures ("**Safe Harbors**") which are exempt from the prospectus requirements of the CO and the authorization requirements of the SFO. Among these, four types of safe harbors which have been commonly relied on to facilitate private placement in Hong Kong are as follows:

(i) Offers to professional investors ("**Professionals Exemption**"). "Professional investor" is defined in the SFO and the Securities and Futures (Professional Investors) Rules and includes the following Type 2 professional investors [315]:

(a) a trust corporation having been entrusted under the trust or trusts of which it acts as a trustee with total assets of not less than HK$40,000,000:

> as stated in the most recent audited financial statement prepared in respect of the trust corporation within 16 months before the relevant date;
> as ascertained by referring to one or more audited financial statements, each being the most recent audited financial statement, prepared in

---

[315] In addition to the following Type 1 Professional Investors:
> An exchange company, clearing house, exchange controller or investor compensation company recognized as such under the SFO, or a person authorized to provide automated trading services under Section 95(2) of the SFO.
> An intermediary (i.e. a corporation licensed under the SFO to conduct any regulated activity), or a person carrying on the business of providing investment services which is regulated under the law of any place outside Hong Kong.
> An authorized financial institution (i.e. a bank, restricted license bank or deposit taking company authorized under the Banking Ordinance (Cap. 155 of Hong Kong), or a bank which is not an authorized financial institution but is regulated under the law of any place outside Hong Kong.
> An insurer authorized under the Insurance Companies Ordinance (Cap. 41) of Hong Kong, or a person carrying on insurance business and regulated under the law of any place outside Hong Kong.
> (i) A collective investment scheme authorized under Section 104 of the SFO; or (ii) A scheme which is similarly constituted under the law of any place outside Hong Kong and, if it is regulated under the law of that place, is permitted to be operated under that law, or a person who operates such scheme.
> A registered scheme as defined in Section 2(1) of the Mandatory Provident Fund Schemes Ordinance (Cap. 485) of Hong Kong, or its constituent fund as defined in Section 2 of the Mandatory Provident Fund Schemes (General) Regulation, or a person who, in relation to any such registered scheme, is an approved trustee or service provider as defined in Section 2(1) of that ordinance, or who is an investment manager of any such registered scheme or constituent fund.
> (i) A registered scheme as defined in Section 2(1) of the Occupational Retirement Schemes Ordinance (Cap. 426) of Hong Kong; or (ii) An offshore scheme as defined in Section 2(1) of that ordinance which, if regulated under the law of the place where it is domiciled, is permitted to be operated under the law of such place, or an administrator as defined in that Ordinance of any such scheme.
> A government (other than a municipal government authority), an institution which performs the functions of a central bank, or a multilateral agency.

respect of the trust or any of the trusts and within 16 months before the relevant date; or
> as ascertained by referring to one or more custodian statements issued to the trust corporation in respect of the trust or any of the trusts within 12 months before the relevant date;

(b) any individual, either alone or with any of his associates on joint account, having an investment portfolio of not less than HK$8,000,000:

> as stated in a certificate issued by an auditor or a certified public accountant of the individual within 12 months before the relevant date; or
> as ascertained by referring to one or more custodian statements issued to the individual (either alone or with the associate) within 12 months before the relevant date;

(c) any corporation or partnership having a portfolio or not less than HK$8,000,000 or total assets of not less than HK$40,000,000:

as ascertained by referring to:

> the most recent audited financial statement prepared in respect of the corporation or partnership (as the case may be) within 16 months before the relevant date; or
> one or more custodian statements issued to the corporation or partnership (as the case may be) within 12 months before the relevant date;

(d) any corporation whose sole business is to hold investments and which is wholly owned by an individual who, either alone or with any of his associates on a joint account, has an investment portfolio of not less than HK$8,000,000.

The above thresholds must be determined in a certain manner and by reference to specific dates.

It is possible to market the shares to the Type 1 and Type 2 professional investors in reliance on this exemption. However, under the Securities and Futures (Professional Investor) Rules (the "**Professional Investor Rules**") the offeror must obtain a documentary proof to establish that the investor qualifies as a professional investor.

(ii) Private Placement Exemption ("**Private Placement Exemption**")[316]. Currently, there is no statutory provision offering a precise definition of private placement in Hong Kong. As a result, the definition of private placement can be examined only in the context of what will not be considered as an "*offer to the public*".

Section 48A of the CO provides that an offer or an invitation is not required to be treated as being made to the public if "*it can properly be regarded, in all the circumstances, as not being calculated to result, directly or indirectly, in the shares or debentures becoming available for subscription or purchase by persons other than those receiving the offer or invitation, or otherwise as being a domestic concern of the persons making and receiving it*". This is the only statutory guide as to what will not constitute an offer to the public and it offers only minimal assistance in construing the definition of private placement, as there remains no precise definition given to the meaning of "*offer to the public*" whilst the term "*public*" is defined in the SFO as meaning "*the public of Hong Kong, and includes any class of that public*".

Due to the lack of case law and legislation on private placements, a body of market practice has developed to govern private placements which includes:

> (a) the offer in Hong Kong should be made to a limited number of offerees and, as a rule of thumb, 50 is taken as the maximum number of persons[317] to whom the offer may be made for the offer to be considered not an offer to the public. The fewer offerees involved, the less likelihood there is of the offer being regarded as an offer to the public;

---

[316] It is possible to combine the Professionals Exemption and the Private Placement Exemption so that documents offering shares in the Company to unlimited numbers of professional investors and to a maximum of not more than 50 other persons (who do not qualify as professional investors) will be exempt from the CO prospectus requirements. If reliance is to be placed on both exemptions, no more than 50 copies of the information memorandum should be issued to persons who do not qualify as professional investors and the steps specified above should also be taken in respect of any offers to such persons.

[317] It is not possible to increase the number of offerees by staggering placements of the shares.

(b) each offer document to be issued should be serial numbered and state clearly that it is not an offer to the public;

(c) each offer document should be individually addressed to a specific offeree and only that offeree should be capable of accepting the offer and taking up the securities;

(d) the offer document should contain appropriate wording indicating the restricted nature of the offering and should expressly note that the offer document should not be passed to any other person;

(e) the minimum number of securities to be acquired should be sufficiently high to make it clear that the offer is intended only for investors of substantial means;

(f) documents which are returned by an offeree should not be reissued in an effort to fill the minimum or maximum subscription levels for a particular offer. This is because the greater the number of people to whom the information memorandum and other information are distributed, the greater the risk will be that the offer will be regarded as being an offer to the public rather than a private placement;

(g) there must be no advertising, press release or press conference relating to the proposed offering or the offer document in Hong Kong;

(iii) Offers in respect of which the total consideration payable for the shares or debentures concerned do not exceed the amount of HK$5,000,000 ("**Small Offer Exemption**").

(iv) Offers in respect of which the minimum denomination of, or the minimum consideration payable by any person for, the shares or, in the case of debentures, the minimum principal amount to be subscribed or purchased, is not less than HK$500,000 (US$64.100). To rely on this exemption ("**Sophisticated investor exemption**"), every investor must pay a minimum of HK$500,000. If they do so, investors do not additionally need to be "professionals" within the definition referred to above.

(v) Offers to persons outside Hong Kong ("**Offers to persons outside Hong Kong**"). Offers to the persons outside Hong Kong can be disregarded in determining whether any exemption applies since those offers do not need to be taken into account. For example, when determining whether the number of offerees is within the 50 persons limit allowed under the Private Placement Exemption, it is only necessary to count the number of offerees in Hong Kong.

Whilst the above types of offers do not require the offer document(s) to comply with the prospectus content and registration requirements of the CO, they must nevertheless contain an appropriate warning in the form stipulated by the CO[318]. Further, offerings exempt from the prospectus requirements under the Companies Ordinance are also exempt from the SFO advertising restrictions under Section 103(2)(ga) of the SFO and Section 2(1)(b)(ii) of the CO.

It is an offence under Section 103 of the SFO for a person to issue in Hong Kong an advertisement, invitation or document which is or contains an invitation to the public to enter into or offer to enter into an agreement to acquire, dispose of, subscribe for or underwrite securities, unless the issue is authorized by the SFC under Section 105(1) of the SFO. It should be noted that the SFO regime covers advertisements and invitations made verbally as well as written documents. In addition, the SFC has stated that the provisions of the SFO and CO relating to the advertisement, offering and dealing of securities apply equally to activities conducted over the internet. The sending of marketing material over the internet is therefore subject to the same restrictions under the CO and the SFO.

There are a number of exemptions from the investment advertisements requirements. Most importantly, any invitation to the public which relates to an offer within the Safe harbors, is also exempt from the prohibition on unauthorized investment advertisements by virtue of Section 103(2)(gaa) of the SFO. Accordingly, the SFC authorization is not required for invitations relating to an offer:

    (i) to investors each paying a minimum consideration of HK$500,000 for the shares; or

---

[318] Required
"WARNING: The contents of this document have not been reviewed by any regulatory authority in Hong Kong. You are advised to exercise caution in relation to the offer. If you are in any doubt about any of the contents of this document, you should obtain independent professional advice".

Suggested
"WARNING: The contents of this [document] have not been reviewed nor endorsed by any regulatory authority in Hong Kong. You are advised to exercise caution in relation to the offer. If you are in any doubt about any of the contents of this [document], you should obtain independent professional advice. This [document] has not been approved by the Securities and Futures Commission in Hong Kong, nor has a copy of it been registered by the Registrar of Companies in Hong Kong. Accordingly, [the securities offered under this document] may not be offered or sold in Hong Kong by means of this or any other document except in circumstances which fall within an exemption from registration or authorization requirements under the Hong Kong Companies Ordinance and the Hong Kong Securities and Futures Ordinance. This [document] may not be reproduced in whole or in part nor may it be passed by you to any other person [and the offer in it is not capable of acceptance by any person other than the named addressee]".

(ii) in circumstances where the total consideration payable for the shares is less than HK$5 million; or

(iii) to unlimited numbers of professional investors, overseas investors and up to a maximum of 50 other investors.

1.2.7 **India**. Some of the key statutes and regulations governing securities offerings in India and the authorities administering them are as follows:

(i) the (India) Companies Act, 2013 ("**2013 Act**") (to the extent notified) and (India) Companies Act, 1956 ("**1956 Act**") (to the extent such enactment is in force) (collectively, "**Companies Act**") – the Companies Act is the principal legislation governing companies in India and sets out the broad framework for the offering of securities by companies, including public offerings and private placements. In addition, the relevant rules under the 2013 Act in relation to allotment of securities, share capital and acceptance of deposits, issue of global depositary receipt ("**the Rules**") are also in force. While the Companies Act is primarily administered by the Ministry of Company Affairs ("**MCA**"), certain specified provisions of the Companies Act, in relation to listed companies and the public offering of securities, are administered by the Securities and Exchange Board of India ("**SEBI**");

(ii) the SEBI (Issue of Capital and Disclosure Requirements) Regulations, 2009 ("**ICDR Regulations**") – the ICDR Regulations, framed by SEBI, are the principal legislation that comprehensively regulate the public offering of securities and other securities offerings by listed companies such as rights offerings. The ICDR Regulations lay down detailed provisions on eligibility, disclosure requirements, restrictions and procedures to be followed in relation to the public offering of securities and other kinds of securities offerings by listed companies. The ICDR Regulations are administered by SEBI;

(iii) the Foreign Exchange Management Act, 1999 ("**Foreign Exchange Act**") – the Foreign Exchange Act, including the rules and regulations framed and the circulars issued thereunder, sets out requirements in relation to foreign investment in securities offerings such as the participation of non-residents, and also regulates foreign currency debt securities. The Foreign Exchange Act, including the rules and regulations framed and the circulars issued thereunder, is administered by the Reserve Bank of India ("**RBI**");

(iv) the Securities Contracts (Regulation) Act, 1956 ("**Securities Contracts Act**") – the Securities Contracts Act, along with the rules and regulations framed thereunder, govern the listing of securities on the stock exchange and certain aspects relating to the public offering of securities. The Securities Contracts Act is administered by the government of India, along with SEBI and the stock exchanges;

(v) the SEBI (Issue and Listing of Debt Securities) Regulations, 2008 ("**Debt Regulations**") – the Debt Regulations, issued by SEBI, govern the offering of debt securities, including public offerings and private placement of listed debt securities. The Debt Regulations are administered by SEBI; and

(vi) the SEBI (Issue and Listing of Non-Convertible Redeemable Preference Shares) Regulations, 2013 ("**RPS Regulations**") – the RPS Regulations, issued by SEBI, govern the offering of non-convertible redeemable preference shares, including public offerings and listing of privately placed non-convertible preference shares. The RPS Regulations are administered by SEBI.

The statutes and regulations applying to the offering of securities[319] and their marketing in India are consistent with best international practices that prohibit accessing public capital unless registration or authorization requirements are complied with or a relevant exemption applies[320].

---

[319] Under the Securities Contracts Act, securities are:
(i) shares, scrips, stocks, bonds, debentures, debenture stock or other marketable securities of a like nature in or of any incorporated company or other body corporate (for the removal of doubts, it is hereby declared that securities shall not include any unit linked insurance policy or scrips or any such instrument or unit, by whatever name called, which provides a combined benefit risk on the life of the persons and investment by such persons and issued by an insurer referred to in Clause (9) of Section 2 of the Insurance Act, 1938);
    (i)(i) derivative;
    (i)(ii) units or any other instrument issued by any collective investment scheme to the investors in such schemes;
    (i)(iii) security receipt as defined in clause (zg) of section 2 of the Securitization and Reconstruction of Financial Assets and Enforcement of Security Interest Act, 2002;
    (i)(iv) units or any other such instrument issued to the investors under any mutual fund scheme.
    (i)(v) any certificate or instrument (by whatever name called), issued to an investor by any issuer being a special purpose distinct entity which possesses any debt or receivable, including mortgage debt, assigned to such entity, and acknowledging beneficial interest of such investor in such debt or receivable, including mortgage debt, as the case may be;
(ii) Government securities;
    (ii)(i) such other instruments as may be declared by the central government to be securities;
(iii) rights or interest in securities.
[320] It is a recently enacted legislation that has, for the most part, replaced the 1956 Act. Until recently, the Companies Act contained detailed provisions regulating various aspects of capital markets, which unfortunately resulted in a multiplicity of rules and regulations. Illustratively, unlike the 1956 Act, a company proposing to make an IPO of its shares or convertible securities, in addition to complying with the ICDR Regulations, was also required to comply with the Rules, which stipulated various additional disclosures, including details pertaining to the source of funds of the promoter's contribution to the IPO. These additional disclosure norms made compliance more onerous and

The 2013 Act prescribes certain requirements in relation to private placements of securities, including shares and debentures. Under the 2013 Act, for an offering to qualify as a private placement, it needs to be ensured that the offer and invitation to subscribe for securities is not made to more than 50 persons. However, under the Rules, this limit has been raised to 200 persons in aggregate in a financial year for each kind of security. Further, these limits do not apply to securities issued to employees under a scheme of employee stock options and to QIBs. Unlike the 1956 Act, under the 2013 Act, even unrelated and independent multiple offers made during a financial year will be combined to determine compliance with the requirement to offer securities to less than the specified number of persons. In other words, for an offer or invitation to subscribe to qualify as a private placement, the "rule of 200" should be adhered to in one financial year, namely, all private placements (other than private placements to QIBs and employees under stock options) in one financial year will be aggregated for the purpose of computing the number of investors. Further, the Rules state that each private placement is to be approved by a special resolution of shareholders. However, for a private placement of debt securities, a single special resolution for all placements in a year may be passed. SEBI has permitted issuers who have sold shares or debentures to persons exceeding 49, but below 200, in number, in a single financial year to avoid penal action, upon carrying out certain remedial measures. This revised regulatory treatment has enabled certain companies and is expected to continue to assist companies in the rectification of private placements that may have been held to be deemed public offerings under the 1956 Act, when such allotments were made in the breach of the "rule of 50".

Under the 2013 Act, private placements are required to be made through an offer letter in the format prescribed under the Rules. The format prescribed under the Rules includes disclosures relating to the business, risk factors and legal action pending or taken by any government department or statutory body against the promoters. Recently, some amendments to the 2013 Act have reduced the burden of compliance and filing of offer letters by unlisted issuers.

Companies offering securities under private placement shall not release any public advertisements or utilize any media, marketing or distribution channels or agents to inform the public at large about such an offer. All

---

cumbersome. However, the Companies Act was amended on May 7, 2018 to eliminate the disclosure requirement under both the Companies Act and the Rules. Nevertheless, the Companies Act continues to stipulate the penalties for untrue statements or material omissions made in a prospectus, which are stringent, and include, in certain instances, mandatory imprisonment. Despite the stringent nature of the penalties under the Companies Act, investors have generally sought recourse against errant companies under the SEBI framework.

private placement offers shall be made to only those persons whose names are recorded by the company prior to the invitation to subscribe and such persons shall receive the offer by name.

1.2.8   *Israel*. The main legislation applicable to securities exchanges is the Securities Law 1968 ("**Securities Law**") and the various regulations issued under it. In addition, the Israeli Companies Law 1999 ("**Companies Law**") features a long list of corporate governance provisions applicable to listed companies. The main regulator of capital markets is the Israeli Securities Authority ("**ISA**"). The Supervisor of Capital Markets in the Ministry of Finance is also a relevant regulator in this field, as this office regulates many aspects of the activities of the institutional investors, which are key players in the Israeli capital market.

The basic position under the Securities Law is that every offer of securities[321] to the public requires, inter alia, the filing of a prospectus with the ISA. However, in order to assist businesses in accessing the capital markets with minimal regulatory involvement, the Securities Law provides several exemptions from such requirement. Section 15 of the Securities Law provides that making an offer to 35 persons or entities or less in Israel during any given 12-month period is exempt from the requirement for publication or delivery of a prospectus. Another important exemption covers offers made to those types of investors which the Securities Law defines as sophisticated investors ("**sophisticated investors**"), being investors in respect of whom there exists a presumption, due to their nature, that they do not require the protection of the Securities Law. The list of such sophisticated investors includes financial institutions, such as insurance companies, banking corporations and mutual funds, it being generally clear whether or not an entity is one of these. The list, though, also includes a corporate entity whose qualification as a sophisticated investor is based on equity value alone (also referred to as a "**qualified corporation**"), and an individual

---

[321] Section 1 of the Israeli Securities Law 1968 ("**Securities Law**") defines securities as "*certificates issued in series by a company, a cooperative society or any other corporation conferring a right of membership or participation in them or claim against them, and certificates conferring a right to acquire securities, all of which whether registered or bearer securities, excluding securities issued by the Government or by the Bank of Israel which comply with one of the following: (i) they do not confer a right of participation or membership in a corporation and are not convertible into, or realizable for, securities conferring such a right; (ii) they are issued under special legislation*". This definition is broad. Case law, however, has ruled that the intention of the legislator was clearly not to paint such a broad stoke. The Israeli Supreme Court has further backed this position by quoting the landmark decision in US, *SEC v. W.J. Howey Co., 328 U.S. 293, 301 (1946)*. However, in a 2015 case before the Supreme Court of Israel (Appeal of Administrative Petition 7313/14 Israel Security Authority v. Kvutzat Kedem Chizuk V'Chidush Mivnim Ltd.) the Honorable Elyakim Rubenstein noted as obiter dictum that the Israeli definition of securities is inherently different from that in the United States, and stated that "*in any case, it is doubtful whether an analogy should be derived from American law to the Israeli one on this issue*".

who qualifies for the list based on a combination of net worth, market expertise and transactional experience (also referred to as a "**qualified individual**").

In particular, sophisticated investors are:

(i) Institutional investors (pension funds, insurance companies, mutual funds, banks, portfolio managers, venture capital funds, etc.);
(ii) large companies with equity exceeding ILS50 million; or
(iii) qualified individual investors that meet one of the following:

(a) Hold liquid assets (cash, deposits, financial assets, and securities) of at least ILS8 million (approximately US$2 million); or
(b) Have received personal income of at least ILS1.2 million (approximately US$308,000) in each of the two most recent years (or ILS1.8 million – approximately US$462,000 – in joint family income); or
(c) Hold liquid assets of at least ILS5 million (approximately US$3 million) and receive personal annual income of at least ILS 600,000 (approximately US$154.000) (or ILS900,000 in joint family income – approximately US$231,000).

The Securities Law provides that in order to be classified as a sophisticated investor, an entity must not only fall within one of the categories in the list, but must also have provided the issuer with a written statement confirming the investor's status as a sophisticated investor, and acknowledging its understanding of the consequences of being classified as such, including the fact that offers made to such investor would be exempt from the prospectus requirement of the Securities Law. The ISA has concluded that issuers must take all reasonable steps to ensure that investors purchasing its securities are indeed sophisticated investors, and in this regard has published more specific guidelines as to what steps as to verification an issuer should take in respect of qualified corporations and qualified individuals. If a potential investor meets the requirements of the verification process, there is a presumption that it is a sophisticated investor, provided that the issuer has no reasonable grounds to believe otherwise. This is a significant development in relation to the types of entities described above which are not financial institutions, in respect of whom little or no public information may exist. While common practice has been to rely on an entity's self-certification by way of a "tick the box" approach, especially in private placement memoranda and prospectuses relating to non-Israeli securities, the new guidelines suggest that this may no longer be sufficient. It should be noted that the guidelines do not have the force of law and are merely advisory. However, it seems highly likely that a regulatory body or a court would be guided by them in determining whether an issuer has met its statutory burden such that it should be entitled to rely on the exemption from the prospectus requirement. Pursuant to the guidelines, in order to verify the amount of equity of a corporation or the scope of liquid assets held by an individual, the issuer should obtain a written confirmation from an accountant or a lawyer that the person providing the confirmation took reasonable measures to ensure that the investor in question indeed meets the relevant qualification criteria. Similarly, in order to satisfy the condition regarding the number of transactions executed by the individual, the issuer will generally need to obtain approval from the broker who executed the relevant transactions or a bank statement regarding such transactions. Finally, with respect to the transactional expertise test, the issuer will need to obtain a detailed statement from the investor supported by external evidence (such as confirmation of employment in a professional position which requires capital market expertise).

Pursuant to the guidelines, the date for verification of the investor's status as a sophisticated investor is the date of actual sale of the securities; at the time of making the offer to purchase the securities, it will be sufficient for the issuer to receive the investor's statement about its compliance with the qualification requirements. In addition, if a sale is made to the same sophisticated investor during a period of one year, it will suffice to obtain a statement from the investor confirming that the investor still satisfies the qualification requirements (assuming, once again, that the issuer has no reasonable reason to believe otherwise).

While, as noted, the new guidelines are not law, it would seem strongly advisable that they be taken into consideration by issuers before offering their securities to sophisticated investors in Israel, particularly if such investors include corporate entities and individuals which are not financial institutions and whose qualification as sophisticated investors is not objectively obvious.

1.2.9 *Japan*. The directly relevant legislation[322] on securities offerings is the Financial Instruments and Exchange Law ("**FIEL**")[323] and the Enforcement

---

[322] In general, it is believed that Japanese laws and regulations do not apply to activities by foreign companies outside Japan as the scope of jurisdiction should be limited to Japanese territory. With respect to cross-border cases, however, there is no provision that specifies the extent of the application of financial laws and regulations, and the scope of the powers of regulatory authorities is still open to interpretation. Even so, it is almost always the case that Japanese laws and regulations apply when a foreign company solicits an investor who resides in Japan, even from outside Japan

Order and related Cabinet Orders thereunder[324]. The Financial Services Agency ("**FSA**") is primarily responsible for the administration of these rules, and delegates its powers under Japanese law to each local finance bureau ("**LFB**") of the Ministry of Finance, for the registration of disclosure documents, including the Securities Registration Statement ("**SRS**"), and to the Securities and Exchange Surveillance Commission for inspections of securities companies, daily market surveillance and investigations of criminal offences. The FSA has issued guidelines concerning corporate disclosure and certain other matters for the interpretation of the FIEL and related regulations.

To conduct a debt or equity offering (whether primary or secondary), a securities registration statement ("**SRS**"), mainly consisting of information about the securities being offered and about the issuer, must be filed with the director-general of the relevant LFB, unless the offering constitutes a private placement that is exempt from disclosure obligations.

Under the FIEL, a private placement of type I securities[325] for a primary offering must satisfy the following requirements:

(i) the number of offerees (not placees) in Japan is fewer than 50 ("**Small Number Placement**");
(ii) offerees are limited to qualified institutional investors ("**QIIs**") as designated under the FIEL ("**QII limited placement**"); or
(iii) offerees are limited to professional investors as designated under the FIEL ("**Professional Investors Limited Placement**").

Certain requirements to ensure the transfer restriction must also be met in order to avail the private placement exemption as described in the three points above. In addition, certain information prescribed by the FIEL and relevant orders thereunder as well as those required by the

---

[323] Act No. 25 of 1948, as amended. The FIEL regulates the financial instruments business and financial transactions, including securities offerings and distributions, for the purpose of maintaining the fairness of capital markets, protecting investors and developing the economy.

[324] There are several other laws and regulations that specifically govern certain types of financial transactions, including derivatives transactions, securitizations, structured products, investment funds, trusts and partnerships, including the Commodity Derivatives Act (Act No. 239 of 1950, as amended), the Act on Investment Trusts and Investment Corporations (Act No. 198 of 1951, as amended), the Limited Partnership Act for Investment (Act No. 90 of 1998, as amended), the Act on Securitization of Assets (Act No. 105 of 1998, as amended), the Trust Act (Act No. 108 of 2006, as amended) and the Companies Act (Act No. 86 of 2005, as amended).

[325] The FIEL contains two broad classifications of securities: type I securities and type II securities. Type I securities include, among others, equity shares of companies, corporate bonds, government bonds and units of investment trusts or investment corporations. Type II securities include, among others, beneficiary interests in trusts and collective investment schemes (as defined in the FIEL). Exemptions to registration requirements are different among these two classifications of securities.

stock exchange in which the securities are or will be traded must be provided to the investors or publicly announced prior to the commencement of the offering.

None of the exemptions above are available to an offering of equity securities issued by a reporting company when the ongoing reporting obligation is triggered in relation to the same type of (underlying) shares. In addition, the Small Number Placement or QII Limited Placement is not available for the same type of securities offered by way of the professional investors limited placement.

The number of offerees of the same kind of securities (as defined in a Cabinet order) offered within six months before the existing offering must be aggregated for the calculation of the number of offerees in a Small Number Placement ("**Integration Rules**"). However, the number of QIIs is disregarded when certain selling restrictions are complied with in respect of such QIIs. An offering of options to subscribe or acquire shares of the issuing company only to directors, corporate auditors, officers and employees of the issuing company or its direct wholly-owned subsidiaries may be made without filing an SRS when certain conditions are met, even if such offering does not constitute a private placement. The Enforcement Order and related Cabinet orders under the FIEL were amended on April 6, 2011, and the exemption described above is now expanded to an offering of options to directors, corporate auditors, officers and employees of a second-tier subsidiary (i.e., an entity that is directly and wholly owned by a direct wholly owned subsidiary) of the issuer, and these options are excluded from the Integration Rules described above.

Before the amendments to the FIEL, which took effect on April 1, 2010 ("**2010 FIEL amendment**"), a secondary offering constituted a private placement unless the number of offerees of securities with uniform terms (such as selling price and closing date) was 50 or more. Under the 2010 FIEL amendment, a private placement of type I securities for a secondary offering must satisfy the requirements of the Small Number Placement, QII Limited Placement or Professional Investors Limited Placement. The respective requirements for each category are mostly the same as those for a primary offering described above, except that the Integration Rules in a Small Number Placement shall apply to offerees for a period of one month and that the total number of holders of the securities may not exceed 1,000 as a result of the Small Number Placement of foreign securities.

In addition, the following secondary offering transactions, among others, are exempted from the requirements for public offerings:

(i) sale of securities through the market;
(ii) sale of securities listed in Japan between securities firms or professional investors (e.g., block trade);
(iii) sale by foreign securities firms to securities firms in Japan or QIIs or sale by securities firms or QIIs to other securities firms for resale of foreign securities not subject to the transfer restriction of private placement;
(iv) sale of securities not subject to the transfer restriction of private placements held by a seller other than insiders of the issuer (including the issuer, its subsidiaries, its principal shareholders and their directors and officers) or securities firms;
(v) sale of securities not subject to the transfer restriction between the insiders described in (iv); and
(vi) sale of securities to the issuer or for resale to the issuer.

Further, for a public offering with a total value of less than ¥100 million (the value of the offering of the same type of securities made within one year before the existing offering must be aggregated for the calculation of such total value of the offering) no SRS needs to be filed. Instead, a simplified form of securities notification must be filed before the commencement of the offering (there is no waiting period for such procedure).

Under the 2010 FIEL amendment, for a secondary offering by securities firms of securities issued abroad or issued in Japan but with respect to which no solicitations were made in Japan (foreign securities), no SRS needs to be filed even if such offering does not constitute a private placement, if the following conditions (foreign securities secondary offering), among other conditions, are met:

(i) information on the sale price of such foreign securities is easily available in Japan through the internet or other methods;
(ii) such foreign securities are listed on a designated foreign exchange or continuously traded overseas, as the case may be; and
(iii) the issuer's information (in Japanese or English) is publicly announced pursuant to regulations of foreign exchange or applicable foreign law, as the case may be, and easily available through the internet or other methods.

In the case of type II securities, the primary or secondary offering of type II securities constitutes a public offering when more than 50 per cent of the capital or assets of the collective investment schemes issuing such type II securities will be invested in securities and the number of purchasers, not offerees, as a result of such offering will be 500 or more, whether they are QIIs or not.

Security Token Offerings

In the case of a private placement of securities, a document must be delivered to each investor at, or prior to, the time of sale, stating certain items prescribed by the FIEL and relevant Cabinet orders. In general, such items include the disclaimer that no SRS has been filed for the placement[326], and the applicable transfer restriction, conditions or restriction of the rights, as required under the FIEL on the relevant securities, unless the total amount of the placement (including private placements made within one month before the existing placement) is less than ¥100 million or disclosure as to the securities placed has already been made. This requirement is not applicable to a Small Number Placement of shares. In respect of the Professional Investors Limited Placement, certain information about the securities as well as issuer information must be provided to the potential investors or publicly announced upon, or prior to, the commencement of the placement. Securities firms that conduct a foreign securities secondary offering must provide to the potential investors or publicly announce certain information about the securities and the issuer upon, or prior to, the commencement of the placement subject to certain exceptions. Such securities firms are continuously required to provide or publicly announce certain information upon request of their customers or occurrence of certain material facts subject to certain exceptions.

There is no other specific requirement under the FIEL on the information to be provided to potential investors in connection with a private placement.

---

[326] **QII Private Placement**
"The Notes have not been and will not be registered in Japan pursuant to Article 4, Paragraph 1 of the Financial Instruments and Exchange Act of Japan (Act No. 25 of 1948, as amended, the **"FIEA"**) in reliance upon the exemption from the registration requirements since the offering constitutes the private placement to qualified institutional investors only as provided for in "i" of Article 2, Paragraph 3, Item 2 of the FIEA. A transferor of the Notes shall not transfer or resell them except where a transferee is a qualified institutional investor under Article 10 of the Cabinet Office Ordinance concerning Definitions provided in Article 2 of the Financial Instruments and Exchange Act of Japan (the Ministry of Finance Ordinance No. 14 of 1993, as amended)".

Small Number Private Placement
"The Notes have not been and will not be registered in Japan pursuant to Article 4, Paragraph 1 of the Financial Instruments and Exchange Act of Japan (Act No. 25 of 1948, as amended, the **"FIEA"**) in reliance upon the exemption from the registration requirements since the offering constitutes the small number private placement as provided for in "ha" of Article 2, Paragraph 3, Item 2 of the FIEA.
[A transferor of the Notes shall not transfer or resell the Notes except where the transferor transfers or resells all the Notes en bloc to one transferee. / The Note is not permitted to be divided into any unit less than the minimum denomination indicated in such certificates]".

NB: In the case of Small Number Private Placement (in which the offerees include QIIs who are subject to a transfer restriction which prohibits any transfer to non-QIIs), if the offering is also made to QIIs who are excluded from the number of the offerees, the wording described in "QII Private Placement" above is to be included in respect of solicitations to such QIIs.

There are transfer restrictions on the securities acquired in a private placement to the effect that the securities offered in a QII Limited Placement or a Professional Investors Limited Placement can only be transferred to QIIs or professional investors, as the case may be, and the securities offered in a Small Number Placement must not be transferred to another, other than as a whole (unless the total number of bond certificates in the placement is less than 50 and cannot be further divided). Shares offered in a Small Number Placement or clause II securities are not subject to any transfer restriction. Similar restrictions are applicable to private placements in a secondary offering under the 2010 FIEL amendment.

1.2.10 *Nigeria*. Securities offerings in Nigeria are governed by the Investments and Securities Act 2007 ("**ISA**") and the Companies and Allied Matters Act chapter C20, Laws of the Federation of Nigeria 2004 ("**CAMA**")[327]. The Securities and Exchange Commission Rules and Regulation 2013 ("**SEC Rules**") issued pursuant to the ISA by the Securities and Exchange Commission ("**SEC**")[328] to regulate the capital market and the Listing Rules issued by the Nigerian Stock Exchange ("**Listing Rules**") are the relevant regulations governing securities offerings[329].

The ISA[330] defines securities as: (i) debentures, stocks or bonds issued or proposed to be issued by a government; (ii) debentures, stocks, shares, bonds or notes issued or proposed to be issued by a body corporate; (iii) any right or option in respect of any such debentures, stocks, shares, bonds, notes; or (iv) commodities futures, contracts, options and other derivatives[331].

As a general rule, every offer of securities to the public requires the filing of a prospectus.

---

[327] It governs most aspects of the incorporation and operations of companies and other corporate bodies requiring incorporation or registration with the Corporate Affairs Commission ("**CAC**").
[328] The SEC is the main regulatory organ of the Nigerian capital market, and has the power, *inter alia*, to: (i) make rules and regulations for the market; (ii) register and regulate securities exchanges and other self-regulatory organizations; (iii) register and regulate the issuance of securities; (iv) intervene in the management and control of failing capital market operators; (v) in appropriate circumstances, impose penalties and levies on defaulting capital market operators.
[329] Foreign issuers can issue, sell or offer for sale or subscription, securities to the public through the Nigerian capital market. Securities may be denominated in naira or any convertible foreign currency. The SEC Rules require foreign issuers to file an application for the registration of their securities with the SEC, and the application must be accompanied by a draft prospectus.
[330] Section 315.
[331] And the term securities includes those securities in the category of the securities listed in points (i) to (iv), which may be transferred by means of any electronic mode approved by the SEC and which may be deposited, kept or stored with any licensed depository or custodian company as provided under the ISA.

Security Token Offerings

The SEC Rules contain specific rules on the private placement of shares by a public company. They provide that no public company may offer for sale or subscription or sell any securities by way of a private placement without obtaining the prior written approval of the SEC. A private placement is defined as any issue of securities not involving a public offering. The provision applies to all public companies, whether their shares are listed on a stock exchange or not. A private placement by a public company is restricted to no more than 50 purchasers. As a condition for approval, an issuer seeking to issue shares by private placement must show evidence of a dire need of fresh funds or technical expertise and must satisfy the SEC that private placement remains the only viable option for achieving its objectives. The private placement must be approved by the shareholders[332] of the issuer by a special resolution. The resolution must also state the price and the number of shares being offered. The notice of a general meeting authorizing the placement by an issuer must be published in two national daily newspapers and evidence of the publications must be filed with the SEC. Other than this, private placements are not permitted to be advertised, mentioned or discussed in the print and electronic media. Listed companies are restricted in the number of shares they can offer by way of a private placement; the SEC Rules provide that, unless a company can show that it is "ailing", the aggregate number of shares that may be offered by such companies should not exceed 30 per cent of their existing issued and paid up capital prior to the offer. Unless otherwise approved by the SEC, the offer may not be open for a period exceeding 10 working days. The issuer is required to file two copies of the placement memorandum with the SEC. The SEC Rules provide that certain mandatory information about the issuer must be included in the placement memorandum. Within 10 working days of the offer closing, the issuer is required to file a report on the offer with the SEC containing names and addresses of the purchasers, the amount purchased by each of them and mode of payment, time of payment, nature of the offeree, and the amount that the company raised.

The SEC does not regulate private placement of shares by private companies. This is governed primarily by the CAMA, the company's articles of association, and any shareholders agreements as well as any arrangements made between the issuer and the potential investor.

The SEC Rules specify the information required to be made available in a placement memorandum that is intended to be issued to potential investors. It provides that a placement memorandum must contain: a summary of the offer, financial summaries of the last five years (or less if the issuer is less than five years old); details of the directors and the

---

[332] It must be approved by 75 per cent of the votes cast at the meeting.

professional advisers; historical financial information about the issuer containing the accounting policies, balance sheets, profit and loss accounts, cash-flow statements and notes on the accounts; statutory and general corporate information about the issuer and any other material information. This information should be such as to enable the investor to have a proper understanding of the issuer, its business and the securities being offered.

There are no restrictions on the transfer of securities acquired pursuant to a private placement. However, where such securities are offered to the public within six months after issuance, the private placement could be deemed to be an offer for sale, for which a prospectus should have been issued.

1.2.11 *Russia*. The securities market and securities transactions within the Russian Federation are primarily regulated by Federal Law No. 39-FZ on the securities market ("**Securities Law**")[333]. The offering of corporate securities is regulated by Federal Law No. 208- FZ on joint-stock companies, dated December 26, 1995 ("**JSC Law**") and by Law No. 395-1 on banks and banking activity, dated December 2, 1990. The issuance of securities in the Russian Federation is also subject to a number of regulations issued by the Central Bank of the Russian Federation and the Federal Service for Financial Markets of the Russian Federation, and other regulatory agencies, as well as the general provisions of the Civil Code. On September 1, 2013 all the powers of the Federal Service for Financial Markets were transferred to the Central Bank of the Russian Federation (together with its predecessors the "**Bank of Russia**").

Particular instruments will not be considered securities unless they are specifically recognized as such under Article 142 of the Civil Code or other relevant securities laws. Generally, all types of securities existing in the Russian Federation can be divided into two main groups: (i) those which should be issued in compliance with a specific issuance procedure prescribed by the Securities Law and which require registration with the Bank of Russia (such securities are referred to as "**mass-issued**"), and (ii) those which don't need to be registered ("**non mass-issued**"). In certain cases, the Securities Law also requires a prospectus to be registered

---

[333] The first version was enacted on April 22, 1996, which has since been amended more than 40 times, including most recently in 2016. The Securities Law: (i) defines the scope and types of regulated market activities; (ii) establishes broad principles applicable to the various categories of regulated market participants; (iii) defines the various types of securities as well as the procedure for their issue and distribution; (iv) sets out the general rules applicable to secondary market trading activities; (v) sets out the standards for continuous disclosure; (vi) regulates exchange trading; (vii) prohibits insider trading; (viii) defines repo transactions and derivative instruments; (ix) sets out the main principles of government regulation of the securities market; and (x) bestows regulatory and supervisory authority on the Bank of Russia.

Security Token Offerings

simultaneously with registration of the securities issue (e.g. when securities are to be distributed through an offering to the public).

The list of exemptions is quite extensive and generally tends to bring Russian offering rules in compliance with international securities offering standards via private placement. In particular, a prospectus is not required if:

> (i) an offering is made solely to Qualified Investors ("**Qis**") provided that the total number of persons who have pre-emptive rights in such offering does not exceed 500 (excluding QIs); or
> (ii) an offering is made to any subscriber, provided that the total number of subscribers does not exceed 150 (excluding QIs[334] and existing shareholders, provided that the total number of existing shareholders does not exceed 500 (excluding QIs)); or

---

[334] An individual may be recognized as a qualified investor if he/she satisfies any of the following criteria:
(i) Holds securities and/or financial derivative contracts entered into for the account of the client, with a total value / total liabilities no less than RUB6,000,000, that meet statutory requirements. Financial instruments put by the individual into a trust are also included in the calculation of total value/total liabilities.
(ii) Has work experience in a Russian and/or foreign organization that has transacted in securities and/or entered into financial derivative contracts:
  (a) no less than two (2) years if such organization(s) is (are) a qualified investor(s) under the Securities Law;
  (b) no less than three (3) years in other cases.
The work experience review will take account of the work performed in the five (5) years preceding the date of filing an application to be recognized as a qualified investor and directly associated with financial instrument transactions, including trade decision-making, preparation of relevant recommendations, transaction control, financial market analysis, risk management.
(iii) Entered into securities transactions and/or financial derivative contracts at an average frequency of at least ten per quarter, but no less frequently than once a month, over the previous four quarters, the total value of such transactions and/or contracts being no less than RUB6,000,000.
(iv) The value of assets owned by the individual is no less than RUB6,000,000. Such assets will only include the following:
  (a) money in the accounts and/or on deposits opened at credit organizations in accordance with the Bank of Russia's regulations, and/or at foreign banks registered in the countries listed in subparagraphs 1 and 2 of paragraph 2 of article 51.1 of the Securities Law, and accrued interest;
  (b) claims to a credit organization to pay the cash equivalent of a precious metal at the book price of such precious metal;
  (c) securities that meet statutory requirements, including those put by the individual into a trust.
(v) Has a higher education degree in economics as evidenced by an official Russian higher education qualification document issued by a higher professional education institution which, at the time of document issue, carried out the certification of individuals in the sphere of professional activity in the securities market; or holds any of the following qualifications or certificates: certified financial markets specialist, certified auditor, certified insurance actuary, Chartered Financial Analyst ("**CFA**"), Certified International Analyst ("**CIIA**"), Financial Risk Manager ("**FRM**").

(iii) proceeds from the offering (obtained either in one or several tranches) do not exceed RUB200 million per year (RUB4 billion for credit organizations); or

(iv) the offering price to be paid by each of the potential subscribers (other than those exercising pre-emptive rights) is RUB4 million or more, provided that the total number of persons exercising pre-emptive rights does not exceed 500 (excluding QIs).

Other exemptions are related to:

(i) offerings of shares or securities convertible into shares solely to existing shareholders, provided that the total number of shareholders does not exceed 500 (excluding QIs), and;

(ii) offerings pursuant to closed subscription, provided that the total number of subscribers does not exceed 500 (excluding QIs)) repeat and further detail the existing rules.

Securities have to be registered within 20 calendar days in case the securities to be offered do not require a registered prospectus. If an offering of securities did not require a prospectus, the offering may commence after registration of the securities to be offered.

1.2.12 **Saudi Arabia**. The primary legislation regulating the offering of securities in the Kingdom of Saudi Arabia ("**Kingdom**") is the law on capital markets (issued by Royal Decree No. M/30 dated 2/6/1424H corresponding to July 31, 2003) ("**Capital Market Law**"), under which the Capital Market Authority ("**CMA**") is tasked with the implementation and enforcement of the Capital Market Law, including by way of issuing implementation regulations. On December 31, 2017, the CMA published the Rules on the Offer of Securities and Continuing Obligations ("**ROSCO**"), which were approved by CMA Board Resolution No. 3-123-2017 dated 9/4/1439H (corresponding to December 27, 2017). In the same Board Resolution, the CMA Board also approved the Listing Rules ("**Listing Rules**") of the Saudi Stock Exchange ("**Tadawul**").

The ROSCO and the Listing Rules are effective as of April 1, 2018 and have replaced:

(i) the Offer of Securities Regulations approved by CMA Board Resolution No. 2-11-2004 dated 20/8/1425H (corresponding to October 4, 2004), as amended;

(ii) the Listing Rules approved by CMA Board Resolution No. 3-11-2004 dated 20/8/1425H (corresponding to October 4, 2004), as amended; and

(iii) the Parallel Market Listing Rules approved by CMA Board Resolution No. 3-151-2016 dated 22/3/1438H (corresponding to December 21, 2016).

The ROSCO contains a detailed legal framework governing the offering[335] of securities[336] in the Kingdom and must be read in conjunction with the Listing Rules and other implementing regulations issued by the CMA such as:

(i) the Authorized Persons Regulations approved by CMA Board Resolution No. 1-83-2005 dated 21/05/1426H (corresponding to June 28, 2005), as amended;
(ii) the Corporate Governance Regulations approved by CMA Board Resolution No. 8-16-2017 dated 16/5/1438H (corresponding to February 13, 2017), as amended; and
(iii) the Instructions of Book Building Process and Allocation Method in Initial Public Offerings approved by CMA Board Resolution No. 2-94-2016 dated 15/10/1437H (corresponding to July 20, 2016), as amended (the "**Book Building Rules**").

Article 6 of the ROSCO lists eight cases that qualify as exempt offers, meaning such cases are not subject to the requirements of the ROSCO (e.g., approval of the CMA or publication of a prospectus). The only legal requirement is for the offeror or the authorized person[337] (if the offer is carried out through an authorized person), when making an exempt offer, to notify the CMA by providing the information set out in Articles 6(b)[338] and 6(c)[339] of the ROSCO.

The following constitute exempt offers:

---

[335] As per Article 1(b) of the ROSCO offering of securities are: (i) issuing securities; (ii) inviting the public to subscribe in securities or the direct or indirect marketing of securities; or (iii) any statement, announcement or communication that has the effect of selling, issuing or offering securities.

[336] Securities, in accordance with the Regulation and Rules of the Capital Market Authority approved by CMA Board Resolution No. 4-11-2004 dated 20/8/1424H (corresponding to 4 October 2004), are: shares; debt instruments; warrants; certificates; units; options; futures; contracts for differences; long-term insurance contracts; any right to or interest in any of the foregoing.

[337] A person authorized by the CMA to carry on securities business (e.g., dealing, managing, arranging, advising or custody) in the Kingdom in accordance with the Authorized Persons Regulations issued by CMA Board Resolution No. 1-83-2005 dated 21/05/1426H (corresponding to June 28, 2005), as amended. The list of the authorized persons can be found at https://cma.org.sa/en/Market/AuthorisedPersons/Pages/default.aspx.

[338] This includes: type of exempt offer, categories of the offerees, amount paid by each offeree category in Saudi Riyals, the start and end dates of the offering, names and nationality of the offeror, price paid for each security, type of security and total size of the offering.

[339] In relation to ongoing offerings, the notification needs to state the expected date of completion of the offering.

(i) where the securities are issued by the government of the Kingdom;

(ii) offers of contractually based securities[340];

(iii) where an issuer whose shares are not listed on Tadawul increases its capital by offering new shares to existing shareholders;

(iv) where the offeree is an affiliate of the issuer, unless it is an offer of a class of shares that is listed on Tadawul;

(v) where all of the offerees are employees of the issuer or of any of its affiliates, unless it is an offer of a class of shares that is listed on Tadawul[341];

(vi) offers in an insolvency situation where shares are offered to creditors;

(vii) where an issuer whose shares are not listed on Tadawul increases its capital by way of debt conversion [342]; and

(viii) where the subscription is limited to sophisticated investors[343] and the total value of the securities being offered is less than

---

[340] These are options, futures, contracts for differences, long-term insurance contracts and any right to or interest in any of the foregoing.

[341] This will cover an offering of shares pursuant to an employee share plan by a Saudi unlisted joint stock company or by a foreign listed parent company to the employees of its Saudi subsidiary.

[342] This will apply, for example, to a capitalization of a debt by a Saudi unlisted joint stock company.

[343] Article 9 of the ROSCO provides that the offering of securities to the following persons will qualify as an offer of securities to sophisticated investors:

(i) the Government of the Kingdom, any supranational authority recognized by the CMA, Tadawul (and any other stock exchange recognized by the CMA) or the Securities Depository Center (which is the sole entity in the Kingdom responsible for providing securities deposit, settlement, clearing and registering ownership of securities traded on Tadawul);

(ii) institutions acting for their own account (institutions are defined as: (a) any company which owns, or which is a member of a group which owns, net assets of not less than SAR 10 million; (b) any unincorporated body, partnership or other organization which has net assets of not less than SAR 10 million; and (c) any person ("**1**") whilst acting in the capacity of director, officer or employee of a person ("**2**") falling within items (a) or (b) above where 1 is responsible for 2 undertaking any securities activity);

(iii) authorized persons acting for their own account;

(iv) clients of an authorized person licensed to carry out management activities, provided that the offer is made to that authorized person and all relevant communications are made through the authorized person and the authorized person has been engaged on terms which enable it to make decisions concerning the acceptance of private offers of securities on the client's behalf without reference to the client;

(v) registered persons (i.e., persons who are registered with the CMA to perform a registrable function (e.g., CEO, finance manager, director or senior officers/managers)) of an authorized person (if the offer was carried out through that authorized person itself);

(vi) professional investors (a professional investor is defined as any individual who fulfils at least one of the following conditions: (a) he/she has carried out at least 10 transactions per quarter over the last 12 months of a minimum total amount of SAR40 million on securities markets; (b) his/her net assets are not less than SAR5 million; (c) he/she works or has worked for at least three years in the financial sector in a professional position which requires knowledge of securities investment; (d) he/she holds a professional certificate that is related to securities business and accredited by an internationally recognized entity; or (e) he/she holds the General Securities Qualification Certificate that is recognized by the CMA and has an annual income of not less than SAR600,000 in the last two years);

SAR10 million or an equivalent amount, provided that the offer is not made more than once during the twelve months after the completion of the offer.

An offer of securities is a private placement where it is not an exempt offer, public offer or a parallel market offer and falls under any of the following categories:

(i) the subscription is restricted to sophisticated investors; or
(ii) the offer is a limited offer. An offer of securities is a limited offer if the subscription is limited to no more than 100 offerees (excluding sophisticated investors) and the minimum amount payable per offeree is not less than SAR1 million or an equivalent amount in other currencies. The minimum amount payable per offeree may be less than SAR1 million where the total value for the offered securities does not exceed SAR5 million.

The ROSCO requires that any private placement must be made through an authorized person licensed to carry out arranging activity and the offeror notifies the CMA at least ten days prior to the proposed offer date and submits a private placement notification[344] and the declarations by the offeror[345] and the authorized person[346] prescribed by Article 11(a)(2) of the ROSCO and copies of any offering documents to be used in the advertising the offer. The offeror is also required to make a post-closing filing (within ten days of the end of the offer period), informing the CMA of the persons who have acquired the securities and the total proceeds of the offer.

1.2.13 **Singapore**. The Securities and Futures Act, Chapter 289 of Singapore ("**SFA**") was enacted in 2001 to be the main statute for the legal and regulatory framework for securities (including the offer of securities) in Singapore. The SFA does not generally distinguish between an offering of

---

or (f) any other persons prescribed by the CMA.

[344] The private placement notification must state, among others: (i) the names of the issuer and the offeror, their principal place of registration and the address of their principal place of the business; (ii) the name and address of the authorized person whom the offer is made through; (iii) the proposed start and end dates of the offer; (iv) the class of securities to be offered; (v) the offer price for each security offered in Saudi Riyals; (vi) the total size of the offer in Saudi Riyals; and (vii) the minimum amount (if any) to be paid by each offeree.

[345] The offeror must submit a declaration in the form set out in Annex 3 of the ROSCO, which essentially contains the offeror's confirmation that all the relevant conditions for the intended private placement have been satisfied and that the information contained in the private placement notification and the offering documents is fair, accurate and not misleading.

[346] The authorized person must submit a declaration in the form set out in Annex 4 of the ROSCO, which essentially contains the authorized person's confirmation that the offeror has satisfied all the relevant conditions for making the intended private placement and has submitted or will submit all the information and documentation required to be provided to the CMA under the ROSCO in connection with the private placement.

securities by a public or private entity or whether the entity is incorporated in Singapore or elsewhere. Entities that are listed in Singapore would either be listed on the Main Board of the SGX-ST or on the sponsor-supervised board, the Catalist, both of which are operated by the SGX-ST. The SGX-ST also regulates and monitors its members as well as market activities, through the issuance of listing rules, practice notes as well as regulatory announcements. There is generally no requirement in Singapore for a foreign issuer (being a company) to be registered in Singapore in order for it to make an offer of securities in Singapore. However, if the offer of securities does not fall within one of the exemptions from the prospectus requirements that is set out in the SFA, the issuer would need to prepare a prospectus to be issued in connection with the offer and the prospectus would need to be registered with the Monetary Authority of Singapore ("**MAS**")[347].

If the issuer is a collective investment scheme ("**CIS**") (whether constituted in Singapore or elsewhere) and the offer comprises units in the scheme, the issuer would in most cases need to register itself with the MAS prior to the commencement of the offer in Singapore, regardless of whether the offer falls within one of the exemptions from the prospectus requirements that is set out in the SFA (unless the offer is made only to institutional investors). Under the SFA, any offer of securities or units in a CIS must be accompanied by a prospectus that is prepared in accordance with the requirements of the SFA and its accompanying regulations, and registered by the MAS.

"Securities" includes (i) shares or units of shares of a corporation; (ii) debentures or units of debentures of an entity; (iii) interests in a limited partnership or limited liability partnership formed in Singapore or elsewhere; or (iv) such other product or class of products as MAS may prescribe. This requirement is regardless of whether the corporation or CIS, whose securities or units are being offered, is constituted in Singapore.

The SFA does exempt offerings made to only institutional and accredited investors or to not more than 50 persons from the prospectus requirements.

In Singapore, accredited investor is defined in Section 4A(1)(a) of the SFA, Chapter 289 as follows:

---

[347] Under the SFA, oversight of securities regulation in Singapore is granted to the MAS which has general rule-making powers and may issue guidelines, codes, practice notes, policy statements and no-action letters. Even though these do not carry statutory effect, they provide non-exclusive guidance to market participants. The MAS also has powers to impose fines and sanctions for breaches of the SFA.

(i) Individuals with net personal assets exceeding SGD2 million (or equivalent in foreign currency)[348], or;
(ii) Individuals with an income in preceding 12 months of not less than SGD300,000 (or equivalent in foreign currency), or;
(iii) A corporation with net assets exceeding SGD10 million in value (or its equivalent in a foreign currency) or such other amount as the MAS may prescribe, in place of the first amount, as determined by – (a) the most recent audited balance-sheet of the corporation; or (b) where the corporation is not required to prepare audited accounts regularly, a balance-sheet of the corporation certified by the corporation as giving a true and fair view of the state of affairs of the corporation as of the date of the balance-sheet, which date shall be within the preceding 12 months;
(iv) The trustee of such trust as the MAS may prescribe, when acting in that capacity; or
(v) Such other person as the MAS may prescribe.

Issuers (whether the issuer is incorporated in or outside Singapore) have to classify their capital markets product before it can be offered in Singapore. The classification must be notified to the SGX-ST (if listed) or to financial institutions operating in Singapore (if not listed). Breach of the section is a criminal offence. Since July 9, 2018, issuers of capital markets products that are being offered in or into Singapore have been required to flag them as being either "prescribed capital markets products"[349] or "capital markets products other than prescribed capital markets products". This involves determining whether they are one of the types of capital markets products listed as "prescribed capital markets products" and notifying the required persons of this classification. The obligation is set out in a new section 309B of the SFA, read together with the Securities and Futures (Capital Markets Products) Regulations 2018 ("**Regulations**") which came into operation on July 9, 2018. The list of the types of capital markets products to be classified as "prescribed capital markets products" is in the Schedule of the Regulations. The types of products in the list include the following:

(i) Shares issued or proposed to be issued by a corporation;

---

[348] To tighten the process of being classified as an accredited investor, the MAS has introduced two main measures: (i) an individual's primary residence can only contribute up to SGD1 million of the required SGD2 million in personal net assets; and (ii) individuals must opt-in for consideration as an Accredited Investor.

[349] Vanilla bonds and shares in companies, for example, are clearly "prescribed capital markets products", while at the other end of the spectrum contracts-for-differences and accumulator notes clearly "not prescribed capital markets products". Other capital markets products, such as covered bonds, are less clearly one or the other.

(ii) Rights, options or derivatives issued or proposed to be issued by a corporation in respect of its own stocks or shares;
(iii) Debentures, other than asset-backed securities or structured notes;
(iv) Units in a business trust; and
(v) Units in a collective investment scheme that is a Real Estate Investment Trust.

If the product is listed on the SGX-ST, the issuer must notify the SGX-ST of the product's classification. If the product is to be offered to investors in Singapore through a financial institution operating in Singapore ("**Singapore FI**"), the issuer must notify that financial institution of the product's classification. The obligation applies so long as the investor is in Singapore, and even if the issuer and the product are outside Singapore.

An issuer/Singapore FI is exempted from these requirements if the offer is to any of the following persons in Singapore ("**Exempted Investors**"):

(i) An accredited investor;
(ii) An expert investor;
(iii) An institutional investor; or
(iv) Any other person that is not an individual.

The categories are similar to the prospectus exemptions set out in sections 274 (offers to institutional investors) and 275 (offers to accredited investors and certain other persons) of the SFA. Section 275, however, exempts offers made to persons other than accredited investors and is also commonly relied on for offers made to an individual for a consideration of at least SGD200,000 for each transaction. As such individuals need not be accredited or expert investors and offers to them would not be exempted from the section 309B obligations.

1.2.14 **South Africa**. The relevant statutes governing securities offerings and trading are the Companies Act 2008 ("**Companies Act**"), the Collective Investment Schemes Control Act 2002 ("**CISCA**"), the Financial Advisory and Intermediary Services Act 2002 ("**FAIS Act**"), the Banks Act 1990 ("**Banks Act**") and the Financial Markets Act 2012 ("**Financial Markets Act**"). This legislation applies to listed and unlisted securities.

In terms of the Companies Act, an offer of securities (including equity and debt securities) to the public can only be made by a South African public company or a foreign company (incorporated outside South Africa) that has lodged its constitution and details of the board of directors with the Commissioner of the Companies and Intellectual Property Commission ("**Commission**"). An offer to the public must

Security Token Offerings

usually be accompanied by a prospectus that is registered with the relevant exchange, in the case of offerings of listed securities; or with the Commission, in the case of offerings of unlisted securities. The "public" includes any section of the public, whether selected as holders of the company's securities, clients of the person issuing the prospectus concerned, or holders of any particular class of property.

The Companies Act provides for the various instances in which the private placement of securities can occur. In a nutshell, a private placement under South African law is any offer for securities that does not constitute an offer to the public in accordance with the Companies Act. IPOs are often done on a private placement basis. The Companies Act only requires public offerings to be accompanied by a prospectus and has no rules or procedures for private placements. If securities (including debt securities) are intended to be listed on the Johannesburg Stock Exchange ("**JSE**")[350] following a private placement, the listing requirements ("**Listings Requirements**") (and in the case of debt securities, the "**Debt Listings Requirements**") set out the specific requirements and documents to be submitted to the JSE by the issuer in order for the listing of the securities to take place. Typically, if an IPO is done by way of a private placement, a pre-listing statement will be required. The Listings Requirements also include rules that regulate vendor private placings (i.e., private placings of shares issued to a vendor of assets to the company, to settle a vendor cash consideration). Privately placed debt securities (whether listed or unlisted) may also need to comply with the Commercial Paper Regulations ("**CP Regulations**") and, in the case of a securitization, the Securitization Regulations. If an existing issuer issues security that are more than 50 per cent of its existing securities, revised listings particulars (effectively a new pre-listing statement) are required.

The Companies Act[351] also contains safe harbors from offers to the public, so that offers can be made without a prospectus to, *inter alia*, persons whose ordinary business it is to deal in securities, or persons who fall into certain categories of institutional investors (person or entity regulated by the Reserve Bank of South Africa, an authorized financial services provider, as defined in the FAIS Act; a financial institution, as defined in the Financial Services Board Act, 1990), or persons who are paying more than a prescribed amount (currently ZAR1 million) for the securities to be acquired by them. An offer is not an offer to the public, also, if it is made in writing, and (i) no offer in the series is accompanied by or made by means of an advertisement and no selling expenses are

---

[350] The JSE has two primary boards: a main board and an alternative exchange ("**AltX**") for small and medium-sized companies.
[351] Section 96 of the Companies Act.

incurred in connection with any offer in the series; (ii) the issue of securities under any one offer in the series is finalized within six months after the date that the offer was first made; (iii) the offer, or series of offers in aggregate, is or are accepted by a maximum of 50 persons acting as principals; (iv) the subscription price, including any premium, of the securities issued in respect of the series of offers, does not exceed, in aggregate, ZAR100,000; and (v) no similar offer, or offer in a series of offers, has been made by the company within 6 months immediately before the offer, or first of a series of offers, as the case may be.

The disclosure requirements are contractual for private placements. If the private placement coincides with an initial listing of securities, then a pre-listing statement containing the prescribed information will need to be prepared.

There are no special rules restricting the transferability of shares acquired in a private placement. This is usually governed by contract.

1.2.15 **South Korea**. Although the Securities and Exchange Act governed securities offerings in the past, the Capital Markets and Financial Investment Services Act ("**CMA**"), which came into effect on February 4, 2009, the Enforcement Decree of the CMA and the Regulation on Securities Issuance and Disclosures ("**RSID**"), published by the Financial Services Commission ("**FSC**"), now govern securities[352] offerings.

The regulatory authority that is primarily responsible for supervising the issuance and trade of securities is the FSC. The Financial Supervisory Service ("**FSS**") implements the matters deliberated and resolved by the FSC. Although the CMA prescribes that the registration statement[353] for a public offering should be filed with the FSC, since the FSC delegates the authority to accept and examine registration statements to the FSS, the FSS is the actual regulatory body. In addition, since a person who intends to list securities issued through a public offering is required to comply with internal regulations of the Korea Exchange ("**KRX**"), the KRX also plays a role as a de facto regulatory body.

There are no specific regulations on private placements. The private placement, however, is defined as follows: a private placement refers to solicitation of the subscription of newly issued securities that do not fall

---

[352] In accordance with the CMA securities are: (i) debt securities; (ii) equity securities; (iii) beneficiary certificates; (iv) investment contract securities; (v) derivatives-combined securities; (vi) securities depositary receipts. The broadest category of securities is the "investment contract security," which is defined as an investor's contractual right to profits and losses arising from the conduct of a joint business with other persons in which the investor has invested money or other property.

[353] An issuer must submit a registration statement prior to publicly offering or selling its securities, and can only solicit investors after the registration statement has been accepted by the FSS.

under the category of public offerings. In other words, in a private placement, securities must be offered to no more than 50 persons in six months and there must be no transferability (i.e., the securities must not be transferred to more than 50 persons in a year). Because securities are typically able to be transferred, in order to prevent a possible transfer, the securities in a private placement are deposited with the Korea Securities Depository ("**KSD**") for one year. Also, a lock-up contract is executed with the KSD to the effect that the relevant securities shall not be withdrawn or sold for one year from the date of deposit, or in cases other than equity securities, the securities are issued in fewer than 50 certificates and each certificate states that it cannot be divided. If the securities already issued are offered for subscription to fewer than 50 persons for six months in total, it does not constitute a sale (secondary offerings).

Delivery of a prospectus is also exempted for the issuance or sales of securities to the following investors (who have a lesser need to be protected) (section 124(1), CMA; section 132, Enforcement Decree of the CMA):

    (i) Professional investors;
    (ii) Accounting firms, credit rating agencies, persons who provide accounting, consulting and similar services to the issuer with an officially recognized qualification certificate (for example, a certified public accountant, appraiser, attorney-at-law, patent attorney, tax accountant) and related parties to the issuer.

The CMA does not specify what information must be provided to potential investors in connection with a private placement. Meanwhile, with respect to small-scale offerings with an amount of less than 1 billion won, which fall under the category of public offerings but are exempted from filing a registration statement, the CMA requires disclosure of the financial conditions of the issuer, solicitation methods for subscription and the contents of the solicitation documents with the FSC in lieu of a registration statement.

An amendment to the Enforcement Decree of the CMA dated June 29, 2012 strengthened the obligation to file a registration statement for issuance of securities by narrowing the scope of exempt transactions. Previously, issuers were exempt from filing a registration statement if the subscription amount per issuance (aggregate of all types of securities for each issuance) was under ₩1 billion. Now, such an exemption is available only if the sum of the subscription amount of all issuances during a one-year period is under ₩1 billion. This amendment aims to prevent harm to investors caused by marginal firms' abuse of the previous rules.

Crypto-assets global corporate finance transactions

Transfer restrictions are required in order for an offer to be considered a private placement. Since securities with respect to which a registration statement has not been filed have limited transferability, their transferability is substantially restricted other than in negotiated transactions. Meanwhile, if debt securities are issued by an issuer with assets of less than ₩500 billion and the initial purchasers from the issuer or underwriter are qualified institutional buyers (QIBs), the securities can be sold in the QIB market to ensure their liquidity.

1.2.16 **Switzerland**. The offering of securities by Swiss or foreign issuers in Switzerland is governed by a variety of rather fragmented rules and regulations[354], the applicability of which depends largely on the specifics of the offering, the securities offered, the issuer and the other parties participating in the offering. For practical purposes, of most relevance are various provisions set forth in the Code of Obligations ("**CO**"), including those providing for the basic prospectus disclosure requirements for public offerings of equity and debt securities, and the Federal Act on Financial Market Infrastructures and Market Conduct in Securities and Derivatives Trading ("**FMIA**") and its implementing ordinances and regulations, such as, in particular, the listing rules adopted by the relevant exchanges[355].

---

[354] Switzerland is neither a member of the European Union ("**EA**") nor the European Economic Area ("**EEA**"). Consequently, the EU prospectus rules and other EU or EEA capital markets rules and regulations are not applicable in Switzerland. Switzerland, however, regularly adapts its legislation to EU equivalence requirements to facilitate market access. As part of Switzerland's efforts to meet EU-equivalent standards, it is in the process of implementing a comprehensive reform package fundamentally changing the Swiss securities regulatory framework, which is expected to enter into force by January 2020. One of the aims of the new rules is the regulatory harmonization with the relevant EU rules (MiFID II, MiFIR, the Prospectus Directive, the PRIIPs Regulation) with adjustments made to reflect the specific Swiss circumstances.

[355] Other relevant Swiss legislation governing securities includes:
(i) Ordinance on Financial Market Infrastructures and Market Conduct in Securities and Derivatives Trading ("**FMIO**") implementing the provisions of the FMIA;
(ii) Ordinance of the Swiss Financial Market Supervisory Authority on Financial Market Infrastructures and Market Conduct in Securities and Derivatives Trading ("**FMIO-FINMA**") implementing the provisions of the FMIA;
(iii) Federal Act on the Swiss Financial Market Supervisory Authority ("**FINMASA**"), stipulating provisions regarding supervision of the financial markets by the Swiss Financial Market Supervisory Authority ("**FINMA**");
(iv) Ordinance of the Takeover Board on Public Takeover Offers providing rules on the requirements for public takeover offers;
(v) Regulations of the Takeover Board, stipulating regulations governing the organization of the Takeover Board;
(vi) the listing rules and all other rules, directives, circulars, prospectus schemes of SIX Swiss Exchange Ltd governing the listing and trading in securities on the SIX Swiss Exchange and laying down the principles for maintaining listings of equity and debt securities on the SIX Swiss Exchange;
(vii) Guideline for Notes issued by Foreign Borrowers dated 1 September 2001 of the Swiss Bankers' Association;
(viii) Federal Act on Collective Investment Schemes ("**CISA**"), governing the issue of structured products;

Swiss law does not provide for specific rules governing the private offering of equity or debt securities. As a general rule, the private placement of securities in Switzerland does not require a prospectus. A placement is deemed to be private if it is not made to the public (i.e., if it is addressed to a limited circle of offerees). While no clear limitation on the permitted number of potential investors to whom securities can be offered by way of a private placement exists under Swiss law, the more conservative view in Switzerland is that an offering directed at or made to 20 or fewer potential investors (irrespective of their sophistication or wealth) qualifies as a private offering under Swiss law. For the purposes of determining the number of potential investors, the number of persons approached is relevant and not the number of persons who eventually purchase the relevant securities. This rule, which is or was used in other areas of Swiss financial legislation, may be viewed as a *safe harbor* rule. However, in light of the amended EU Prospectus Directive (although not applicable in Switzerland), pursuant to which an offering addressed to fewer than 150 persons per member state does not trigger an obligation to prepare a prospectus, the above-mentioned 20 offeree rule has been criticized as being too stringent. It is at the same time not disputed that the legal concept of a "limited circle of offerees" has not only a quantitative, but also a qualitative aspect. Arguing that the focus should not primarily be on the number of offerees approached, but on the manner in which potential investors are being approached, an offering to more than 20 potential investors should be currently permissible (without triggering an obligation to prepare a prospectus), provided that: (i) the prospective investors are hand-picked and are being approached on an individual basis (e.g., through personal letters or by invitation only presentations); (ii) and the offering is directed at or made to a predefined circle of potential investors that share common qualifying criteria that distinguish them from the public at large. However, this latter approach is still untested, and an offering of equity or debt securities directed at or made to more than 20 potential investors may not, in the present state of law and practice, be considered to be a safe harbor. A significant change in this regard will be brought in by the incoming Federal Financial Services Act (**"FinSA"**)[356].

(ix) Federal Ordinance on Collective Investment Schemes, implementing the provisions of the CISA;
(x) Federal Act on Intermediated Securities, governing the custody, transfer and related issues of securities held with regulated custodians;
(xi) Federal Act on Banks and Savings Banks (**"Banking Act"**);
(xii) Federal Ordinance on Banks and Savings Banks; and
(xiii) Federal Act on Combating Money Laundering and Terrorist Financing (**"AML Act"**) and the corresponding implementing ordinances.

[356] The FinSA – adopted by both chambers of Parliament and currently expected to enter into force as of January 1, 2020 – introduces a comprehensive and harmonized prospectus regime to meet EU equivalence requirements while reflecting specific Swiss circumstances. Among other things, it embraces the codification of the private placement exemption and other exemptions to publish a prospectus in line with the EU Prospectus Directive.

No prior approval of FINMA is required for the offering of shares or interests in a non-Swiss collective investment scheme or from Switzerland if such offering is directed at and made exclusively to qualified investors (as defined in the Federal Act on Collective Investment Schemes ("**CISA**") and its implementing ordinance and guidelines). However, under CISA such offering may trigger regulatory requirements such as the appointment of a Swiss representative and a Swiss paying agent.

The concept of qualified investors encompasses, *inter alia*:

(i) financial intermediaries that are subject to a prudential supervision (i.e., banks, securities dealers, fund management companies, asset managers of collective investment schemes and central banks);
(ii) supervised insurance companies;
(iii) pension funds with professional treasury management;
(iv) corporate investors with professional treasury management;
(v) high-net-worth individuals (i.e., individuals that are holding, directly or indirectly, a minimum net wealth of 5 million swiss francs in financial assets or holding a minimum net wealth of 500,000 swiss francs and having sufficient technical knowledge), provided such individuals or, in the case a private investment structure has been set up for one or more high-net-worth individuals, the person responsible for managing the investment structure, have expressly requested, on a written basis ("**opt-in**"), to be considered as qualified investors;
(vi) investors having entered into a written discretionary asset management agreement, provided that they do not exercise their right to opt-out ("**opt-out**") of the qualified investors status and the written discretionary asset management agreement is entered into with a regulated financial intermediary or with an independent asset manager that is subject to anti-money laundering supervision, rules of conduct meeting certain minimum requirements, and the relevant management agreement complies with the directives of a recognized professional organization (e.g., Swiss Bankers' Association guidelines); and
(vii) independent asset managers (if the relevant independent asset manager meets the requirements of the CISA and undertakes in writing to exclusively use the fund-related information for clients who are themselves qualified investors).

No specific information is required to be made available to potential investors. Notwithstanding the above, information submitted to potential investors must be accurate and not be misleading. If false or

Security Token Offerings

misleading statements are made in connection with a private placement, the issuer or the persons involved in preparing the relevant offering documents and the offering may become liable.

No restrictions apply to the transfer of securities acquired in private placements, but any private offering of securities made with an aim to ultimately offer or distribute the relevant securities to the public is deemed to be a public offering.

1.2.17 **United Arab Emirates**. This section sets out the legal framework for offers of securities in "onshore" United Arab Emirates ("**UAE**")[357], i.e. in Abu Dhabi or Dubai rather than in the "free zones" of the country, e.g. the Dubai International Financial Centre ("**DIFC**")[358], which has its own separate regulatory framework[359]. While the UAE is growing rapidly and developing in all business sectors, the regulations governing the issue of shares are currently not clear-cut. Similarly, there is still only a very limited system of precedent in the UAE meaning the interpretation of regulations very much depends upon the decision of the relevant authorities in the particular circumstances at the relevant time[360].

All onshore UAE companies are governed by Federal Law No. 2 of 2015 concerning Commercial Companies ("**Companies Law**"), as amended. The basic law relating to securities is the Federal Law No. 4 of 2000 ("**Securities and Commodities Exchange Law**"). The UAE's onshore stock exchanges[361] are regulated by the Securities and Commodities Authority

---

[357] The UAE was established in 1971 and comprises the seven emirates of Abu Dhabi, Ajman, Dubai, Fujairah, Ras Al Khaimah, Sharjah and Umm Al Quwain. Abu Dhabi is the capital and the site of a number of federal ministries, the Central Bank of the United Arab Emirates ("**Central Bank**") and other government institutions and agencies.

[358] The DIFC is a financial free zone established in the emirate of Dubai. It should not be confused with the emirate of Dubai itself. The DIFC has its own laws and regulations, which differ considerably from the laws and regulations applicable to capital markets and securities transaction outside the DIFC. The DIFC regulatory scheme applies only within the DIFC. The UAE federal regulatory scheme applies everywhere in the UAE (i.e., in all seven emirates) except the DIFC (and *vice versa*). The DIFC has its own regulator, the Dubai Financial Services Authority ("**DFSA**").

[359] Regulation of capital markets is generally a matter of UAE federal law, but there is a second regulatory scheme applicable in the DIFC (and to a lesser extent, the Abu Dhabi Global Market ("**ADGM**")). With regard to the laws and regulations affecting securities, the DIFC and the ADGM are effectively different jurisdictions altogether, with rules and regulations that differ significantly from the UAE federal regulatory scheme.

[360] In the absence of the doctrine of binding judicial precedent, the results of one court case do not necessarily offer a reliable basis for predicting the outcome of a subsequent case involving similar facts. Consequently, the UAE legal system may generally be regarded as offering less predictability than more developed legal systems.

[361] In the UAE, there are three financial exchange markets, two of which are onshore, being the Abu Dhabi Securities Exchange ("**ADX**") and Dubai Financial Market ("**DFM**"), while the third financial market is located within the jurisdiction of the DIFC, being NASDAQ Dubai. ADX and DFM are subject to the supervisory authority of the ESCA, while the DFSA regulates NASDAQ Dubai in its capacity as the

("**ESCA**"). In addition, each exchange has its own set of rules and regulations with which the companies listed on them must comply.

A prospectus is required where: (i) there is an offer of securities[362] to the public; (ii) there is an application for listing on one of the exchanges.

In order for a company to offer its shares to the public, the said company must be or take up the legal form of a public joint stock company. Accordingly, a company wishing to execute an IPO will be either a newly incorporated public joint stock company, or a company assuming the legal form of a private joint stock company or a limited liability company that undergoes a conversion process to become a public joint stock company.

There are no published ESCA rules or guidelines defining an offer to the public or which securities transactions may qualify as private placements exempt from the prospectus requirement[363]. Generally, offers and issues to federal and local Emirate governments, governmental agencies or to licensed banks in the UAE are exempt from any prospectus requirement.

Where the relevant offer shares will be issued, transferred and traded outside the UAE, then some types of low-profile marketing activities of foreign securities have traditionally been tolerated by the Central Bank

---

securities supervisory authority within the DIFC. As at the time of writing, there is no financial market that is located in the ADGM.

[362] The Securities Law and (most) regulations issued thereunder define Securities as *"shares, bonds and notes (...) and any other domestic or non-domestic financial instruments accepted by the Authority"*.

[363] In January 2017, the ESCA issued Chairman of the SCA Board of Directors' Decision No. 3/RM of 2017 Concerning the Regulation of Promotion and Introduction ("**Promotion Regulations**"). While the Promotion Regulations relate only to the promotion of foreign funds (and reconfirm that any marketing of interests in foreign funds to investors in the UAE requires that such interests be registered with the ESCA), specifying a further exemption whereby a foreign fund need not be marketed by way of a private offering in the UAE by an ESCA-licensed promoter if offered to a qualified investor, introduced concepts that are already being used in private placement activities outside the funds sector. A qualified investor is:

(i) an investor that is capable of managing its investments by itself and on its own accord, such as: (a) the federal government and local governments, government institutions and authorities, or the companies fully owned by any of the aforementioned; (b) international bodies and organizations; (c) a person licensed to engage in a commercial business in the UAE, provided that one of the purposes of its business is investment; or (d) a natural person with an annual income of no less than 1 million UAE dirhams, or with his or her net equity, with the exception of his or her main residence, valued at 5 million UAE dirhams and declaring that he or she has the adequate knowledge and experience – whether solely or through a financial consultant – to assess the offering documents, the advantages and the risks associated with or arising from the investment; and

(ii) represented by an investment manager licensed by the SCA.

as falling below the threshold for requiring licensing by the Central Bank[364]. Examples include:

> (i) responding to requests for information received from potential investors;
> (ii) short visits with potential institutional investors known or introduced to the offeror's representative;
> (iii) passing information to a UAE resident through their existing financial adviser who is located abroad;
> (iv) advertisements in newspapers published abroad that circulate in the UAE, provided that no reference is made to specific presentations or meetings that will be held in the country, and provided that any specific address to which potential investors are referred for inquiries is outside the UAE; and
> (v) inviting journalists from the UAE press to news conferences and road shows held outside the UAE.

Therefore, whether or not the "marketing" of the relevant offer shares in the UAE will attract the Central Bank's regulatory attention will be a matter of degree.

1.2.17.1 **Dubai International Financial Centre**. This section contains an overview of the regulatory system of the Dubai International Financial Centre Free Zone (the "**DIFC**") with regard to the offering of securities within the DIFC. The DIFC is a separate jurisdiction from the UAE and mainland Dubai with its own securities offering rules.

The relevant statutes governing the offering of securities in the DIFC are:

> (i) Markets Law, DIFC Law No. 12/2004 (the "**ML**");
> (ii) Offered Securities Rules (the "**OSR**") issued by the DFSA; and
> (iii) the NASDAQ Dubai Listing Rules (detailing the application procedure and continuing obligations of those entities who wish to list and trade on the NASDAQ Dubai).

---

[364] If an offer of foreign securities is deemed not to require approval from the UAE Central Bank, we suggest including the following legend in the offer document:
"This prospectus does not constitute an offer to sell or the solicitation of an offer to buy any Shares in the United Arab Emirates to any person to whom it is unlawful to make the offer or solicitation in the United Arab Emirates or in respect of whom there may be a legal requirement to obtain prior approval of this prospectus from the regulatory authorities and/or to appoint a local broker. The distribution of this prospectus and the offer or sale of the Shares may be restricted by law in the United Arab Emirates. The Company does not represent that this prospectus may be lawfully distributed, or that any Shares may be lawfully offered, in compliance with any applicable registration or other requirements in the United Arab Emirates, or pursuant to an exemption available thereunder, nor does it assume any responsibility for facilitating any such distribution or offering. No transaction relating to the Shares will be concluded in the United Arab Emirates. Investors wishing to obtain Shares should apply to [address]".

Exempt offers from the prospectus requirements are defined in the ML as offers of securities:

>(i) by recognized governments or other persons on the list of exempt offerors ("**Exempt Offerors**")[365];
>(ii) maintained by the DFSA in the OSR;
>(iii) made to and directed at professional investors ("**Professional Investors**")[366];
>(iv) made in connection with a takeover offer; or
>(v) as may be prescribed by the OSR.

An offer may be an exempt offer under the OSR where it satisfies one of the following conditions:

>(i) the securities are either commercial paper, certificates of deposits or bills of exchange;
>(ii) the offer is made to no more than 50 offerees in the DIFC in any 12 months period;
>(iii) the total amount paid for the securities does not exceed US$1 million; or
>(iv) the securities are debentures and the minimum paid by any person is US$50,000.

In many respects, the rules regarding prospectus exemption are structured to fall within the principles set out in the EU Directive 2003/71/EC on the prospectus to be published when securities are offered to the public or admitted to trading (the so-called Prospectus Directive).

A person making an exempt offer must ensure that the offeree is provided with an exempt offer statement. The minimum information which must be included in the exempt offer statement includes:

>(i) the name of the issuer and address of its principal place of business and registered office;
>(ii) if different from the issuer, the name and address of the offeror;

---

[365] The OSR lists Exempt Offerors properly constituted governments, government agencies, central banks or other national monetary authorities of the following countries or jurisdictions:
(i) Organization for Economic Co-operation and Development ("**OECD**") member countries;
(ii) Member countries of the Gulf Co-operation Council ("**GCC**"); or
(iii) The Emirate of Dubai;
(iv) The International Monetary Fund and the World Bank; and
(v) Any other country, jurisdiction or supranational organization that may be approved as an Exempt Offeror by the DFSA for the purpose of that offer.
[366] Professional Investors are those whose normal business activities involve them acquiring, holding, managing or disposing of investments.

> (iii) the name and address of any professional advisors in relation to the exempt offer; and
>
> (iv) the nature and rights attached to the securities.

If the offer is not an exempt offer, it must be made by way of a prospectus offer.

1.2.18 **United States**. Two statutes primarily govern the US securities markets at the federal level:

> (i) the Securities Act of 1933 ("**Securities Act**"), which was designed to regulate offerings of securities to the public; and (ii) the Securities Exchange Act of 1934 ("**Exchange Act**"), which was designed to regulate subsequent trading of those securities in secondary market transactions.

These statutes regulate the securities markets through disclosure requirements as opposed to any requirements for regulatory approval of the merits of an offering[367].

---

[367] In planning to negotiate, effect, clear or settle transactions involving securities, market participants should evaluate whether their activities may trigger registrations and related requirements under the framework of the Exchange Act. In particular, market participants should be aware of the definitions of broker (15 U.S.C. § 78c(a)(4) (2012)), dealer 15 U.S.C. § 78c(a)(5) (2012), exchange (15 U.S.C. § 78c(a)(1) (2012)), alternative trading system (ATS) (17 C.F.R. § 242.300(a) (2017)), clearing agency (15 U.S.C. § 78c(a)(23) (2012) and transfer agent 15 U.S.C. § 78c(a)(25) (2012).

(i) Broker-dealer. Registration with the SEC is generally required for any entity that meets the statutory definition of a broker or dealer. A securities broker includes any person who is engaged in the business of effecting transactions in securities for the accounts of others (15 U.S.C. § 78c(b)(4) (2012)). A securities dealer includes any person engaged in the business of buying and selling securities for such person's own account, regardless of whether through a broker or otherwise. However, the definition also includes an exception for persons who are not in the business of dealing in securities. Specifically, the dealer-trader exception states that a person is generally not acting as a dealer where that person trades for her or his own account but not as part of a regular business. Section 15(a)(1) of the Exchange Act generally requires registration of any person who acts as a broker or dealer, as described above, and who uses instrumentalities of interstate commerce (15 U.S.C. § 78c(a)(17) (2012)) to effect any transaction in, or to induce or attempt to induce the purchase or sale of, any security (other than an exempted security or commercial paper, bankers acceptances or commercial bills) (15 U.S.C. § 78o(a)(1) (2012)). Registration with the SEC requires the submission of Form BD (Uniform Application for Broker-Dealer Registration) through the Central Registration Depository, which is currently the central licensing and registration system operated by the FINRA. Unless a broker-dealer is a member of a US national securities exchange and generally limits its securities activities to trading on that exchange, it must also become a member of FINRA, which is the national securities association in the United States for broker-dealers that, among other things, has surveillance and enforcement authority over its members. To apply to become a member of FINRA, broker-dealers must complete a detailed new membership application that requires an applicant to provide FINRA with, among other things, detailed written supervisory and compliance procedures. Among other considerations regarding acting as a broker-dealer in respect of virtual currencies that are securities, market participants should consider the compatibility of their planned activities with the existing requirements of the SEC's financial responsibility rules.

The Securities Act requires that every offer[368] and sale of a security in the United States be registered with the SEC unless an exemption is available

(ii) Exchanges and alternative trading system. In general, under the Exchange Act, an exchange is defined to mean a system that brings together the orders for securities of multiple buyers and sellers, and uses established, non-discretionary methods (whether by providing a trading facility or by setting rules) under which such orders interact with each other (15 U.S.C. § 78c(a)(1) (2012); 17 C.F.R. § 240.3b-16(a) (2017)). Under the regulatory framework administered by the SEC, an ATS is a national securities exchange; however, it is exempt from such registration provided that it complies with the requirements of Regulation ATS (17 C.F.R. § 240.3a1-1(a)(2) (2017)). The regulatory burdens associated with registering and operating as a national securities exchange are significantly greater than those associated with an ATS. For example, the registration process for an exchange involves completing and submitting Form 1 to the SEC, which is published for public notice and comment. By contrast, the submission of Form ATS to the SEC is not subject to the same public notice and comment process.

(iii) Clearing agencies. The term clearing agency under Section 3(a)(23)(A) of the SEA is defined broadly to generally include any person who: (a) acts as an intermediary in making payments or deliveries, or both, in connection with transactions in securities; (b) provides facilities for the comparison of data regarding the terms of settlement of securities transactions, to reduce the number of settlements of securities transactions or for the allocation of securities settlement responsibilities; (c) acts as a custodian of securities in connection with a system for the central handling of securities whereby all securities of a particular class or series of any issuer deposited within the system are treated as fungible and may be transferred, loaned or pledged by bookkeeping entry, without physical delivery of securities certificates; or (d) otherwise permits or facilitates the settlement of securities transactions or the hypothecation or lending of securities without physical delivery of certificates. In practice, this reaches firms that operate as a central counterparty to novate, net and guarantee securities settlement obligations or that operate as a central securities depository (e.g., DTC) to transfer ownership by book entry. However, it may capture firms performing other common types of functions in the securities markets (including collateral management activities – involving calculating collateral requirements and facilitating the transfer of collateral between counterparties and trade matching services – whereby an intermediary compares trade data to reduce the number of settlements or to allocate settlement responsibilities). The registration and operation of a registered clearing agency involves significant regulatory requirements that include, but are not limited to, the submission of proposed rule changes to the SEC and compliance with Regulation SCI. Accordingly, market participants who believe that their activities may come within the clearing agency definition may wish to consider whether they nonetheless qualify for certain exclusions from the clearing agency definition in Section 3(a)(23)(B) of the Exchange Act, or whether it would be appropriate to pursue an exemption from registration. The SEC has authority to provide conditional or unconditional exemptions from registration pursuant to Section 17A(b)(1) of the Exchange Act.

(iv) Transfer agents. The definition of a transfer agent in Section 3(a)(25) of the Exchange Act includes any person who engages on behalf of a securities issuer in: (a) countersigning such securities upon issuance; (b) monitoring the issuance of such securities with a view to preventing unauthorized issuance; (c) registering the transfer of the issuer's securities of the issuer; (d) exchanging or converting the securities; or (e) transferring record ownership of the securities by bookkeeping entry without physical issuance of securities certificates. In turn, Section 17A(c)(1) requires that, except as otherwise provided in the Exchange Act, it is unlawful for any transfer agent, unless registered, to use US instrumentalities of interstate commerce to perform the function of a transfer agent with respect to any security registered under Section 12 or which would be required to be registered except for the exemption from registration provided by subsections (g)(2)(B) or (g)(2)(G) of that section.

[368] Section 2(a)(3) of the Securities Act defines the term "offer" expansively to include *"every attempt or offer to dispose of, or solicitation of an offer to buy, a security or interest in a security, for value"*. The SEC long ago stated that any publicity that may *"contribute to conditioning the public mind or arousing public interest"* in the offering can itself constitute an offer under the Securities Act (see SEC, *Publication of Information Prior to or After the Effective Date of a Registration Statement*, Release No.

(e.g., offers and sales not involving a "public offering"). The Securities Act has two basic objectives: (i) to provide investors with material financial and other information regarding the securities to be offered, and (ii) to prevent fraud in connection with sales of securities. To achieve these objectives, the Securities Act requires that, in the absence of an exemption, a statutory prospectus that has been filed with the SEC as part of the registration process be furnished in advance to purchasers of securities and imposes statutory liability for material omissions or misstatements in such documents or any other documents that may be furnished to purchasers of securities under the Securities Act.

The Exchange Act requires US and non-US companies with a security listed on a US stock exchange (including the New York Stock Exchange and NASDAQ), meeting certain asset amount and shareholder number requirements or making public offerings of securities in the United States, to register such securities with the SEC and to file with the SEC annual reports, quarterly reports (in the case of US companies) and certain other reports containing information similar to that required in a registration statement under the Securities Act.

33-3844 (Oct. 8, 1957)). Some communications are far enough afield from an offer of securities. Depending on your specific facts and circumstances, examples of things that may fall outside the definition include:
(i) Product Advertising and Factual Business Communications. Just because a securities offering is planned or ongoing, a company need not stop advertising its products or refrain from issuing press releases regarding factual developments in the business (the opening of a new office, for example). See SEC, *Guidelines for the Release of Information by Issuers Whose Securities are in Registration*, Release No. 33-5180 (Aug. 16, 1971). As the SEC put it in the context of securities offering reform in 2005, "*in general, as we recognized many years ago, ordinary factual business communications that an issuer regularly releases are not considered an offer of securities (...). Such communications will not be presumed to be offers, and whether they are offers will depend on the facts and circumstances*". See SEC, *Securities Offering Reform*, Release No. 33-8591 (July 19, 2005) at 82 n. 122.
(ii) The Collision Principle. As a general matter, where a company faces an obligation under the Exchange Act to make a public statement, or where good corporate citizenship calls for disclosure of important events to existing public security holders, the required disclosure should not be considered an offer. In a collision between the requirements of the Exchange Act and those of the Securities Act, the Exchange Act's ongoing disclosure requirements ought to prevail over the Securities Act's close regulation of offers. As the SEC has explained: "*we do not believe that it is beneficial to investors or the markets to force reporting issuers to suspend their ordinary course communications of regularly released information that they would otherwise choose to make because they are raising capital in a registered offering*". See SEC, *Securities Offering Reform*, Release No. 33-8591 (July 19, 2005) at 58-59.
(iii) Release of Material Non-Public Information to Satisfy Regulation FD. The SEC Staff has recognized that a reporting company engaged in a private offering may have obligations under Regulation FD to publicly disclose material non-public information it provides to potential investors in the private offering. If so, the SEC Staff has indicated that it is permissible to release the material non-public information on a Form 8-K, so long as the entire private offering memorandum is not included in the filing (see SEC Division of Corporation Finance, *Securities Act Sections Compliance and Disclosure Interpretations* (C&DI), Question 139.32). Arguably, this is simply an application of the Collision Principle discussed above.

Offerings of securities are also subject to state "blue sky" laws, although the National Securities Markets Improvement Act of 1996 has largely pre-empted state securities laws.

In addition, companies that complete a securities offering that is registered with the SEC or otherwise become subject to the reporting obligations of the Exchange Act also need to comply with the provisions of the Sarbanes-Oxley Act of 2002, including the provisions with respect to internal control over financial reporting, prohibitions on loans made to executive officers and directors, auditor independence and independent audit committees, certifications by executive officers of financial reports and increased civil and criminal penalties for violations of the securities laws and also the Dodd-Frank Wall Street Reform and Consumer Protection Act of 2010 ("**Dodd-Frank**"), which introduced important changes to the corporate governance and executive compensation landscape for public companies.

On April 5, 2012, the US adopted a capital formation reform bill known as the Jumpstart Our Business Startups Act ("**JOBS Act**"). The JOBS Act significantly eases restrictions under the Securities Act relating to the initial public offering process for equity securities of a newly designated class of smaller companies and to the private placement capital raising process for virtually all issuers. The JOBS Act also provides ongoing relief, mainly for these smaller companies, from certain requirements under the Exchange Act as well as from certain existing (and potentially future) accounting and auditing rules.

The SEC is the primary administrative authority charged with administering the Securities Act, the Exchange Act and the other federal securities laws. In addition to enforcing these statutes, the SEC is charged with promulgating rules and regulations under such statutes.

Section 4(a)(2) (formerly 4(2)) of the Securities Act exempts "transactions by an issuer not involving any public offering". A substantial body of case law and SEC regulatory practice has developed concerning private placements under section 4(a)(2). The availability of the exemption turns on a factual analysis of several factors, including the number and sophistication of the offerees, the relationship between the issuer and the offerees, the minimum denomination of the securities being offered and the relative bargaining power between them. To ensure compliance with section 4(a)(2), issuers often have purchasers make certain representations as to their sophistication as investors and their receipt of all requisite information in connection with the offering.

In order to provide issuers with certainty regarding the section 4(a)(2) exemption, the SEC adopted Regulation D[369], which provides three regulatory exemptions from the registration requirements of the Securities Act for offers and sales by issuers. Rule 504 and rule 505 of Regulation D provide exemptions from the registration requirements of the Securities Act for certain securities offerings limited in aggregate dollar amount (e.g., offerings not exceeding $1 million or $5 million, depending on the parameters of the offering). Rule 506 of Regulation D (by far the most widely used Regulation D exemption) provides issuers with a non-exclusive "unlimited" safe harbor under section 4(a)(2) of the Securities Act, that exempts offerings of an unlimited amount of securities, to an unlimited number of "accredited investors" (e.g., institutions and certain wealthy individuals) and to no more than 35 non-accredited investors. The previous prohibition on general solicitation and advertising in rule 506 offerings was eliminated by rules adopted by the SEC pursuant to the JOBS Act. As required by the JOBS Act, the SEC adopted amendments that took effect in June 2015, which created a new exemption from registration pursuant to section 3(b) of the Securities Act for up to $50 million of securities (referred to as "**Regulation A+**"). Under another requirement of the JOBS Act, the SEC adopted rules in October 2015 to create by rule a substantial regulatory framework providing for a crowdfunding exemption from registration, whereby small aggregate amounts of securities of an issuer can be sold through brokers or internet "funding portals" to investors in small individual accounts.

If a sale is made to a non-accredited investor, Regulation D requires that certain information be provided to the purchaser within a reasonable time before the sale. The information to be provided varies according to whether or not the issuer is a reporting company under the Exchange Act, but in either case such information is similar to that which would be required in a registration statement in the case of a registered offering under the Securities Act. Regulation D does not require that any specific information be provided to accredited investors. Nonetheless, in practice issuers generally provide potential purchasers with information similar to that provided to non-accredited investors. In addition, rule 144A and Regulation S have limited information requirements. However, issuers offering securities via section 4(a)(2) private placements coupled with resales pursuant to rule 144A and Regulation S typically provide

---

[369] Over the period 2009-2014, an average of $660 billion per annum in fresh equity was issued using Regulation D offers, nearly three times as much as was raised each year using public (registered) equity offers. Of this, approximately twenty per cent was raised by foreign issuers. Regulation D offers tend to be very small in comparison to offers via public markets, with the mean capital raising being only $28 million. See S. Bauguess, R. Gullapalli, V. Ivanov, *Capital Raising in the US: An Analysis of the Market for Unregistered Securities Offerings* 2009-2014, SEC Division of Economic and Risk Analysis Working Paper (2015).

information that is similar to what would be required in a registration statement in the case of a registered offering under the Securities Act.

Unregistered securities purchased in a private offering may not be resold except pursuant to a registration statement under the Securities Act or pursuant to an exemption contained in the Securities Act or the rules and regulations thereunder. Several mechanisms exist to facilitate the resale of these "restricted" securities. One such mechanism is the "section 4(1-1/2)" exemption, now "4(a) (1-1/2)", which allows investors who purchased restricted securities in a valid private placement to resell those securities in a further private placement following the procedures set forth in section 4(a)(2) without being deemed an underwriter engaged in a distribution of securities (who would not be exempt from the registration requirements of section 5 of the Securities Act). A similar but more commonly used mechanism for resales of restricted securities is rule 144 under the Securities Act, which defines the circumstances under which an owner of restricted securities or an affiliate of the issuer may offer and sell such securities to the public without being deemed an underwriter engaged in a distribution of securities. Following rule amendments that became effective on February 15, 2008, rule 144 provides a non-exclusive safe harbor for the resale of restricted securities of a reporting issuer beginning six months after issuance of such securities, subject to requirements as to the public availability of certain information regarding the issuer and, in the case of resales by affiliates only, to limitations as to the manner and volume of such sales. With respect to the restricted securities of a non-reporting issuer, rule 144 provides a non-exclusive safe harbor for resales beginning one year after issuance of such securities. Under rule 144, after a one-year holding period, public resales of restricted securities of reporting and non-reporting issuers may now be made by non-affiliates without any restriction. Another important mechanism for reselling restricted securities is pursuant to rule 144A under the Securities Act, which permits an investment bank or other financial intermediary who has purchased restricted securities from an issuer in a private placement to make resales of those securities to an unlimited number of "qualified institutional buyers" without being deemed an underwriter engaged in a distribution of securities. Generally speaking, qualified institutional buyers ("**QIBs**") consist of large institutions that own or invest on a discretionary basis, in aggregate, at least US$100 million in securities of unaffiliated issuers. Sales under rule 144A can take place immediately after a valid private placement under section 4(a)(2), and securities acquired by QIBs pursuant to rule 144A are deemed to be "restricted securities" for purposes of the resale restrictions. Rule 144A may not be used to offer securities that are fungible (i.e., of the same class) with a listed security, and therefore it is not available in connection with equity offerings (other than convertible offerings with a conversion premium of at least 10 per cent) of companies whose shares are listed on a US stock exchange. Finally, Regulation S under the Securities Act enhances liquidity for holders of restricted securities by allowing them to resell restricted securities in offshore transactions.

1.2.18.1 **Rule 506 of Regulation D in detail.** Rule 506 of Regulation D provides two distinct exemptions from registration for companies when they offer and sell securities. Companies relying on the Rule 506 exemptions can raise an unlimited amount of money.

(i) Under Rule 506(b), a "safe harbor" under Section 4(a)(2) of the Securities Act, a company can be assured it is within the Section 4(a)(2) exemption by satisfying certain requirements, including the following:

(a) The company cannot use general solicitation or advertising to market the securities.
(b) The company may sell its securities to an unlimited number of "accredited investors" and up to 35 other purchasers. All non-accredited investors, either alone or with a purchaser representative, must be sophisticated – that is, they must have sufficient knowledge and experience in financial and business matters to make them capable of evaluating the merits and risks of the prospective investment.
(c) Companies must decide what information to give to accredited investors, so long as it does not violate the antifraud prohibitions of the federal securities laws. This means that any information a company provides to investors must be free from false or misleading statements. Similarly, a company should not exclude any information if the omission makes what is provided to investors false or misleading. Companies must give non-accredited investors disclosure documents that are generally the same as those used in Regulation A or registered offerings, including financial statements, which in some cases may need to be certified or audited by an accountant. If a company provides information to accredited investors, it must make this information available to non-accredited investors as well.
(d) The company must be available to answer questions by prospective purchasers.

(ii) Under Rule 506(c), a company can broadly solicit and generally advertise the offering and still be deemed to be in compliance with the exemption's requirements if:

(a) The investors in the offering are all accredited investors; and
(b) The company takes reasonable steps to verify that the investors are accredited investors, which could include reviewing

documentation, such as W-2s, tax returns, bank and brokerage statements, credit reports and the like.

Purchasers of securities offered pursuant to Rule 506 receive "restricted" securities, meaning that the securities cannot be sold for at least six months or a year without registering them.

1.2.18.2 **Regulation S in detail.** Regulation S[370] consists of a general statement and two safe harbors. The general statement indicates that the registration requirements of the Securities Act apply only to offers and sales of securities made in the United States. Of course, the general statement alone generally is insufficient for purposes of structuring an offering; however, it is worth noting as an indication of the SEC's response to the problems leading up to the regulation, as well as the regulation's generally territorial approach. The first safe harbor covers offers and sales by issuers and other distribution participants, as well as their affiliates. The second covers resales by others, such as investors acquiring the securities in a US private placement (*e.g.*, pursuant to Rule 144A).

To facilitate discussion of the safe harbors, a brief overview of key concepts used in Regulation S is helpful:

> *Directed Selling Efforts* > Any activity undertaken for the purpose of, or that could reasonably be expected to have the effect of, conditioning the market in the United States for any of the securities being offered in reliance on Regulation S. Examples include the following: (i) sending promotional materials (including research reports not satisfying the requirements of Rules 138 or 139)9 to US investors; (ii) holding promotional seminars for US investors; and (iii) placing advertisements in publications with a general circulation in the United States. However, activities that are countenanced by the securities laws or are otherwise routine and unconnected with the offering should not constitute directed selling efforts. Examples include the following: (i) meeting with QIBs) in roadshows in a simultaneous U.S. private placement; (ii) issuing press releases under Rule 135, Rule 135c or Rule 135e; (iii) press conferences outside the United States open to U.S. and non-US journalists, as permitted by Rule 135e; (iv) customary marketing activities conducted offshore and permitted by local

---

[370] The annual amount of capital (both debt and equity) raised by using Regulation S over the period 2009-2014 was approximately $140 billion, slightly less than the total of $200 billion per year raised by foreign issuers using Regulation D over the same period. See S. Bauguess, R. Gullapalli, V. Ivanov, *Capital Raising in the US: An Analysis of the Market for Unregistered Securities Offerings* 2009-2014, SEC Division of Economic and Risk Analysis Working Paper (2015).

law; and (v) routine press releases, even including results announcements.

Offshore transaction > In general, an offer or sale of securities is made in an "offshore transaction" if the offer is not made to a person in the United States, and either:

> (i) at the time the buy order is originated, the buyer is outside the United States, or the seller and any person acting on its behalf reasonably believe that the buyer is outside the United States; or
> (ii) for purposes of an offering by an issuer, an underwriter or other distribution participants, the transaction is executed on or through a physical trading floor of an established foreign securities exchange located outside the United States; or
> (iii) for purposes of resales, the transaction is executed in, on or through the facilities of a designated offshore securities market, and neither the seller nor any person acting on its behalf knows that the transaction has been pre-arranged with a buyer in the United States.

In addition, offers and sales to any discretionary or similar account (other than an estate or trust) held for the benefit or account of a non-US person by a dealer or other professional fiduciary organized, incorporated or resident in the United States are deemed to be "offshore transactions".

Substantial US Market Interest > A determination of whether there is Substantial US Market Interest ("**SUSMI**") is based on the issuer's reasonable belief at the commencement of an offering. For a class of equity securities, there is SUSMI if, in the shorter of the issuer's prior fiscal year or the period since the issuer's incorporation: (i) US securities exchanges and inter-dealer quotation systems (including the "pink sheets" over-the-counter market) constituted the single largest market for that class; or (ii) 20% or more of all trading in such class took place in, on or through the facilities of US exchanges or inter-dealer quotations systems and less than 55% of such trading took place in, on or through securities markets of a single foreign country.

US Person > Any natural person resident in the United States. Any partnership or corporation organized or incorporated under the laws of the United States. "US person" excludes, among other persons, US citizens resident in other countries.

(i) The first safe harbor: offers and sales by issuers and distribution participants under Rule 903. The first safe harbor applies to issuers, underwriters, selling group members and others that participate in the distribution of the securities pursuant to a contractual arrangement. Two conditions must be satisfied for an offer or sale to qualify: (a) the offer and sale must be an "offshore transaction," and (b) there may be no "direct selling efforts."

If the offerings of securities of foreign private issuers do not have SUSMI, Regulation S does not impose any requirements beyond the offshore transaction requirement and the prohibition on directed selling efforts.

(ii) The second safe harbor: resales under Rule 904. The second safe harbor covers offshore resale of securities initially placed offshore or by private placement in the United States by persons other than the issuer, a distributor or any of their affiliates (except officers and directors that are affiliates merely by virtue of their position). Such persons generally can resell their securities outside the United States immediately, provided the "offshore transaction" requirement is satisfied and directed selling efforts are not used in the United States. By contrast with the first safe harbor, where one way to satisfy the offshore transaction requirement is to execute the transaction in, on or through a physical trading floor of an established foreign securities exchange, the second safe harbor relies on the broader concept of the transaction being executed in, on or through the facilities of a "designated offshore securities market" and also requires that neither the seller nor anyone acting on its behalf know that the transaction has been pre-arranged with a buyer in the United States.

Notwithstanding the availability of Rule 904, in practice, most resales of securities are covered by another exemption from registration, such as Section 4(a)(1), which provides an exemption for transactions by any person other than an issuer, underwriter or dealer. The safe harbor of Rule 904 generally is used only when the securities being offered or sold are restricted or when the seller is an officer or director of the issuer who is not otherwise affiliated with the issuer. For example, QIBs that purchase securities pursuant to Rule 144A may resell the securities pursuant to Rule 904 during the Rule 144 restricted period.

1.2.18.2.1 *Resales into the United States*.

(i) Resales following a Rule 903 offering. Aside from equity securities of US issuers (discussed below), Regulation S does not explicitly address when securities placed offshore pursuant to the first safe harbor may be resold in the United States. However, the SEC staff has confirmed the generally held view that such securities, other than unsold allotment securities and equity securities of US issuers, may be resold into the United States immediately, subject to the restrictions imposed on dealers by Section 4(a)(3) (and possibly those imposed on distributors and their affiliates under the applicable distribution compliance period). Caution nonetheless may be appropriate in certain cases, as there is no safe harbor for such resales and a person falling within the definition of "underwriter" under Section 2(a)(11) of the Securities Act – a facts and circumstances-based determination – would not be entitled to rely on Section 4(a)(1). Rule 905 of Regulation S explicitly treats equity securities of US issuers placed pursuant to the first safe harbor as "restricted securities", as defined in Rule 144 (discussed further below), even if they are resold pursuant to Rule 904 (as discussed further below). This rule was added in 1998 to provide investors with clarity about permissible resales in this context. Thus, once the one-year (or six- month, in the case of a current reporting issuer) distribution compliance period has ended, limited resales pursuant to Rule 144 should be permissible, with unlimited resales becoming possible for non-affiliates after one year (or six months in the case of a current reporting issuer). Compliance with Rule 905 may result in practical difficulties for an issuer, as Section 4(a)(2) procedures, such as legending, should be applied during the restricted period; these procedures may pose problems with the listing requirements of non-US markets, which may not accept legended, certificated securities.

(ii) Resales following a Rule 904 resale. In adopting Rule 905, the SEC made clear that the resale of restricted securities (*e.g.,* equity securities of a domestic issuer placed pursuant to Regulation S) under Rule 904 would not "wash off" the restricted status of the securities and thereby allow them to be freely resold into the United States by the purchaser. However, the SEC also noted that it was taking a targeted approach to addressing the abuses prompting the 1998 amendments to Regulation S and declined to extend Rule 905 to the securities of foreign private issuers.

1.2.18.3 *Rule 144A in detail*. Regulation S offerings, whether public or private in the issuer's home jurisdiction or elsewhere outside the United States, often feature a concurrent private placement in the United States pursuant to Rule 144A. Rule 144A allows such issuers to tap the deep institutional investor base in the United States, while avoiding the time constraints and regulatory demands of SEC review.

The policy underlying the rule is that sophisticated institutions do not need the protections afforded by the Securities Act registration process.

Securities sold in accordance with the rule's terms will not be considered distributions or to involve a public offering. However, securities acquired under Rule 144A are "restricted securities" as defined in Rule 144 and subject to limitations on their public resale, as discussed further below.

The availability of Rule 144A turns on several conditions being met:

(i) Qualified Institutional Buyers. The seller must reasonably believe that the purchaser is a QIB. To qualify, an institution generally must own or invest on a discretionary basis at least $100 million of securities and be an institution falling within a list of specified types (which includes corporations, insurance companies, registered investment advisers, registered investment companies, employee benefit plans, broker-dealers and banks, among others).

(ii) Notice. The seller and any person acting on its behalf must take reasonable steps to ensure that the purchaser is aware that the seller may be relying on Rule 144A. Typically, such steps would include a statement to this effect in the offering memorandum, as well as the sale confirmation.

(iii) Fungibility. The securities, when issued, cannot have been of the same class as securities listed on a US securities exchange or quoted in a US automated inter-dealer quotation system. Securities convertible or exchangeable into securities so listed or quoted at the time of issuance that have an effective conversion premium of less than 10% are considered securities of the class into which they are convertible or exchangeable for this purpose.

(iv) Information. The issuer must be a Securities Exchange Act-reporting company or exempt from reporting under Rule 12g3-2(b) under the Securities Exchange Act. Otherwise, it must agree to provide certain financial and other information upon request to holders and prospective holders of the securities.

On July 10, the SEC adopted final rules under Section 201(a) of the JOBS Act removing the ban against general solicitation and general advertising in private offerings made in reliance on Rule 144A and Rule 506 of Regulation D under the Securities Act of 1933. The amendment to Rule 144A permits offers of securities to persons other than QIBs, as long as the securities are sold only to persons reasonably believed to be QIBs[371].

---

[371] The amendment to Rule 506 permits an issuer to engage in general solicitation or general advertising, provided that all purchasers are accredited investors and the issuer takes reasonable steps to verify that the purchasers are accredited investors.

1.2.18.3.1 **Restricted securities**. Securities sold under Rule 144A are "restricted securities" (as defined in Rule 144)[372]. They cannot be resold publicly with the benefit of the Rule 144 safe harbor for public resales of privately placed securities until the applicable conditions of that rule are satisfied (*e.g.*, the six-month or one-year holding period relating to resale without restrictions by non-affiliates).[373] Accordingly, until those conditions are met, resales of the securities must be limited or carried out pursuant to Regulation S.

Rule 144A does not require purchasers to sign any documentation under which they agree to adhere to applicable transfer restrictions. QIBs are considered sophisticated and capable of self-policing.

Offering memoranda typically will contain deemed representations under which QIBs are considered, merely by virtue of purchasing the securities, to have represented and agreed that they satisfy the conditions for purchasing the securities initially and that they will comply with applicable transfer restrictions on reselling them. In particular, the purchaser typically will be deemed to agree on its own behalf and on behalf of any investor account for which it is purchasing the securities, and each subsequent holder of the securities will be deemed to agree, to offer, sell or otherwise transfer the securities so long as they are restricted under Rule 144 only:

(i) to the issuer or any of its subsidiaries;
(ii) pursuant to a registration statement that has been declared effective under the Securities Act;
(iii) to a person it reasonably believes is a QIB that purchases for its own account or for the account of a QIB to whom notice is given that the transfer is being made in reliance on Rule 144A;
(iv) in an offshore transaction in accordance with Regulation S; or
(v) pursuant to another available exemption from the registration requirements of the Securities Act, subject to the right of the issuer (and, in the case of a debt offering, the trustee) to require the delivery of an opinion of counsel,

---

[372] Unlike Regulation D offerings, however, almost all (over 99%) Rule 144A transactions involve debt securities. See S. Bauguess, R. Gullapalli, V. Ivanov, *Capital Raising in the US: An Analysis of the Market for Unregistered Securities Offerings* 2009-2014, SEC Division of Economic and Risk Analysis Working Paper (2015).

[373] In December 2007, the SEC adopted amendments to Rule 144 that substantially reduced the holding periods applicable to the sale of restricted securities, among other things. In particular, the revised rule allows non-affiliates to resell freely the securities of a Securities Exchange Act-reporting company six months after issuance, so long as the issuer continues to report.

certifications and/or other information satisfactory to the issuer (and the trustee).

As these restrictions indicate, shares acquired under Rule 144A may be resold offshore in compliance with Regulation S and generally will no longer be restricted once resold outside the United States.

Chapter 5
HOW TO REGULATE A MERE MARKET RESPONSE TO OVERREGULATION

1.1 A starting point for regulators to think about ICO regulations: 1.1.1 Investor protection: 1.1.1.1 Investor losses; *1.1.2 Asymmetric information and moral hazard:* 1.1.2.1 ICO rating platforms and secondary sources; 1.1.2.2 Strong corporate governance and ethics count; *1.1.3 Some actual proposals to balance support for innovation and investor protection; 1.1.4 An International Convention for crypto finance transactions? 1.1.5 Should regulators take a proactive approach about crypto finance transactions?*

1.1 *A starting point for regulators to think about ICO regulations*. A research on the effects of legislations that required small firms on the over-the-counter bulletin board (hereinafter "**OTCBB**") to register with the SEC[374] found that the new rules had a "crowding out" effect on stocks, with nearly 75 percent of the shares targeted by the rules moving off the OTCBB to avoid the SEC registration. The result shows that overregulation ends up pushing many companies further off the grid, where funding may be less available. According to a piece from the Heritage Foundation, not only do these regulations overburden predominantly small and start-up companies, but too much disclosure can also obfuscate rather than inform[375]. The surfeit of information can be overwhelming to investors and hide red flags.

In addition, the cost of centralized financial market regulations likely outweighs potential benefits, as compliance costs are far from trivial. The SEC estimates that the average initial cost of complying with its regulations for stock offerings is $2,5 million, with ongoing annual compliance costs of $1,5 million. These costs could be prohibitive for many firms, especially small startups.

The rapid rise of ICOs is nothing else than a mere market response to overregulation.

ICOs, anyway, involve high asymmetries of information existing between crypto-assets holders and issuers (due to the complexity of the technology)[376], the risk of irrational behavior[377] (as a result of the market

---

[374] B.J. Bushee, C. Leuz, *Economic Consequences of Sec Disclosure Regulation: Evidence from the OTC Bulletin Board*, Journal of Accounting & Economics, 39(2) (2005).
[375] See D. Burton, *Reducing the Burden on Small Public Companies Would Promote Innovation, Job Creation, and Economic Growth*, The Heritage Foundation (June 20, 2014), available at: https://www.heritage.org/jobs-and-labor/report/reducing-the-burden-small-public-companies-would-promote-innovation-job.
[376] It is generally believed that the recent financial crisis is in large part attributable to the complexity of modern financial instruments. When faced with complex structured products, investors are more inclined to use emotional responses and make decisions based on trust or existing relationships (such as going by the reputation of the issuer or financial brand, relying on newspaper articles or advice

euphoria that is characterizing the crypto market), and the lack of governance mechanisms to protect crypto-assets holders, subject to the risk of opportunism by issuers (due to the lack of corporate law rules usually in place to protect shareholders)[378]. Therefore, ICOs should be regulated properly.

While we think that regulations of ICOs are necessary, it has to be noted anyway that:

(i) overregulation could kill innovation at birth, economic liberty, dynamism and outweigh potential benefits[379];

(ii) many modern innovations are being created to get around what seem like protectionist and inhibiting regulations;

(iii) regulations should be technologically neutral, and in order to become so, address the actors and not the products themselves;

(iv) far too often (non-accredited, non-qualified, non-sophisticated) investors are denied the opportunity to invest in new and promising technologies and in new companies — all which undermine productive capital formation and economic growth[380];

---

from an acquaintance with similar investment interests and a similar lack of information) than analyze the risks for themselves.

[377] See with regard to behavioral economics J.R. Nofsinger, *The Psychology of Investing,* Routled (2017).

[378] Innovation, excessive speculation, and dubious behavior are often closely linked. Financial bubbles have historically been associated with various forms of fraud. For example, the Mississippi Bubble of 1719-1720, like the 1719-1720 South Sea Bubble, experienced inflated valuations around subsequent issuances and margin lending on the securities themselves (see R. Dale, *The First Crash: Lessons from the South Sea Bubble*, Princeton University Press ("2004")). The company also engaged in false marketing about the potential in its income generating assets, price support by the stock itself, and paper money that was not fully backed by gold as claimed (R.Z. Aliber, C.P. Kindleberger, *Manias, Panics, and Crashes*, Palgrave Macmillan (2015)). Other famous bubbles, such as the 1840s Railroad bubble, roaring 1920s stock, the dot-com, and 2008 financial crisis, contained substantial evidence of misinformation, false accounting, price manipulation, collusion, and fraud, often in sophisticated forms. The dot-com bubble of 1997 to 2000, in particular, contained strong elements of stock promotion through inflated analysts' forecasts from affiliated analysts (see H.W. Lin, M.F. McNichols, *Underwriting relationships, analysts' earnings forecasts and investment recommendations*, Journal of Accounting and Economics 25, 101-127 (1998)), pushing or "laddering" prices through implicit agreements to purchase more IPO shares in the aftermarket (J.M. Griffin, J.H. Harris, S. Topaloglu, *Why are IPO investors net buyers through lead underwriters?*, Journal of Financial Economics 85, 518-551 (2007)), and accounting fraud, the most notable being Enron.

[379] While adequate regulations and supervision are necessary, excessive regulations and supervision can lead to unnecessarily high transaction costs, distortions and a stifling of innovation. Regulations and supervision should add value. No regulation, otherwise, might be superior to a badly-implemented regulatory structure.

[380] Investors protection and the promotion of economic liberty should always be meticulously weighted because history already told us that regulators are generally unable to outperform the

(v) crypto finance transactions are part of a self-contained system and this unique context requires to carefully weigh competing goals – protecting investors (that can lead to a larger and healthier crypto finance environment) while promoting capital raising and economic liberty.

Hence, we believe that a light touch regulatory approach is to prefer. Whole, the regulatory approach should be based on addressing primarily actors and behaviors, rather than the very technical matters, and more resources should be spent to investigate fraudulent issuance of crypto-assets[381].

The final part of this chapter sketches some proposals – based on a weighted approach – that, if adopted, would enhance legal certainty and seek to balance support for innovation and investor protection.

1.1.1 **Investor protection**. Investor protection encourages the development of financial markets. When investors are protected, they pay more for securities, making it more attractive for entrepreneurs to issue these securities. Shareholder rights encourage the development of equity markets, as measured by the valuation of firms, the number of listed firms (market breadth), and the rate at which firms go public. Protection includes not only the rights written into the laws and regulations but also the effectiveness of their enforcement. Countries that protect shareholders have more valuable stock markets, larger numbers of listed securities per capita, and a higher rate of IPO activity[382]. Several studies have also established a link between investor protection, insider ownership of cash flows, and corporate valuation. Higher ownership by the large shareholders is associated with higher valuation of corporate assets[383]. Greater insider cash flow ownership is associated with higher valuation of corporate assets, whereas greater insider control of voting

---

market in evaluating the quality and the potentiality of financial products. One such example was when Apple Computer went public in 1980. Although it obtained registration of its stock from the SEC, the offering was still subject to merits review in some US states. Massachusetts prohibited the offering of the Apple shares because they were too risky. Texas approved the sale after an extensive review, but its securities regulator called his decision "a close call". Apple did not even bother to offer its shares in Illinois due to strict state laws on new issues (See P.S. Atkins, *Is Excessive Regulation and Litigation Eroding U.S. Financial Competitiveness?* (Washington D.C., April 20, 2007), available at: http://www.sec.gov/news/speech/2007/spch042007psa.htm). Needless to say, Apple has proved one of the most successful enterprises in the world today, and investors in Massachusetts and Illinois missed out on investing in it because of the strict requirements under their state's merits-based securities regulation.

[381] This is essential to avoiding a potentially overzealous regulatory response which would result in a market collapse and the potential discrediting of the structure (see the South Sea Bubble and the Bubble Act of 1720 and their stifling impact on the early development of the joint stock company).

[382] R. La Porta, F. Lopez-de-Silanes, A. Shleifer, R. Vishny, *Legal determinants of external finance*, Journal of Finance 52, 1131-1150 (1997).

[383] G. Gorton, F. Schmid, *Universal banking and the performance of German firms*, Journal of Financial Economics 58, 29-80 (2000).

rights is associated with lower valuation of corporate assets[384]. Firms in countries with better shareholder protection have higher Tobin's Q^{385}. Higher insider cash flow ownership is (weakly) associated with higher corporate valuation, and that this effect is greater in countries with inferior shareholder protection[386]. These results support the roles of investor protection and cash flow ownership by the insiders in limiting expropriation.

A study draws an ingenious connection between investor protection and financial crises[387]. In countries with poor protection, the insiders might treat outside investors well as long as future prospects are bright and they are interested in continued external financing. When future prospects deteriorate, however, the insiders step up expropriation, and the outside investors are unable to do anything about it. This escalation of expropriation renders security price declines especially deep in countries with poor investor protection. To test this hypothesis, the authors examine the depreciation of currencies and the decline of the stock markets in 25 countries during the Asian crisis of 1997-1998. They find that governance variables, such as investor protection indices and the quality of law enforcement, are powerful predictors of the extent of market declines during the crisis. These variables explain the cross-section of declines better than do the macroeconomic variables that have been the focus of the initial policy debate.

Through its effect on financial markets, investor protection influences the real economy[388]. Financial development can accelerate economic

---

[384] S. Claessens, S. Djankov, J. Fan, L. Lang, *Expropriation of minority shareholders in East Asia*, Unpublished working paper. The World Bank, Washington, DC (1999).

[385] R. La Porta, F. Lopez-de-Silanes, A. Shleifer, R. Vishny, *Investor protection and corporate valuation*. NBER Working Paper 7403. National Bureau of Economic Research, Cambridge, MA (1999).

[386] R. La Porta, F. Lopez-de-Silanes, A. Shleifer, R. Vishny, *Investor protection and corporate valuation*. NBER Working Paper 7403. National Bureau of Economic Research, Cambridge, MA (1999).

[387] S. Johnson, P. Boone, A. Breach, E. Friedman, *Corporate governance in the Asian financial crisis*, Journal of Financial Economics 58, 141-186 (2000).

[388] UK's Alternative Investment Market (AIM), launched in 1995 is a secondary market, with the primary market component operating as a private placement. However, unlike US private placements, thanks to the absence of meaningful resale restrictions, retail as well as sophisticated investors can participate in AIM's secondary market. It was deliberately structured in this way to take advantage of then-EU rules that exempted a 'multilateral trading facility' (MTF) from compliance with issuer securities law rules. In its first decade, AIM was highly successful in attracting issuers, so much so that in 2006, its 'IPOs' raised more funds than those on NASDAQ. See J. Gerakos, M. Lang, M. Maffett, *Post-listing performance and private sector regulation: The experience of London's Alternative Investment Market*, Journal of Accounting and Economics 56, 189 (2013). In so doing, it drew the ire of US regulators, with an SEC commissioner labelling it a *"casino"* where 30 per cent of new listings were *"gone in a year"* and the then-head of the NYSE saying AIM *"did not have any standards at all"*. See J. Gapper, *Thain lambasts AIM standards*, Financial Times (Jan. 26, 2007), available at: https://www.ft.com/content/beb09508-ad27-11db-8709-0000779e2340. Subsequent empirical research reports that AIM-listed firms have underperformed those listed on traditional regulated exchanges. Firms with a higher proportion of retail investors were particularly badly affected,

growth in three ways[389]: (i) it can enhance savings; (ii) it can channel these savings into real investment and thereby foster capital accumulation; (iii) to the extent that some controls are exercised over the investment decisions of the entrepreneurs, financial development allows capital to flow toward the more productive uses, and thus improves the efficiency of resource allocation. All three channels can in principle have large effects on economic growth.

1.1.1.1 **Investor losses**. While the effective impact of investor protection as we have just seen is unquestionable, it should be noted that investor losses in the crypto context are probably more acceptable. Crypto finance transactions, indeed, are part of a self-contained system. Crypto-assets may only be purchased by exchanging other crypto-assets such as Bitcoin. In an ICO, the issuer sells a pre-functional crypto-asset that is a smart-contract activated when a deposit of a more established crypto-asset such as Bitcoin or Ether has been received. Thus, ICOs do not directly raise funds in the form of more traditional currencies such as dollars.

While many investors purchase Bitcoin or Ether on exchanges using dollars at current market prices, many investors obtained it by mining it or purchasing it before it rose exponentially in price. Much of the wealth stored in these crypto-assets represents abnormal capital gains by early investors. Regardless of whether it is invested in crypto-assets, such gains could dissipate at any time if the price of Bitcoin and Ether were to collapse (indeed the price of both have declined significantly over the last year). If the main investment in ICOs represents speculative gains that are being reinvested, it is unclear whether there are strong policy reasons to protect such investments. Most ICOs raise relatively small amounts from investors and are not listed on exchanges, making it less likely that a wide range of investors will purchase the crypto-assets[390]. Though significant amounts have been raised through ICOs, the total amount is a small percentage of the $300 billion market capitalization of Bitcoin and Ether.

However, if these investments are increasingly made by late investors who purchase crypto-assets for cash, there would be a stronger reason for regulators to heavily step in.

---

suggesting investor protection concerns are a real issue. See J. Gerakos, M. Lang, M. Maffett, *Post-listing performance and private sector regulation: The experience of London's Alternative Investment Market*, Journal of Accounting and Economics 56, 189 (2013).
[389] T. Beck, R. Levine, N. Loayza, *Finance and the sources of growth*, Journal of Financial Economics 58, 261-300 (2000).
[390] H. Benedetti, L. Kostovetsky, *Digital Tulips? Returns to Investors in Initial Coin Offerings* (May 2018).

1.1.2 **Asymmetric information and moral hazard.** Traditional financial markets are rapidly evolving to a situation where very often the buyer and the seller have roughly equal knowledge. One of the salient features of the crypto finance transactions market, instead, is considerable information asymmetry between entrepreneurs and investors. Unlike VCs, who tend to perform thorough due diligence, ICO investors need to rely mainly on the contents of the whitepaper and the terms of the ICO when making their investment decisions. Although it is likely that the tighter regulation that is being considered will reduce the extent of information asymmetry in the ICO market, VCs are likely to be always better informed than potential ICO investors. In the presence of high information asymmetry, ICOs are expected to be less prevalent and of lower quality on average.

Moral hazard is a kind of asymmetric information problem which very often can be tolerably overcome with cheap, ubiquitous information. By moral hazard we mean the tendency of a better-informed party to exploit its information advantage in an undesirable or dishonest way. The scandals, the fraud and the dark headlines often associated with moral hazard, have all helped erode the trust in the crypto finance transactions market.

Hence, it is highly recommended to promote a system of smart disclosure and the imposition of some minimum requirements[391] for whitepapers. The disclosure should cover details such as the nature of the business, properties, contributors or founders, budgets, plans for distribution and running of the ICO, and governance details (bylaws, disclosure to auditors, etc.). The issuers should also state clearly that no-one of the key people has experienced disqualifying events, such as being convicted of, or subject to court or administrative sanctions for security, financial and white-collar frauds and crimes.

For private companies looking to register an IPO, the SEC requires: (i) a description of the company's business, properties, and competition; (ii) a description of the risks of investing in the company; (iii) a discussion and analysis of the company's financial results and financial condition as seen through the eyes of management; (iv) the identity of the company's officers and directors and their compensation; (v) a description of material transactions between the company and its officers, directors, and significant shareholders; (vi) a description of material legal proceedings involving the company and its officers and directors; (vii) a

---

[391] The lack of standardization needs to be solved in order to avoid several problems, including selective disclosure, lack of comparability, and adverse selection problems. These asymmetries of information might be corrected by either setting which elements should be included as a minimum in the whitepapers, or letting markets decide the best way to guarantee a certain degree of standardization, for example using analysts or law firms as advisors in structuring ICOs or through peer reviews.

description of the company's material contracts; (viii) a description of the securities being offered; (ix) the plan for distributing the securities; (x) the intended use of the proceeds of the offering; (xi) important facts about its business operations, financial condition, results of operations, risk factors, and management; (xii) audited financial statements; (xiii) copies of material contracts.

For crowdfunding companies that fall under the Securities Act exemption, the SEC requires: (i) information about officers, directors, and owners of 20 percent or more of the issuer; (ii) a description of the issuer's business and the use of proceeds from the offering; (iii) the price to the public of the securities or the method for determining the price; (iv) the target offering amount and the deadline to reach the target offering amount; (v) whether the issuer will accept investments in excess of the target offering amount; (vi) certain related-party transactions; (vii) a discussion of the issuer's financial condition and financial statements.

A reasonable balance that provides investors with necessary disclosure while not placing excessive burdens on smaller ICO issuers seeking to innovate could be something in the middle. Therefore, a good whitepaper should be very clear and structured as follow: (i) a description of the entity's business, properties, and competition; (ii) a description of the corporate structure (e.g. separation between ICO issuing entity and OpCo? Foundation or corporation?) and the reasons behind the adoption of the jurisdiction(s); (iii) a description of the risks of investing in the project; (iv) the identity of the entity's key people and management; (v) the statement that no-one of the key people has experienced disqualifying events; (vi) a description of legal proceedings involving the entity and its key people; (vii) a description of the crypto-assets being offered; (viii) the plan for distributing the crypto-assets; (ix) the intended use and handling of the proceeds of the offering and the purchaser's return on investment.

1.1.2.1 ***ICO rating platforms and secondary sources***. Whitepapers are difficult for non-technical people to analyze, leading many to rely primarily on secondary sources and peer review[392]. Newcomers and inexperienced investors are especially trusting ICO rating platforms when looking for information for their investment decisions. Peer reviews vary widely and are potentially biased. In many cases the research / review is commissioned and paid for directly by the projects that are being reviewed. Companies listing and rating ICOs accept very often payments in Ether but also accept part of the total fee in the project's crypto-asset.

---

[392] ICObench is one of the most popular websites listing and rating ICOs. Its pages are among the top hits in any Google search for a specific crypto project and the word ICO, making it a key site for crypto-assets operators to appear on.

The risk of conflict of interest is high. It is also evident that most rating platforms are nothing more than marketing tools hawking visibility to the highest bidders under the guise of supposedly legitimate and expert ratings. Therefore, this area should be regulated properly. Regulators should impose, for example, at least specific disclosure about whether a payment was made by the client whose project is being assessed, and if so, how much. As crypto finance transactions move into the mainstream, research and rating of crypto finance transactions should mimic the standards of traditional Wall Street analysis.

1.1.2.2 **Strong corporate governance and ethics count**. Corporate governance refers to the structures and processes in place to direct and control companies (or other large, complex institutions), including relationships between stakeholders, oversight and supervision of the company, the rights of investors, risk mitigation and ethical behavior. It is intended to increase the company's transparency and to balance powers between founders, investors and the wider applicable community.

The origins of corporate governance can be found in the first companies that were formed sometime around the 1600s, namely companies trading with India [East India Company]. As a complex, multi-party organization, they implemented the first trifecta of corporate governance layers – the three main levels of authority – which included:

> (i) The participants – individuals that funded the building of a ship in the company. They would be compensated by the returns made on a trade voyage. Today these are the shareholders.

> (ii) The governors – a group of individuals chosen by the participants to represent their interests and ensure profitable trade when they arrived at their destination. Today these are the board of directors.

> (iii) The captain – who steers the ship, who manages a crew and gets the ship from A to B. Today it's the CEO.

For most corporations, the basic governance structure today is: shareholders vote for, and hence empower, a board of directors, who then have a fiduciary responsibility to look out for shareholders' interests. The board hires a CEO, who is accountable to the board. The CEO (sometimes with input from the board) hires a management team, and so on. At each step, there is a flow of power down the chain (from shareholders through to front-line employees), and a flow of accountability back up that chain. And there are all sorts of rules – including various policies and principles of good governance – that establish how that power and accountability is to be implemented. There will be internal rules, for example (partly determined by relevant corporate law), about how board elections are to be carried out. There are also governance principles that apply to things like the inclusion of external, independent directors on the board.

Ethics have an important role in governance. Complex corporate structures and opaque corporate governance have led to headline-grabbing scandals (think Enron) in our recent history of business. The company's reputation demands the highest ethics from the people who lead an organization. Therefore, the corporate governance should be out-and-out a matter of ethics. The primary objective of a corporation is to increase shareholder value. Successful corporations must operate within society; to that end, they must maintain the values and norms of the society in which they operate. And governance is also legal matter (for example, the Sarbanes-Oxley Act of 2002 includes a number of requirements about corporate governance). Governance is properly a legal matter because (at least arguably) shareholders need protection from unscrupulous or merely lazy boards of directors and executives, and because the public interest is at stake when large companies are mis-governed. Enron used to be the prime example of poor governance practices having a devastating effect on shareholders and the broader public. The law and ethics are not one and the same, however. Although the law can guide ethical behavior by laying out a framework, the law should be thought of as the bare minimum of an ethical framework. Complying with the law and behaving ethically are not necessarily synonymous.

In ICOs the governance is often centralized. Nothing is explicitly disclosed. Thinks about financials, that are closely held. The vast majority of whitepapers has unstated governance structures. Projects with stated governance generally grant crypto-assets holders limited rights, but ultimately vest control power with founders. Many projects have made promises about assigning rights to stakeholders; few have delivered. Almost no ICO has offered blockchain-based equity in the company. Instead, crypto-assets are either a pre-sold access key to a future service, or investments tied in some nebulous way to the success of the platform. Crypto-assets, in the vast majority of cases, do not imply ownership of the platform or a claim to cash-flows of the underlying. Founders can promise some capital-return mechanisms to crypto-assets holders[393], but these are in practice barely enforceable (the most basic principle of law – *pacta sunt servanda*, agreements must be respected – is not very

---

[393] A recent empirical study (surveying 253 ICOs) found that only 26% of crypto-assets offer profit rights, and that the existence of profit rights is a good predictor of ICO success. See S. Adhami, G. Giudici, S. Martinazzi, *Why Do Businesses Go Crypto? An Empirical Analysis of Initial Coin Offerings*, Journal of Economics and Business (Jan. 6, 2018).

effective here). Thus, most ICOs are structured not as equity purchases (as developers rarely seek to register with local securities regulators), but rather as contributions or donations, often to a foundation.

Crypto-assets holders very often are speculative investors into a crypto-asset whose value is still yet undetermined. Adding this layer into the trifecta of corporate governance is no simple task. Anyway, meritocratic, non-hierarchical, reputation-based, stakeholders open corporate governance systems should be applied, not only to lead to better post ICOs' entities and protect investors, but also because governance decentralization is one means of avoiding being qualified a security[394].

1.1.3 *Some actual proposals to balance support for innovation and investor protection.* First of all, we propose a definition of the crypto-assets based on the legal nature, categorizing between non-speculative (crypto-assets with real intrinsic usage) and speculative crypto-assets (crypto-assets without real intrinsic usage). Speculative crypto-assets are issued speculatively (with little backing, no community backing, and no viable product at the time of the crypto finance transaction) and could represent significant risks for non-accredited, non-qualified, non-sophisticated investors (investors with no depth of experience and market knowledge). The legal classification of the crypto-assets should be based on a test that puts substance over form when considering: (i) soliciting a broad base of investors, including retail investors; (ii) using the internet, including public websites and discussion boards, to reach a large number of potential investors; (iii) attending public events, including conferences and meetups, to actively advertise the sale of the crypto-assets; and (iv) raising a significant amount of capital from a large number of investors. This test (hereinafter the "**speculative crypto-assets test**") should be self-assessed by ICO issuers – other than used by regulators – and disclosed in the whitepaper[395].

---

[394] In the DAO investigation report, the [decentralized] Bitcoin protocol and the Ethereum distributed computing platform were considered not to be securities. Indeed distributed, not centrally-controlled platforms such as Bitcoin and Ethereum do not easily fit the definition of a regulated security, in contrast with centrally-organized and questionably marketed crypto-assets.

[395] ICO whitepapers are inconsistent regarding the applicable law, the regulatory status of the ICO – which means whether the functional crypto-asset or even the pre-sale should be considered as securities under the applicable securities regulation –, and the location of the funds once received by the issuer. Only 31% of the ICOs in a sample of 450 ICOs mention the law applicable to the ICO. In 37.7% of the cases the whitepaper excluded investors from certain countries from participation. In 86.5% of the cases there is no information at all as to the regulatory status of the ICO. See D.A. Zetzsche, R.P. Buckley, D.W. Arner, L. Föhr, *The ICO Gold Rush: It's a scam, It's a bubble, It's a super challenge for regulators*, European Banking Institute Working Paper Series 2018 – NO. 18 (2018). These elements are avoided in whitepapers probably because companies believe that, as financial contributions to an ICO are made in cryptocurrencies (and benefits returned to participants are instrumented through tokens or digital assets), these instruments exist beyond the jurisdictions or laws.

Second, regulators should promote a system of non-excessively burdensome disclosures[396]. More generally, prospectuses tend to be technical[397] and are considered to provide little information that can be fruitfully processed by retail clients[398]. As a matter of fact, a system of smart disclosure and the imposition of some minimum requirements for whitepapers – in relation to which regulators should establish a legal presumption stating that any ambiguous provision in the whitepaper should be interpreted in favor of non-speculative crypto-assets – could protect crypto-assets holders[399], while avoiding excessive costs and

---

[396] Reliance on current applicable untailored securities disclosure forms could prove not only potentially burdensome, but also inadequate for investor protection in case of crypto finance transactions. See C. Brummer, T. Kiviat, J. Massari, *What Should be Disclosed in an Initial Coin Offering*, Cryptoassets, (Nov 29, 2018 forthcoming).

[397] It is generally believed that the recent financial crisis is in large part attributable to the complexity of modern financial instruments and that disclosure documents like prospectuses are close to impenetrable for many investors. See e.g., S.L. Schwarcz, *Disclosure's Failure in the Subprime Mortgage Crisis*, Utah Law Review, 1109 (2008); F. Partnoy, *Historical Perspectives on the Financial Crisis: Ivar Kreuger, the Credit-Rating Agencies, and Two Theories about the Function, and Dysfunction, of Markets*, Yale Journal on Regulation 26(2), 431 (2009); J. Crotty, *Structural Causes of the Global Financial Crisis: A Critical Assessment of the 'New Financial Architecture'*, Cambridge Journal of Economics 33, 563 (2009); A.J. Schwartz, *Origins of The Financial Market Crisis of 2008*, Cato Journal 29(1), 19 (2008); D. Arner, *The Global Credit Crisis of 2008: Causes and Consequences*, Working Paper No.3, Asian Institute of International Financial Law, University of Hong Kong (Jan. 2009); J.H. Farrar, *The global financial crisis and the governance of financial institutions*, Australian Journal of Corporate Law 24(3), 227 (2010).

[398] See D. Langevoort, *Taming the Animal Spirits of the Stock Markets: A Behavioral Approach to Securities Regulation*, Northwestern University Law Review 97, 135 (2002); J. Choi, *Behavioral Economics and the Regulation of Public Offerings*, Lewis & Clark Law Review, 85 (2006). A cognitive research in the UK on risk disclosure has revealed poor retail investor appreciation of risk and its consequences – investors tend to read risk information as disclaimers rather than warnings. See J. Hamilton, L.E. Gillies, *The Impact of E-Commerce Developments on Consumer Welfare – Information Disclosure Regimes*, Journal of Financial Regulation and Compliance 11(4), 329, 336 (2003). Another research has suggested that even in the US, retail investors have limited knowledge of finance and are not capable of fully understanding disclosures. See L.E. Willis, *Against Financial Literacy Education*, Iowa Law Review 94, 197-201 (2008). Added to this are the intricacies of modern accounting practices which determine how corporate financial matters are reported.

[399] The recent Lehman Minibonds saga in Hong Kong provides a vivid example of how the disclosure-based regulation may break down. The Minibonds, despite being innocuously branded as "bonds", were actually very complex structured debt instruments, completely different from normal corporate bonds in that, under the terms of the Minibonds, payments of interest, principle or both, were credit-linked to the financial condition of each of seven "reference entities" and their ability to avoid certain "credit events" such as insolvency. With the nominal purchase price of only US$5000 together with "gifts" of inexpensive consumer products or supermarket coupons upon purchase, the Minibonds were clearly targeted at retail investors (see P. Lejot, *Dictum Non Meum Pactum: Lehman's Minibond Transactions*, Hong Kong Law Journal 38, 585-587 (2008)). What happened then was that many retail investors bought Lehman Minibonds without appreciating the real nature of the product, and when Lehman Brothers filed for bankruptcy on September 15, 2008, investors lost most, if not all, of the initial amount they had paid for the Minibonds. Days after the bankruptcy filing, those that lost substantial sum due to the Minibonds took to the street, lashing out at banks that had sold them Minibonds as well as demanding governmental investigation and intervention. However, the investigation conducted by the securities regulator, the Hong Kong Securities and Futures Commission ("**SFC**"), found that the Minibonds prospectus actually complied with relevant information disclosure requirements both in form and substance (Hong Kong Securities and Futures Commission, *Issues*

bureaucracy. On the contrary, a more traditional empowerment of crypto-assets holders is not the best option, because it could lead to detrimental governance problems, such as the risk of crypto-assets holders becoming as actual directors if they were given strong rights to make key managerial decisions.

Hence, ICOs, regardless of the legal nature of the crypto-asset, should be required to file a light offering statement to Financial Market Authorities electronically. The filing should have the purpose to disclose and facilitate the collection of information about ICOs and to run *ex post* fraud controls by the Financial Market Authorities.

The filing of ICOs issuing non-speculative crypto-assets (hereinafter "**Non-speculative ICOs**") to raise a maximum aggregate amount of $5,000,000 in a 12-months period should require the submission of a summary of the following key information (and a whitepaper containing them extensively): (i) a description of the entity's business; (ii) a description of the risks of purchasing the crypto-assets; (iii) the identity of the project's key-people with the statement that no-one of the them has experienced disqualifying events; (iv) the self-assessment of the speculative crypto-assets test and a description of the legal nature of the crypto-assets being offered; (v) the intended use of the proceeds of the offering. The purchaser's purchase should be limited to 10% of the GDP per capita of the country in a 12-month period (principle of the "**Proportional income investment**"[400]) if the purchaser is a non-accredited, non-qualified, non-sophisticated investor[401]. There should be no restriction on the resale after a (30 days) "cooling off" period that allows non-accredited, non-qualified, non-sophisticated investors to return the crypto-assets without cost. The purchase of crypto-assets in Non-speculative ICOs should be prohibited to pension funds and commercial banks, since they invest money from the general

---

Raised by the Lehman Minibonds Crisis – Report to the Financial Secretary (Dec. 2008), available at: https://www.sfc.hk/web/doc/EN/general/general/lehman/Review%20Report/Review%20Report.pdf). For instance, the risks section of the Minibonds prospectus contained a clear general warning that "our Notes are not principle protected; you could lose part, and possibly all, of your investment" in addition to other specific risks. The SFC did identify several problems contributing to the crisis, including improper selling practices and inadequate advice, but none of them related to any deficiency in the prospectus information disclosure regime. In short, there was no breach of the information disclosure regulation and thus no legal liability could be pursued in that regard. The important point to note is that information disclosure regulation failed to provide adequate protection for investors in the Minibonds crisis in Hong Kong.

[400] Proportional income investments are investments that are minor in light of the income of the investor. Anyone should be allowed to invest up to X% of his or her income or X% of his or her total amount of capital.

[401] For instance, US non-accredited investor could invest up to $5950 yearly (10% of $59,500, that is GDP per capita in the US) and cumulatively in Non-speculative ICOs.

public and a potential failure could have consequences for the stability of the financial system.

The filing of ICOs issuing speculative crypto-assets (hereinafter "**Speculative ICOs**") to raise a maximum aggregate amount of $40,000,000 in a 12-month period – or Non-speculative ICOs exceeding the limit of $5,000,000 in a 12-months period or the purchaser's purchase limit of 10% of the GDP per capita of the country in a 12-month period[402] – should require the submission of a summary of the following key information (and a whitepaper containing them extensively): (i) a description of the entity's business, properties, and competition; (ii) a description of the corporate structure and the reasons behind the adoption of the jurisdiction; (iii) a description of the risks of investing in the project; (iv) the identity of the entity's key people and management with the statement that no-one of the key people has experienced disqualifying events; (v) the self-assessment of the speculative crypto-assets test and a description of the legal nature of the crypto-assets being offered; (vi) a description of legal proceedings involving the company and its key people; (vii) the plan for distributing the crypto-assets; (viii) the intended use and handling of the proceeds of the offering and the investor's return on investment; (ix) the conflicts of interest policy; (xii) a code of conduct (substantially aligned with the conduct regulation as per point four below) complemented by an affirmation that key people and management will not breach it; (xiii) information about the to be engaged third-party financial auditor. The purchaser's purchase should be limited to 10%[403] of the GDP per capita of the country in a 12-month period if the purchaser is a non-accredited, non-qualified, non-sophisticated investor. There should be no restriction on the resale after a (30 days) "cooling off" period that allows non-accredited, non-qualified, non-sophisticated investors to return crypto-assets without cost. The purchase of crypto-assets in Speculative ICOs should be prohibited to pension funds and commercial banks.

Speculative ICOs looking to raise a maximum aggregate amount greater than $50,000,000 in a 12-months period should be subject, in addition to the filing above, to: (i) a control *ex ante* by the Financial Market Authority; (ii) the filing of additional biannual progress updates; (iii) the

---

[402] Non-speculative ICOs exceeding the limit of $5,000,000 in a 12-months period or the purchaser's purchase limit of 10% of the GDP per capita of the country in a 12-month period should also be required to have at least X% of their initial raise from professional investment firms who perform due diligence on the project. In order to qualify, initial investments must proceed at a price that is close to ICO price (e.g. no less than 33% of VWAP (volume-weighted average price) in the first 6 months of crowdfunding and no less than 66% of the initial price at outset).

[403] Or up to 20% if at least X% of their initial raise comes from professional investment firms who perform due diligence on the project. In order to qualify, initial investments must proceed at a price that is close to ICO price (e.g. no less than 33% of VWAP (volume-weighted average price) in the first 6 months of crowdfunding and no less than 66% of the initial price at outset).

filing of annual reports; (iv) the compliance with OECD guidelines on tax transparency. The purchaser's purchase limit should be set by the Financial Market Authority. The purchase of crypto-assets in Speculative ICOs by pension funds and commercial banks could be possible if permitted by the Financial Market Authority. The Financial Market Authorities could impose "cooling off" periods that allow crypto-asset holders to return crypto-assets within a given period and without cost.

Third, Know Your Customer ("**KYC**") is a universal concept that's broadly understood in global finance. Know Your Customer/Anti-Money Laundering is a due diligence process by which a company can verify the identity of its customers, making sure that the money they wish to move was acquired legitimately and that the customer is not a part of a sanctioned list, a criminal, a terrorist, or a corrupt organization. While the unnecessary collection of personal information should be avoided, comply with customized but effective KYC / AML light controls (to be introduced) should be required to any crypto finance transaction.

Four, regulators should impose a conduct regulation – i.e. standards of behavior aiming to prevent expropriation by founders and incentivize to do the business in a responsible and transparent way, and do not engage in practices which would be potentially or factually damaging to the image and interests of the ecosystem. The adoption of industry-wide minimum standards on crypto-assets listings, and the restriction of unfair trade practices like insider trading should also be adopted.

Five, the code that governs the ICO process could be programmed in such a way to provide investors with protection from fraud and theft by founders. A recent study finds that many ICOs do not contain such protections even though they could[404]. Financial Market Authorities should announce that the existence of protective code would weigh against the initiation of enforcement proceedings against a project.

To finish, regulators should pay attention to abnormal fluctuations of the market value of the listed crypto-assets[405]. Otherwise, we might observe

---

[404] S. Cohney, D. Hoffman, J. Sklaroff, D. Wishnick, *Coin-Operated Capitalism* (2018).

[405] The vast majority of crypto-assets transactions occur on centralized exchanges that offer varying levels of limited transparency. Trading on unregulated exchanges could leave crypto-assets vulnerable to gaming and manipulation. Recent examples of apparently manipulated markets include Libor manipulation (see C. Mollenkamp, M. Whitehouse, *Study casts doubt on key rate*, The Wall Street Journal (May 29, 2008), available at: https://www.wsj.com/articles/SB121200703762027135), FX manipulation (L Vaughan, G Finch, *Currency spikes at 4 pm in London provide rigging clues*, Bloomberg (Aug. 27, 2013), available at: https://www.bloomberg.com/news/articles/2013-08-27/currency-spikes-at-4-p-m-in-london-provide-rigging-clues), gold (C. Denina, J. Harvey, *E-trading pulls gold into forex units as commodity desks shrink*, Reuters (Apr. 22, 2014), available at: https://www.reuters.com/article/banks-gold-forex/e-trading-pulls-gold-into-forex-units-as-commodity-desks-shrink-idUSL6N0NE3K920140422), and the VIX index (J.M Griffin, A. Shams,

unexpected declines that may undermine the stability of the financial system.

1.1.4 **An International Convention for crypto finance transactions?** The regulatory landscape surrounding crypto finance transactions would significantly benefit from an international convention determining which investor protection regimes are applicable, and at which venues victims of fraud or misrepresentation may sue issuers of crypto-assets. The conditions for such a convention are arguably in place. Despite some frictions, there is significant convergence between the securities regulation regimes worldwide[406]. This particularly holds if one looks at law from a purposive and functional rather than a merely formalist point of view.

1.1.5 **Should regulators take a proactive approach about crypto finance transactions?** Crypto-assets are early today, but will transform the world tomorrow.

We believe, without overstatement, that crypto-assets-based networks hold the potential to create value on an order of magnitude far bigger to that of the internet[407]. Crypto finance transactions play a critical role in unlocking the value inherent in these networks. Countries, issuers, investors, and users alike could stand to gain tremendously from this innovation if it is broadly adopted.

Government regulations can have both positive and negative effects on the innovation process. The ability of a country to provide effective regulations is an important determinant of how an economy performs. In this context experience shows, moreover, that regulators are often unable to outperform the market in evaluating financial products[408].

Access to finance, particularly for startups, is a crucial element in the innovation process. Crypto finance transactions are an alternative source

---

Manipulation in the VIX?, The Review of Financial Studies 31, 1377-1417 (2018)). With regard to conditions that may facilitate manipulation see P. Kumar, D.J. Seppi, *Futures manipulation with "cash settlement"*, The Journal of Finance 47, 1485-1502 (1992); C. Spatt, *Security market manipulation*, Annual Review of Financial Economics 6, 405-418 (2014).

[406] Convergence in securities law has reduced, but not eliminated, differences in substantive securities laws, and there remain substantial differences in enforcement styles and intensity. See J. C. Coffee Jr., *Law and the Market: The Impact of Enforcement*, University of Pennsylvania Law Review 156, 229 (2007).

[407] Consider how much has changed since the internet was first introduced to mainstream. Today society relies on it as a resource for almost everything. Use of the Internet as a percentage of the world's population has grown from 0.049% in 1990 to almost 45.80 percent in 2016. See *Individuals Using the Internet*, The World Bank, available at: https://data.worldbank.org/indicator/it.net.user.zs.

[408] See M. Jennings, *The Efficacy of Merit Review of Common Stock Offerings: Do Regulators Know More than the Market*, BYU Journal of Public Law 7, 211-222 (1992).

of early stage funding to traditional venture capital and can support high-risk investments in small, technology-based firms, which are often passed over by traditional financial institutions. Regulatory reform in financial markets is a prerequisite to improving the supply of capital.

As we have seen, projects based originally and organically in ICO banned[409] or ICO unfriendly countries have made the difficult decision to relocate the project to foreign jurisdictions with proactive approach. This is a loss of intellectual capital for the countries which seek to lead the world in technology innovation. This also could lead to a "race to the bottom"[410], with potentially severe consequences for the stability of the financial markets. Well-developed domestic standards for crypto-assets corporate finance transactions could provide the certainty that keeps innovators at home and attracts talent from all over the world, effectively promoting country's entrepreneurship spirit and innovation.

---

[409] Bans are usually highly ineffective. With regard to the ICO ban in China, for instance, citizens in China are using various types of evasion to continue investing in ICO's and crypto despite a comprehensive ban there. See M. Huillet, *Skirting the Great Wall: The Chequered Saga of Crypto in China, 2018*, Cointelegraph (Nov. 4, 2018), available at: https://cointelegraph.com/news/skirting-the-great-wall-the-chequered-saga-of-crypto-in-china-2018.

[410] The "race to the bottom" was an argument that was raised in the wake of the internationalization of securities markets in the 1990s, criticizing the idea of countries competing for foreign investment by framing their securities laws in a particular fashion that would be excessively beneficial to investors; for an overview, see R. Bollen, *International Standard-Setting and the Regulation of Hedge Funds: Part II*, Company and Securities Law Journal 28, 370-377 (2010); E.C. Chaffee, *Finishing the Race to the Bottom: An Argument for the Harmonization and Centralization of International Securities Law*, Seton Hall Law Review 40, 1581 (2010).

Chapter 6
THE EVOLVING LANDSCAPE

Below a timeline in reverse chronological order (from newest to oldest) about the evolving landscape in terms of new regulations, regulatory actions and enforcements with regard to the crypto industry.

APRIL 10, 2019	The Financial Services Commission of Mauritius ("**FSC**") issues guidance for Security Token Offerings[411].
APRIL 3, 2019	The US Securities and Exchange Commission ("**SEC**") issues a framework for analyzing whether a digital asset is offered and sold as an investment contract, and, therefore, is a security[412].
MARCH 28, 2019	Hong Kong's Securities and Futures Commission ("**SFC**") issues detailed guidance for Security Token Offerings[413].
MARCH 19, 2019	The Italian Companies and Exchange Commission ("**CONSOB**") publishes a discussion document about ICOs and crypto-assets exchanges that may lead to the introduction of specific regulation in this field. CONSOB, in particular, proposes that crypto-assets that don't qualify as financial instruments or investment products should be considered as an autonomous asset class[414].
MARCH 13, 2019	The Thai Securities and Exchange Commission approves the first ICO portal[415].

---

[411] See FSC, *Guidance Note 2 Securities Token Offerings* (STOs), (Apr. 10, 2019), available at: https://www.fscmauritius.org/media/70864/guidance-note-on-securities-tokens.pdf.

[412] See SEC, *Framework for "Investment Contract" Analysis of Digital Assets*, (April 3, 2019), available at: https://www.sec.gov/corpfin/framework-investment-contract-analysis-digital-assets; B. Hinman, V. Szczepanik, *Statement on Framework for "Investment Contract" Analysis of Digital Assets*, (April 3, 2019), available at: https://www.sec.gov/news/public-statement/statement-framework-investment-contract-analysis-digital-assets.

[413] See SFC, *Statement on Security Token Offerings*, (Mar. 28, 2019), available at: https://www.sfc.hk/web/EN/news-and-announcements/policy-statements-and-announcements/statement-on-security-token-offerings.html.

[414] See CONSOB, *Initial Coin Offerings and Crypto-Assets Exchanges*, (Mar. 19, 2019), available at: http://www.consob.it/documents/46180/46181/doc_disc_20190319_en.pdf/e981f8a9-e370-4456-8f67-111e460610f0.

[415] See D. Chudasri, *SEC approves first ICO portal, still unnamed*, Bangkok Post (Mar. 13, 2019), available at: https://www.bangkokpost.com/business/news/1643532/.

Crypto-assets global corporate finance transactions

MARCH 1, 2019	The Thai Securities and Exchange Commission announces that Bitcoin Cash, Ethereum Classic, and Litecoin are banned from use in initial coin offerings[416].
FEBRUARY 22, 2019	The US Securities and Exchange Commission ("**SEC**") issues updated guidelines and warnings concerning ICOs[417].
	The National Legislative Assembly in Thailand approves a Securities and Exchange Act amendment that allows blockchain-based securities to be issued and traded[418].
FEBRUARY 20, 2019	The US Securities and Exchange Commission ("**SEC**") encourages self-reporting in case of unregistered ICOs. The SEC charges Gladius Network LLC with conducting an unregistered initial coin offering, but doesn't impose a penalty because the company self-reported the conduct, agreed to compensate investors, and registered the tokens as a class of securities[419].
	The UK Financial Conduct Authority ("**FCA**") publishes draft guidance for market players in the developing crypto-assets sector[420].
FEBRUARY 19, 2019	The US Federal Bureau of Investigation ("**FBI**") releases details on what they believe to be warning signs of fraudulent ICO activity. The FBI also warned investors to conduct due diligence[421].
	The US Securities and Exchange Commission ("**SEC**") announces plans to expand the *"Test-the-Waters"* accommodation to all issuers. The new expansion

---

[416] See Y. Khatri, *Thai SEC Bans Three Cryptocurrencies from ICO Investment, Trading Pairs*, Coindesk (Mar. 1, 2019), available at: https://www.coindesk.com/thai-sec-bans-three-cryptocurrencies-from-ico-investment-trading-pairs.
[417] See SEC, *Spotlight on Initial Coin Offerings*, (Feb. 22, 2019), available at: https://www.sec.gov/ICO.
[418] See N. Polkuamdee, *NLA nod clears path for scripless issuance, tokenisation*, Bangkok Post (Feb. 22, 2019), available at: https://www.bangkokpost.com/business/news/1632926/nla-nod-clears-path-for-scripless-issuance-tokenisation.
[419] See SEC, *Company Settles Unregistered ICO Charges After Self-Reporting to SEC*, (Feb. 20, 2019), available at: https://www.sec.gov/news/press-release/2019-15.
[420] See FCA, *Guidance on Cryptoassets – Consultation Paper CP19/3*, (Jan. 2019), available at: https://www.fca.org.uk/publication/consultation/cp19-03.pdf.
[421] See M. Huillet, *FBI Outline Key Features of Scam ICOs, Warns Investors to Be Vigilant*, Cointelegraph (Feb. 19, 2019), available at: https://cointelegraph.com/news/fbi-outline-key-features-of-scam-icos-warns-investors-to-be-vigilant.

	would allow any prospective issuer to test market interest prior to filing a registration statement[422].
FEBRUARY 14, 2019	The US Securities and Exchange Commission ("**SEC**") obtains *"preliminary injunction against Blockvest LLC"* and its founder Reginald Buddy Ringgold III. The SEC is charging Blockvest LLC with *"making fraudulent offers of securities"* as well as unauthorized use of the SEC logo in order to mislead investors[423].
FEBRUARY 10, 2019	US Securities and Exchange Commission ("**SEC**") commissioner Heister Peirce states in a speech that the delay in establishing crypto regulation may allow more freedom for the industry to move on its own[424].
JANUARY 24, 2019	The Monetary Authority of Singapore ("**MAS**") reminds investors of the risks of investing in ICOs. The MAS also warned an ICO issuer not to proceed until compliant with their regulations[425].
JANUARY 13, 2018	The Cyberspace Administration of China announces regulations requiring all companies utilizing blockchain technology to adhere to anti-anonymity regulations[426].
JANUARY 10, 2018	Thailand issues licenses to its first four crypto exchanges. The four approved exchanges are Bx, Bitkub, Coins and Satang Pro[427].
	Florida's Congressman Darren Soto says that digital assets should not be regulated by the US Securities and

---

[422] See SEC, *SEC Proposes to Expand "Test-the-Waters" Modernization Reform to All Issuers*, (Feb. 19, 2019), available at: https://www.sec.gov/news/press-release/2019-14.

[423] See SEC, *SEC Obtains Preliminary Injunction Against Blockvest LLC and Its Founder for Making Fraudulent Offers of Securities in Reconsideration of Earlier Order*, (Feb. 14, 2019), available at: https://www.sec.gov/litigation/litreleases/2019/lr24400.htm.

[424] See H. M. Pierce, *Regulation: A View from Inside the Machine*, Remarks at Protecting the Public While Fostering Innovation and Entrepreneurship: First Principles for Optimal Regulation – University of Missouri School of Law (Feb. 8, 2019), available at: https://www.sec.gov/news/speech/peirce-regulation-view-inside-machine.

[425] See MAS, *MAS halts Securities Token Offering for regulatory breach*, (Jan. 24, 2019), available at: http://www.mas.gov.sg/News-and-Publications/Media-Releases/2019/MAS-halts-Securities-Token-Offering-for-regulatory-breach.aspx.

[426] See J. Wall, *China Introduces New Anti-Anonymity Regulations To Enable "Orderly Development" In Their Blockchain Industry*, Invest in Blockchain (Jan. 13, 2019), available at: https://www.investinblockchain.com/china-introduces-new-anti-anonymity-regulations/.

[427] See J. Russel, *Thailand issues its first licenses to 4 crypto exchanges*, TechCrunch (Jan. 10, 2019), available at: https://techcrunch.com/2019/01/09/thailand-crypto-exchange-license/.

Crypto-assets global corporate finance transactions

	Exchange Commission ("**SEC**"). He proposes that digital assets should answer to the Commodity and Futures Trading Commission[428].
JANUARY 9, 2018	The European Securities and Markets Authority ("**ESMA**"), publishes their "Advice" on ICOs and crypto-assets[429].
JANUARY 4, 2018	The Capital Market Authority of Kenya warns public against investing in an ICO or trading coins offered by the Kenyan based Wiseman Talent Ventures[430].
JANUARY 3, 2019	The Philippine Securities and Exchange Commission ("**PSEC**") announces that the release of ICO regulations will be delayed. The PSEC says that they were pressured by "different shareholders" into delaying publishing the regulations in order to allow them more time to review the drafts of the regulations before publishing[431].
DECEMBER 20, 2018	US Representatives Warren Davidson and Darren Soto introduce the "Token Taxonomy Act". The new bill aims to remove digital currencies from being classified as securities[432].
DECEMBER 8, 2018	The Securities Commission Malaysia and Bank Negara Malaysia announce that they will tighten scrutiny of ICOs via expanded rules which are intended to

---

[428] See T. Macheel, *Cryptocurrencies Don't Belong Under SEC's Authority: Rep Soto*, Cheddar (Jan. 10, 2019), available at: https://cheddar.com/videos/cryptocurrencies-dont-belong-under-secs-authority-rep-soto.

[429] See J.D. Alois, *European Securities and Markets Authority Tells European Commission that ICOs and Crypto Assets Need an EU Wide Regulatory Approach*, Crowdfund Insider (Jan. 9, 2019), available at: https://www.crowdfundinsider.com/2019/01/143130-european-securities-and-markets-authority-tells-european-commission-that-icos-and-crypto-assets-need-an-eu-wide-regulatory-approach/.

[430] See APA, *Kenya's Capital Markets Authority cautions public against participating in coin offerings*, Political Analysis South Africa (Jan. 4, 2019), available at: https://www.politicalanalysis.co.za/kenyas-capital-markets-authority-cautions-public-against-participating-in-coin-offerings/.

[431] See R. McIntosh, *Philippine SEC Delays ICO Regulations at Shareholders' Request*, Finance Magnates (Jan. 3, 2019), available at: https://www.financemagnates.com/cryptocurrency/news/philippine-sec-delays-ico-regulations-at-shareholders-request/.

[432] See K. Rooney, *Lawmakers look to change SEC's 72-year-old securities definition to exclude cryptocurrencies*, CNBC (Dec. 20, 2010), available at: https://www.cnbc.com/2018/12/20/lawmakers-look-to-change-secs-72-year-old-securities-definition-to-exclude-cryptocurrencies.html.

The evolving landscape

	eradicate issues of money laundering and unfair trade practices[433].
DECEMBER 4, 2018	The Municipal Bureau of Finance's bureau chief Huo Xuewen announces that security token fundraising is illegal[434]. China also aims to ban airdrops.
DECEMBER 3, 2018	Japan's Financial Services Agency ("**FSA**") prepares to enact regulations regarding ICOs. The new regulations will require registration with the FSA for businesses planning to offer their own cryptocurrencies[435].
	US Representative Warren Davidson of Ohio announces plans for federal government to regulate ICOs and cryptocurrencies. The goal of the bill is to classify tokens in their own asset class, thus exempting them from being classified as securities[436].
NOVEMBER 29, 2018	The US Securities and Exchange Commission ("**SEC**") announces charges against Floyd Mayweather Jr. and DJ Khaled for failure to disclose payments they received to promote the Centra Tech Inc. ICO. Mayweather will have to pay upwards of $600,000 in fines, while Khaled will have to pay approximately $150,000. Both celebrities have agreed not to promote any digital securities for three years[437].
NOVEMBER 16, 2018	Two ICOs, Airfox and Paragon Coin agree to settle US Securities and Exchange Commission ("**SEC**") registration charges and will return funds to investors, register the tokens as securities, pay penalties and file

---

[433] See J. Gogo, *Malaysian Financial Regulators to Intensify Scrutiny of ICOs, Cryptocurrencies*, Bitcoin.com (Dec. 8, 2018), available at: https://news.bitcoin.com/malaysian-financial-regulators-to-intensify-scrutiny-of-icos-cryptocurrencies/.
[434] See D. Ren, *Central bank deputy governor: STO business 'essentially an illegal financial activity in China'*, South China Morning Post (Dec 9, 2018), available at: https://www.scmp.com/business/banking-finance/article/2177134/central-bank-deputy-governor-sto-business-essentially.
[435] See K. Helms, *Japan Unveils Plans to Regulate Initial Coin Offerings*, Bitcoin.com (Dec. 3, 2018), available at: https://news.bitcoin.com/japan-plans-regulate-initial-coin-offerings/.
[436] See E. Bamforth, *U.S. Rep. Warren Davidson announces legislation to regulate initial coin offerings at Blockchain Solutions conference*, Cleveland.com (Dec. 3, 2018), available at: https://www.cleveland.com/news/2018/12/us-rep-warren-davidson-announces-legislation-to-regulate-initial-coin-offerings-at-blockchain-solutions-conference.html.
[437] See SEC, *Two Celebrities Charged With Unlawfully Touting Coin Offerings*, (Nov. 29, 2018), available at: https://www.sec.gov/news/press-release/2018-268.

reports periodically with the SEC. Both ICOs failed to register their offerings under federal securities laws[438].

NOVEMBER 15, 2018   Maksim Zaslavskiy, pleads guilty to fraud involving the REcoin ICO offering. This is the first ICO fraud case to be prosecuted[439].

NOVEMBER 10, 2018   The US Securities and Exchange Commission ("**SEC**") tweets out *"five things you need to know about ICOs"* in order to remind investors of the potential risk of investing and that ICOs may fall under the umbrella of securities[440].

NOVEMBER 8, 2018   The US Securities and Exchange Commission ("**SEC**") announces that charges against EtherDelta founder Zachary Coburn have been settled. Coburn was ordered to pay hundreds of thousands of dollars in penalties and his cooperation was noted by the SEC[441].

Colorado's Division of Securities of the US State issues four cease-and-desist orders *"directing the cessation of unregistered securities in the state of Colorado"*[442].

NOVEMBER 4, 2018   The US Securities and Exchange Commission ("**SEC**")'s annual Enforcement Report is released. The report prominently features ICOs and addresses the SEC's crackdown on the relatively new form of fundraising[443].

OCTOBER 27, 2018   The Thai Securities and Exchange Commission issues warnings against nine not accredited ICO and token offerings. The Thai Securities and Exchange

---

[438] See SEC, *Two ICO Issuers Settle SEC Registration Charges, Agree to Register Tokens as Securities*, (Nov. 16, 2018), available at: https://www.sec.gov/news/press-release/2018-264#.W-7slCLOyKE.facebook.

[439] See P. Hurtado, *First Initial Coin Offering Fraud Case Ends in Guilty Plea*, Bloomberg (Nov. 15, 2018), available at: https://www.bloomberg.com/news/articles/2018-11-15/first-fraud-case-for-initial-coin-offering-set-for-guilty-plea.

[440] See SEC, Initial Coin Offerings (ICOs), available at: https://www.sec.gov/ICO.

[441] See SEC, *SEC Charges EtherDelta Founder With Operating an Unregistered Exchange*, (Nov. 8, 2018), available at: https://www.sec.gov/news/press-release/2018-258.

[442] See K. Helms, *Colorado Takes Action Against Four More ICOs – 12 in Total*, Bitcoin.com (Nov. 10, 2018), available at: https://news.bitcoin.com/colorado-takes-action-against-icos/.

[443] See SEC, *2018 Annual Report – Division of Enforcement*, (Nov. 4, 2018), available at: https://www.sec.gov/files/enforcement-annual-report-2018.pdf.

	Commission warns investors to beware of fraudulent raises and Ponzi schemes[444].
OCTOBER 26, 2018	Taiwan's securities regulatory agency announces that it will introduce a legal framework for ICOs. Taipei Times predicts that the regulations regarding tokens should be finalized by June 2019[445].
OCTOBER 9, 2018	Austria's Financial Market Authority issues guidelines regarding its views on ICOs from a financial regulatory perspective. The new guidelines are meant to give further clarification on crypto-assets such as tokens and virtual currencies. The new guidelines address what constitutes an ICO, regulatory requirements that should be considered when launching an ICO, as well as a further explanation of the types of tokens[446].
OCTOBER 8, 2018	The United Arab Emirates Securities and Commodities Authority ("**ESCA**") announces that it will introduce ICOs next year as a viable source of fundraising[447].
SEPTEMBER 27, 2018	The Capital Markets Board of Turkey issues statement that they do not regulate or supervise ICOs or companies utilizing blockchain technology, including cryptocurrencies and token offerings[448].
SEPTEMBER 20, 2018	US Securities and Exchange Commission ("**SEC**") co-director Stephanie Avakian states in a speech that the SEC aims to recommend *"more substantial remedies"* against those ICOs are who fail to meet registration requirements[449].

---

[444] See P. Sangwongwanich, *SEC issues warning on renegade ICOs*, Bangkok Post (Oct. 27, 2018), available at: https://www.bangkokpost.com/business/news/1565406/.
[445] See K. Shih-ching, *FSC says it is drafting ICO regulations*, Taipei Times (Oct. 26, 2018), available at: http://www.taipeitimes.com/News/biz/archives/2018/10/23/2003702843.
[446] See FMA, *FMA Focus on Initial Coin Offerings*, (Oct. 9, 2018), available at: https://www.fma.gv.at/en/fma-thematic-focuses/fma-focus-on-initial-coin-offerings/.
[447] See S. Carvalho, *UAE plans initial coin offerings to boost capital markets – regulator*, Reuters (Oct. 8, 2018), available at: https://www.reuters.com/article/emirates-ico/uae-plans-initial-coin-offerings-to-boost-capital-markets-regulator-idUSL8N1WO2QI.
[448] See G. Gürkaynak, C. Yildiz, N. Gürün, *Capital Markets Board Issues an Official Announcement on Initial Coin Offerings and Crowdfunding*, Mondaq (Oct. 3, 2018), available at: http://www.mondaq.com/turkey/x/742304/Securities/Capital+Markets+Board+Issues+an+Official+Announcement+on+Initial+Coin+Offerings+and+Crowdfunding.
[449] See S. Avakian, *Measuring the Impact of the SEC's Enforcement Program*, (Sept. 20, 2018), available at: https://www.sec.gov/news/speech/speech-avakian-092018.

Crypto-assets global corporate finance transactions

SEPTEMBER 13, 2018	Gaws Miners' CEO Homero Joshua Garza is sentenced to 21 months of imprisonment for defrauding investors. Garza was also ordered to pay $9.2M in restitution related to the *"creation and sale of a cryptocurrency called PayCoin"*[450].
SEPTEMBER 12, 2018	A judge from the US District Court for the Eastern of New York issues an order which confirms that a federal indictment against Maksim Zaslavskiy for promoting digital tokens through an ICO, was adequately pled[451].
SEPTEMBER 11, 2018	The US Securities and Exchange Commission (**"SEC"**) and Financial Industry Regulatory Authority (**"FINRA"**) each announce three "first of their kind" enforcements related to the digital token market. The actions targeted a token sale website for being unregistered broker-dealer, a digital asset hedge fund manager for failure to register as an investment company, and finally a complaint against a firm which violated federal security laws by offering a blockchain token as an unregistered security[452].
SEPTEMBER 10, 2018	The United Arab Emirates Securities and Commodities Authority (**"ESCA"**) plan to recognize ICOs as securities, as well as to increase regulation[453].
AUGUST 27, 2018	Gerald Rome, the Colorado Securities Commissioner, issues orders to three companies conducting unregistered ICOs. The three companies under investigation are Bionic Coin, Sybrelabs Ltd., and Global

---

[450] See SEC, *Connecticut-Based Bitcoin Mining Fraudster Sentenced to Prison*, (Sept. 20, 2018), available at: https://www.sec.gov/litigation/litreleases/2018/lr24281.htm.
[451] D. Meshulam, B. Klein, R. Kelley, *EDNY: U.S. Securities Laws Can Be Used to Prosecute ICO Fraud*, New York Law Journal (Sept. 18, 2018), available at: https://www.law.com/newyorklawjournal/2018/09/18/edny-u-s-securities-laws-can-be-used-to-prosecute-ico-fraud/.
[452] See SEC, *SEC Charges ICO Superstore and Owners With Operating As Unregistered Broker-Dealers*, (Sept. 11, 2018), available at: https://www.sec.gov/news/press-release/2018-185; SEC, *SEC Charges ICO Superstore and Owners With Operating As Unregistered Broker-Dealers*, (Sept. 11, 2018), available at: https://www.sec.gov/news/press-release/2018-186; FINRA, *FINRA Charges Broker with Fraud and Unlawful Distribution of Unregistered Cryptocurrency Securities*, (Sept. 11, 2018), available at: http://www.finra.org/newsroom/2018/finra-charges-broker-fraud-and-unlawful-distribution-unregistered-cryptocurrency.
[453] See B. Debusmann Jr, *UAE's SCA to regulate initial coin offerings*, Arabian Business (Sept. 10, 2018), available at: https://www.arabianbusiness.com/banking-finance/404039-uaes-sca-to-regulate-initial-coin-offerings.

	Pay Net. The Division of Securities, which is a task force created by Rome, are in charge of the investigations[454].
AUGUST 16, 2018	The Financial Industry Regulatory Authority ("**FINRA**") warns investors that they should not consider ICOs that promote SAFTs, or Simple Agreement for Future Tokens, as safe investments, nor does the promotion of a SAFT contract mean that the offering is compliant[455].
AUGUST 14, 2018	The US Securities and Exchange Commission ("**SEC**") announces *"permanent officer-and-director and penny stock bars"* against David T. Laurance, who is *"the founder of a company who perpetrated a fraudulent initial coin offering (ICO) to fund oil exploration and drilling in California"*[456].
JULY 18, 2018	The Australian Securities and Investment Commission ("**ASIC**") releases additional guidelines regarding compliance for ICOs and cryptocurrencies via Information Sheet 225. The new guidelines provide clarity on the legal status of ICOs, as well as other issues relating to ICOs such as social media promotion and disclosing of information[457].
JULY 11, 2018	The Gibraltar Stock Exchange announces plans to apply for an extension to its license from the Gibraltar Financial Services Commission. The extension would then allow the trading of security tokens on the GBX exchange[458].
JULY 10, 2018	The Financial Industry Regulatory Authority ("**FINRA**") sends reminder urging firms to *"consider all applicable federal and state laws, rules and regulations, including those of FINRA and the SEC"*. The notice went on to say

---

[454] See Colorado Department Of Regulatory Agencies, *Securities Commissioner issues orders to three companies as part of cryptocurrency investigation*, (Aug. 27, 2018), available at: https://www.colorado.gov/pacific/dora/cryptocurrency-investigation-orders-to-show-cause.
[455] See FINRA, *Initial Coin Offerings (ICOs)—What to Know Now and Time-Tested Tips for Investors*, (Aug. 16, 2018), available at: http://www.finra.org/investors/alerts/initial-coin-offerings-what-to-know.
[456] See SEC, *SEC Bars Perpetrator of Initial Coin Offering Fraud*, (Aug. 14, 2018), available at: https://www.sec.gov/news/press-release/2018-152.
[457] See ASIC, *Information Sheet 225*, (July 18, 2018), available at: https://asic.gov.au/regulatory-resources/digital-transformation/initial-coin-offerings-and-crypto-currency/.
[458] P. Baker, *Gibraltar Stock Exchange Confirms Move Into Security Tokens*, Crypto Briefing (July 11, 2018), available at: https://cryptobriefing.com/gibraltar-stock-exchange-security-tokens/.

	that firms should disclose involvement in cryptocurrency products and production[459].
JULY 4, 2018	Delaware announces that the Delaware Blockchain Amendments *"do not provide blanket authority for shares of stock of a Delaware corporation to be tokenized"*[460].
	The Thai Securities and Exchange Commission announces that its ICO regulations will go into effect on July 16th. The regulations utilize a *"two tier form vetting procedure"* which requires applicants to pass a final SEC screening[461].
JULY 1, 2018	Thailand unveils new Digital Asset Business Decree law which respectively defines cryptocurrencies and digital tokens as a *"medium of exchanging goods"* and *"rights to participate in an investment or receive specific goods"*. The new law also provides rules for exchanges, brokers and dealers, as well as a formalized process for ICOs[462].
JUNE 14, 2018	The US Securities and Exchange Commission ("**SEC**") announces it will not consider Bitcoin or Ether as securities[463].
JUNE 13, 2018	Thailand's Securities and Exchange Commission expects five initial coin offering projects to register for fund-raising procedures after the organic law of the digital asset decree takes effect[464].

---

[459] C. Haal, *FINRA "Encourages" Investment Broker-Dealers to Disclose Crypto Activities*, Crowdfund Insider (July 10, 2018), available at: https://www.crowdfundinsider.com/2018/07/136053-finra-encourages-investment-broker-dealers-to-disclose-crypto-activities/.

[460] See A. Tinianow, *Tokenized Securities Are Not Secured By Delaware Blockchain Amendments*, Forbes (July 4, 2018), available at: https://www.forbes.com/sites/andreatinianow/2018/07/04/tokenized-securities-are-not-secured-by-delaware-blockchain-amendments/#7787ce3e792e.

[461] See W. Suberg, *Thai Regulator Confirms July Start Date for Regulated ICOs*, Cointelegraph (July 5, 2018), available at: https://cointelegraph.com/news/thai-regulator-confirms-july-start-date-for-regulated-icos.

[462] See *Thailand leads in crypto by skipping the big debate*, Bangkok Post (July 1, 2018), available at: https://www.bangkokpost.com/opinion/opinion/1495614/thailand-leads-in-crypto-by-skipping-the-big-debate.

[463] See F. Wolff-Mann, *SEC announces cryptocurrency ether is not a security*, Yahoo Finance (June 14, 2018), available at: https://finance.yahoo.com/news/sec-announces-ether-not-security-162658147.html.

[464] See N. Polkuamdee, *SEC expects 5 ICOs in the pipeline once law enacted*, Bangkok Post, (June 13, 10, 2018), available at: https://www.bangkokpost.com/business/finance/1483753/sec-expects-5-icos-in-the-pipeline-once-law-enacted.

JUNE 12, 2018	Lithuania's Ministry of Finance announces new guidelines for ICOs which address regulations, taxation, accounting and AML[465].
JUNE 4, 2018	The US Securities and Exchange Commission ("**SEC**") appoints Valerie Szczepanik to the position of associate director of the Division of Corporation Finance and senior advisor for digital assets and innovation. Szczepanik's role will be to "coordinate efforts across all SEC Divisions and Offices regarding the application of US securities laws to emerging digital asset technologies and innovations, including initial coin offerings and cryptocurrencies[466].
MAY 24, 2018	The Monetary Authority of Singapore ("**MAS**") warns 8 cryptocurrency exchanges that trading of tokens which are regarded as securities or futures contracts are not permitted without permission from the MAS[467].
MAY 22, 2018	Overstock.com's company tZero and BOX Digital Markets announce plans to open the first regulated exchange for security tokens[468].
MAY 21, 2018	Regulators in the US and Canada announce they have opened investigations into more than 70[469] cryptocurrencies and ICOs in a wide-ranging crackdown named "Operation Crypto Sweep"[470].
MAY 10, 2018	Ontario's chartered professional accountants urges chartered accountants to avoid "participating in

---

[465] See K. Helms, *Lithuania Unveils Detailed Cryptocurrency and ICO Guidelines*, Bitcoin.com (June 12, 2018), available at: https://news.bitcoin.com/lithuania-cryptocurrency-ico-guidelines/.
[466] See SEC, *SEC Names Valerie A. Szczepanik Senior Advisor for Digital Assets and Innovation*, (June 4, 2018), available at: https://www.sec.gov/news/press-release/2018-102.
[467] See MAS, *MAS warns Digital Token Exchanges and ICO Issuer*, (May 24, 2018), available at: http://www.mas.gov.sg/News-and-Publications/Media-Releases/2018/MAS-warns-Digital-Token-Exchanges-and-ICO-Issuer.aspx.
[468] See G. Chavez-Dreyfuss, *Overstock.com unit, BOX to launch security token exchange*, Reuters (May 22, 2018), available at: https://www.reuters.com/article/us-crypto-currency-tzero/overstockcom-unit-box-to-launch-security-token-exchange-idUSKCN1IN22G.
[469] See NASAA, *Operation Cryptosweep*, (May 21, 2018), available at: http://www.nasaa.org/regulatory-activity/enforcement-legal-activity/operation-cryptosweep/.
[470] See G.T. Rubin, *State and Provincial Regulators in U.S. and Canada Target Initial Coin Offerings*, The Wall Street Journal (May 21, 2018), available at: https://www.wsj.com/articles/state-and-provincial-regulators-in-u-s-and-canada-target-initial-coin-offerings-1526918512.

unregulated cryptocurrency offerings" and to avoid any ICOs which don't treat their tokens as securities[471].

MAY 1, 2018 — The Australian Securities and Investments Commission ("**ASIC**") says that it is taking aim at fraud in the initial coin offering market[472].

APRIL 30, 2018 — US Securities and Exchange Commission ("**SEC**") commissioner Robert Jackson issues criticism of ICOs saying, "*investors are having a hard time telling the difference between investments and fraud (...) If you want to know what our markets would look like with no securities regulation, what it would look like if the SEC didn't do its job? The answer is the ICO market*"[473].

APRIL 28, 2018 — The US House of Representatives holds hearing regarding whether or not ICOs could be regulated with a "*balanced approach*"[474].

APRIL 27, 2018 — Bermuda's House Assembly passes the Companies and Limited Liability Company Amendment Act 2018 (ICO Act) which, if approved by the Senate, will regulate all aspects of digital assets (including ICOs)[475].

APRIL 26, 2018 — The Australian Securities and Investments Commission ("**ASIC**") announces that ICOs will be a key focus as it expands its guidance and regulations[476].

---

[471] See A. Posadzki, *Ontario accountants advised to avoid unregulated initial coin offerings*, The Globe and Mail (May 10, 2018), available at: https://www.theglobeandmail.com/business/article-ontario-accountants-advised-to-avoid-unregulated-initial-coin/.

[472] K. Helms, *Australia Cracks Down on Misleading and Deceptive Initial Coin Offerings*, Bitcoin.com (May 3, 2018), available at: https://news.bitcoin.com/australia-cracks-down-misleading-deceptive-initial-coin-offerings/.

[473] See K. Rooney, *SEC is cautiously open to initial coin offerings, commissioner says*, CNBC (Apr. 30, 2018), available at: https://www.cnbc.com/2018/04/30/sec-is-cautious-but-open-to-crypto-fundraising-commissioner-says.html.

[474] See M.J. Zuckerman, *US: SEC Official Says ICO Regulation Should Be 'Balanced', Congressman Suggests Ban*, Cointelegraph (Apr. 28, 2018), available at: https://cointelegraph.com/news/us-sec-official-says-ico-regulation-should-be-balanced-congressman-suggests-ban.

[475] See T. Faries, S. Rees Davies, J. Eve, *Bermuda Innovates With New Initial Coin Offering (ICO) Legislation*, Mondaq (May 2, 2018), available at: http://www.mondaq.com/x/698116/fin+tech/Bermuda+Innovates+With+New+Initial+Coin+Offering+ICO+Legislation.

[476] See *Initial coin offerings a "key focus" for Australian regulator*, Reuters (Apr. 26, 2018), available at: https://www.reuters.com/article/crypto-currencies-australia/initial-coin-offerings-a-key-focus-for-australian-regulator-idUSL3N1S34DM.

APRIL 23, 2018	Gary Gensler, the former chairman of the US Commodity Futures Trading Commission ("**CFTC**"), says that government officials should take a closer look at the largest coins by market capitalization, not just at tokens sold in ICOs. Ethereum's Ether and Ripple's XRP could probably be classified as securities, Gensler said[477].
APRIL 20, 2018	US Securities and Exchange Commission ("**SEC**") officials file fraud charges against a third "mastermind" in in Centra Tech's allegedly fraudulent initial coin offering[478].
APRIL 19, 2018	Tezos cofounder Arthur Breitman is fined $20,000 by the Financial Industry Regulatory Authority ("**FINRA**") and is barred from broker-dealer interaction until 2020 due to a failure to disclose outside business activities[479].
APRIL 9, 2018	The Ontario Securities Commission ("**OSC**") announces that platforms offering cryptocurrency trading must determine if they are a marketplace. The OSC went on to say that cryptocurrencies may qualify as securities[480].
APRIL 3, 2018	Australia announces that Australian cryptocurrency exchanges are required to abide by anti-money laundering (AML) rules[481].
APRIL 2, 2018	The US Securities and Exchange Commission ("**SEC**") charges two co-founders of Centra Tech Inc., a Miami startup, for orchestrating a fraudulent initial coin

---

[477] See C. Russo, *Former CFTC Head Says Big Cryptocurrencies Could Be Classified as Securities*, Bloomberg (Apr. 23, 2018), available at: https://www.bloomberg.com/news/articles/2018-04-23/ether-ripple-may-be-securities-former-cftc-head-gensler-says.

[478] See SEC, *SEC Charges Additional Defendant in Fraudulent ICO Scheme*, (April 20, 2018), available at: https://www.sec.gov/news/press-release/2018-70.

[479] See A. Irrera, S. Stecklow, J. McCrank, *Wall Street regulator sanctions Tezos cryptocurrency project co-founder*, Reuters (April 19, 2018), available at: https://www.reuters.com/article/us-cryptocurrency-tezos/wall-street-regulator-sanctions-tezos-cryptocurrency-project-co-founder-idUSKBN1HQ38F.

[480] See K. Hanly, *Province of Ontario examining cryptocoin trading platforms*, Digital Journal (April 9, 2018), available at: http://www.digitaljournal.com/tech-and-science/technology/ontario-securities-commission-examining-cryptocoin-trading/article/519428.

[481] See AUSTRAC, *Digital currency exchange providers: register online with AUSTRAC*, (April 26, 2018), available at: http://www.austrac.gov.au/news/digital-currency-exchange-providers-register-online-austrac.

offering that raised more than $32 million from investors last year[482].

The US Securities and Exchange Commission ("**SEC**") charges Michael Liberty, the founder of Mozido Inc., with defrauding investors of more than $48 million by tricking investors into investing in shell companies[483].

APRIL 1, 2018 Russia's Ministry of Telecom and Mass Communications announces new set of regulations for ICOs. The new regulations state that companies conducting ICOs are required to guarantee that tokens can be bought back at a nominal price[484].

MARCH 27, 2018 Massachusetts regulator orders the halting of five ICOs due to being unregistered securities[485].

MARCH 11, 2018 Tennessee government proposes bills to ban retirement funds from investing in cryptocurrencies. The state's government also proposed bills that would legalize the use of blockchain for electronic transactions[486].

MARCH 9, 2018 South Carolina lawmakers request that Genesis Mining, a cryptocurrency cloud mining platform, leave the state "due to selling unlicensed securities"[487].

The Praetorian Group files with the US Securities and Exchange Commission to hold the "first ever SEC-registered ICO"[488].

---

[482] See SEC, *SEC Halts Fraudulent Scheme Involving Unregistered ICO*, (Apr. 2, 2018), available at: https://www.sec.gov/news/press-release/2018-53.

[483] See SEC, *SEC Charges Fintech Company Founder With Scheme to Defraud Investors and Misappropriate Funds*, (Apr. 2, 2018), available at: https://www.sec.gov/news/press-release/2018-52.

[484] See L. Tasser, *Strict Rules for ICOs Prepared in Russia*, Bitcoin.com (Apr. 2, 2018), available at: https://news.bitcoin.com/strict-rules-for-icos-prepared-in-russia/.

[485] See E. Dilts, A. Irrera, *Massachusetts regulator blocks ICOs by five firms*, Reuters (Mar. 27, 2018), available at: https://www.reuters.com/article/us-crypto-currencies-massachusetts/massachusetts-regulator-blocks-icos-by-five-firms-idUSKBN1H32PC.

[486] See M.J. Zuckerman, *Tennessee: New Legislation Prevents Crypto Retirement Funds While Legalizing Blockchain*, Cointelegraph (Mar. 11, 2018), available at: https://cointelegraph.com/news/tennessee-new-legislation-prevents-crypto-retirement-funds-while-legalizing-blockchain.

[487] See W. Suberg, *South Carolina Wants To Ban Genesis Mining Over Unregistered Securities*, Cointelegraph (Mar. 12, 2018), available at: https://cointelegraph.com/news/south-carolina-wants-to-ban-genesis-mining-over-unregistered-securities.

[488] See M.J. Zuckerman, *Praetorian Group Files To Be First ICO To Sell Registered Security Tokens In US*, Cointelegraph (Mar. 9, 2018), available at: https://cointelegraph.com/news/praetorian-group-files-to-be-first-ico-to-sell-registered-security-tokens-in-us.

The evolving landscape

MARCH 18, 2018   South Korea reverses view on cryptocurrencies and announces it is working on creating policy guidelines for ICOs[489].

MARCH 7, 2018   Japan's Financial Services Agency issues punishment notices and business improvement orders to 7 cryptocurrency exchanges due to a lack of required internal control systems related to anti-money laundering and counter terrorism financing[490].

The US Securities and Exchange Commission ("**SEC**") publishes statement regarding cryptocurrency exchanges / online trading platforms that states that the mechanism for trading assets meets the definition of a security under federal securities laws[491].

MARCH 6, 2018   The Financial Crimes Enforcement Network ("**FinCEN**") publishes a letter Tuesday that indicates the US agency will apply its regulations to those who conduct initial coin offerings.

FEBRUARY 28, 2018   The US Securities and Exchange Commission ("**SEC**") issues dozens of subpoenas and information requests to technology companies and advisers involved in the red-hot market for cryptocurrencies, according to people familiar with the matter[492].

FEBRUARY 27, 2018   Malaysia announces that all cryptocurrency exchanges must verify identities of traders due to new AML legislation going into effect[493].

FEBRUARY 26, 2018   A cease-and-desist letter is issued by the Texas State Securities Board to Leadinvest.com due to accusations of fraudulently selling unlicensed securities[494].

---

[489] See K. Yoo-chul, Korea to allow ICOs with new regulations, The Korea Times (Mar. 8, 2018), available at: https://www.koreatimes.co.kr/www/biz/2018/03/367_245242.html.

[490] See *Japanese authorities issue punishments to several cryptocurrency exchanges*, CNBC (Mar. 7, 2018), available at: https://www.cnbc.com/2018/03/07/japanese-authorities-issue-punishments-to-several-cryptocurrency-exchanges.html.

[491] See SEC, *Statement on Potentially Unlawful Online Platforms for Trading Digital Assets*, (Mar. 7, 2018), available at: https://www.sec.gov/news/public-statement/enforcement-tm-statement-potentially-unlawful-online-platforms-trading.

[492] See J. Eaglesham, P. Vigna, *Cryptocurrency Firms Targeted in SEC Probe*, The Wall Street Journal (Feb. 28, 2018), available at: https://www.wsj.com/articles/sec-launches-cryptocurrency-probe-1519856266.

[493] See BNM, *Bank Negara Malaysia issues policy document for digital currencies* (Feb. 27, 2018), available at: http://www.bnm.gov.my/index.php?ch=en_press&pg=en_press&ac=4628&lang=en.

Crypto-assets global corporate finance transactions

	The Israeli Supreme Court decides that banks must allow crypto trading and may not prohibit company accounts associated with the industry[495].
FEBRUARY 19, 2018	Israel announces it will tax cryptocurrencies as property. Individuals will not have to pay the value-added tax, however businesses will[496].
FEBRUARY 16, 2018	The US Securities and Exchange Commission ("**SEC**") suspends trading in three companies amid questions surrounding similar statements they made about the acquisition of cryptocurrency and blockchain technology-related assets[497].
FEBRUARY 13, 2018	The US Treasury releases letter stating that companies must report suspicious transactions to authorities in order to combat money laundering and financing of terrorism.
FEBRUARY 12, 2018	Thailand's central bank prohibits financial institutions from investing or trading cryptocurrency, offering cryptocurrency exchanges, and creating cryptocurrency-based platforms. Banks are also banned from allowing credit card transactions to buy cryptocurrencies[498].
	Russia's Ministry of Communications unveils new licensing rules for ICOs. New regulations include a required $1.7M nominal capital, specific licensed bank

---

[494] See M.J. Zuckerman, *Texas Regulator Orders Another Crypto Scam To Stop Selling Fraudulent Securities*, Cointelegraph (Feb. 27, 2018), available at: https://cointelegraph.com/news/texas-regulator-orders-another-crypto-scam-to-stop-selling-fraudulent-securities.

[495] See R. Mashraky, *Israeli Supreme Court Backs Crypto, Forces Banks to Allow Trading*, Finance Magnates (Feb. 26, 2018), available at: https://www.financemagnates.com/cryptocurrency/news/israeli-supreme-court-backs-crypto-forces-banks-allow-trading/.

[496] A. Milano, *Israel Confirms It Will Tax Bitcoin as Property*, Coindesk (Feb. 19, 2018), available at: https://www.coindesk.com/israel-confirms-will-tax-bitcoin-property.

[497] See SEC, *SEC Suspends Trading in Three Issuers Claiming Involvement in Cryptocurrency and Blockchain Technology*, (Feb. 16, 2018), available at: https://www.sec.gov/news/press-release/2018-20.

[498] See *Thai central bank bans banks from cryptocurrencies*, Reuters (Feb. 12, 2018), available at: https://www.reuters.com/article/thailand-economy-cenbank/thai-central-bank-bans-banks-from-cryptocurrencies-idUSL4N1Q234I.

The evolving landscape

accounts, as well as a license for the development, production, and issuance of tokens[499].

The European Supervisory Authorities ("**ESAs**") for securities ("**ESMA**"), banking ("**EBA**"), and insurance and pensions ("**EIOPA**") warns customers that virtual currencies (cryptocurrencies) are highly risky, not backed by tangible assets and unregulated under EU law[500].

FEBRUARY 9, 2018 Hong Kong's Securities and Futures Commission alerts investors to the potential risks of dealing with cryptocurrency exchanges and investing in ICOs[501].

China's National Internet Finance Association ("**NIFA**") announces plans to increase oversight of ICOs and cryptocurrencies[502].

Gibraltar officials look to develop regulations and a framework for companies utilizing ICOs[503].

FEBRUARY 5, 2018 China announces plans to cut off internet access for citizens to sites which trade cryptocurrency and permit ICO investments[504].

FEBRUARY 4, 2018 The Securities and Commodities Authority of the United Arab Emirates ("**ESCA**") issues a warning regarding the risk of investing in ICOs, advising that

---

[499] See H. Partz, *Russia: Ministry of Communications Requires ICO Issuers To Have $1.7 Mln Nominal Capital*, Cointelegraph (Feb. 12, 2018), available at: https://cointelegraph.com/news/russia-ministry-of-communications-requires-ico-issuers-to-have-17-mln-nominal-capital.
[500] See EBA, *ESAs warn consumers of risks in buying virtual currencies*, (Feb. 12, 2018), available at: https://eba.europa.eu/-/esas-warn-consumers-of-risks-in-buying-virtual-currencies.
[501] See SFC, *SFC warns of cryptocurrency risks*, (Feb. 9, 2018), available at: https://www.sfc.hk/edistributionWeb/gateway/EN/news-and-announcements/news/doc?refNo=18PR13.
[502] See R. Mashraky, *Ying & Yang: Weighing Contradictory Moves on Cryptos, ICOs in China*, Finance Magnates (Feb. 12, 2018), available at: https://www.financemagnates.com/cryptocurrency/news/ying-yang-weighing-contradictory-moves-cryptos-icos-china/.
[503] See H. Jones, *Gibraltar moves ahead with world's first initial coin offering rule*, Reuters (Feb. 9, 2018), available at: https://www.reuters.com/article/us-gibraltar-markets-cryptocurrencies/gibraltar-moves-ahead-with-worlds-first-initial-coin-offering-rules-idUSKBN1FT1YN.
[504] See X. Yu, *China to stamp out cryptocurrency trading completely with ban on foreign platforms*, South Chinas Morning Post (Feb. 5, 2018), available at: https://www.scmp.com/business/banking-finance/article/2132009/china-stamp-out-cryptocurrency-trading-completely-ban

Crypto-assets global corporate finance transactions

	legal protection is not available since the agency doesn't regulate ICOs[505].
JANUARY 28, 2018	Philippines' Securities and Exchange Commission announces it is crafting rules to regulate cryptocurrency transactions to protect investors and reduce the risk of fraud[506].
JANUARY 25, 2018	Wyoming lawmakers propose bill that would exempt creators and sellers of utility tokens from securities regulations[507].
	South Korea announces plans to create a task force to oversee local cryptocurrency exchanges and enforce compliance with regulations for cryptocurrency-based businesses[508].
JANUARY 20, 2018	India's top banks suspend and severely limit functions of Bitcoin exchange accounts[509].
JANUARY 19, 2018	The US Commodity Futures Trading Commission ("**CFTC**") targets two allegedly fraudulent cryptocurrency investment schemes with lawsuits[510].
JANUARY 17, 2018	Bermuda Monetary Authority issues statement regarding the risks of ICOs which warns investors about

---

[505] See SCA, *SCA issues circular warning investors against digital, token-based fundraising activities*, (Feb. 4, 2018), available at: https://www.sca.gov.ae/English/News/Pages/Articles/2018/2018-2-4.aspx.

[506] See *Philippines to develop rules on cryptocurrency trading*, Reuters (Jan. 29, 2018), available at: https://www.reuters.com/article/us-philippines-cryptocurrency/philippines-to-develop-rules-on-cryptocurrency-trading-idUSKBN1FI0NK

[507] See S. Higgins, *Wyoming Lawmakers Want Exemptions for ICO Utility Tokens*, Coindesk (Jan 25, 2018), available at: https://www.coindesk.com/utility-token-exemption-sought-in-new-wyoming-blockchain-bill.

[508] See J. Young, *South Korea Intelligence Creates Task Force to Oversee Local Cryptocurrency Exchanges*, Cointelegraph (Jan. 25, 2018), available at: https://cointelegraph.com/news/south-korea-intelligence-creates-task-force-to-oversee-local-cryptocurrency-exchanges.

[509] See S. Dave, S. Shukla, *Top banks suspend accounts of major Bitcoin exchanges in India*, The Economic Times (Jan. 20, 2018), available at: https://economictimes.indiatimes.com/industry/banking/finance/banking/top-banks-suspend-accounts-of-major-bitcoin-exchanges-in-india/articleshow/62576882.cms?from=mdr.

[510] See CFTC, *CFTC Charges Patrick K. McDonnell and His Company CabbageTech, Corp. d/b/a Coin Drop Markets with Engaging in Fraudulent Virtual Currency Scheme*, (Jan. 19, 2018), available at: https://www.cftc.gov/PressRoom/PressReleases/pr7675-18.

the lack of investor protections in the unregulated space[511].

Israel's Tax Authority publishes a draft circular addressing the possibility of taxing ICO profits[512].

JANUARY 15, 2018   China's National Internet Finance Association ("**NIFA**"), a self-regulatory organization in the field of Internet finance, issues a warning against risks from the so-called "initial miner offerings" ("**IMO**"). NIFA claimed in a statement that IMOs are disguised initial coin offerings (ICO), which are completely banned in the China. The warning is in compliance with the Notice on ICO issued by the Chinese government in September, 2017[513].

Bank Indonesia teams up with the National Police to enforce Indonesia's ban on cryptocurrencies. Police announce they will target Bali. Indonesia's ban on cryptocurrencies require that all transactions be made in Rupiah[514].

JANUARY 9, 2018   The Philippines' Securities and Exchange Commission warns investors to exercise caution when invited to participate in initial coin offerings (ICOs) involving cryptocurrencies[515].

The Swiss government announces support for Taskforce Blockchain, a new group which will review legal guidelines for blockchain companies[516].

JANUARY 8, 2018   The Swiss Crypto Valley Association unveils code of conduct for ICOs[517].

---

[511] See BMA, *Risks Of Initial Coin Offerings (ICOs)*, (Jan. 17, 2018), available at: http://www.bma.bm/BMANEWS/Risks%20of%20Initial%20Coin%20Offerings.pdf.

[512] See S. Golstein, *Israel to Tax Cryptocurrency, Publishes Draft of Legislation*, Finance Magnates (Jan 17, 2018), available at: https://www.financemagnates.com/cryptocurrency/news/israeli-tax-authority-publishes-draft-cryptocurrency-taxation-legislation/.

[513] See NIFA, *Risk Alert on Disguised ICO Activities*, (Jan 15, 2018), available at: http://www.nifa.org.cn/nifaen/2955875/2955895/2970216/index.html.

[514] See *Bank Indonesia, police prevent bitcoin transactions in Bali*, The Jakarta Post (Jan 15, 2018), available at: https://www.thejakartapost.com/news/2018/01/15/bank-indonesia-police-prevent-bitcoin-transactions-in-bali.html.

[515] See SEC, *SEC Advisory*, (Jan 9, 2018), available at: http://www.sec.gov.ph/wp-content/uploads/2018/01/2017Advisory_InitialCoinOffering.pdf.

[516] See N. De, *Swiss Government Supports Launch Blockchain Task Force*, Coindesk (Jan 9, 2018), available at: https://www.coindesk.com/swiss-government-launches-blockchain-task-force.

JANUARY 4, 2018	The North American Securities Administrators Association ("**NASAA**") reminds investors to be cautious of cryptocurrency investments, while also having previously identified ICOs as emerging investor threats last month[518].
DECEMBER 27, 2017	A new bill that would limit the raises of ICOs to a maximum of $17.3 million, as well as limit the individual investment amount per person to $864, has been proposed by the Russian Ministry of Finance[519].
DECEMBER 21, 2017	The US Securities and Exchange Commission ("**SEC**") begins to seriously crackdown on suspicious cryptocurrencies[520].
	Russia announces plans to regulate cryptocurrencies by imposing limits on investment amounts in ICOs[521].
	The Caribbean nation of Anguilla proposes the AUTO Act which would aim to register and monitor ICOs while at the same time avoid securities regulations[522].
DECEMBER 15, 2017	The UK Financial Conduct Authority ("**FCA**") announces it will take closer look at ICOs to determine if more regulations are needed to protect retail consumers[523].
DECEMBER 11, 2017	Bitcoin futures begin trading on Chicago's Cboe Global Market[524].

---

[517] See CVA, *CVA Policy Framework*, available at: https://cryptovalley.swiss/codeofconduct/.

[518] See NAASA, *NASAA Reminds Investors to Approach Cryptocurrencies, Initial Coin Offerings and Other Cryptocurrency-Related Investment Products with Caution*, (Jan 4, 2018), available at: http://www.nasaa.org/44073/nasaa-reminds-investors-approach-cryptocurrencies-initial-coin-offerings-cryptocurrency-related-investment-products-caution/.

[519] See K. Helms, *Russia Unveils Proposed Regulation Putting Limits on ICOs and Investors*, Bitcoin.com (Dec. 27, 2017), available at: https://news.bitcoin.com/russia-proposed-regulation-limits-icos-investors/.

[520] See M. Sheetz, *The SEC's crackdown on cryptocurrencies is about to get serious, former chairman says*, CNBC (Dec. 21, 2017), available at: https://www.cnbc.com/2017/12/21/sec-crackdown-on-cryptocurrencies-is-about-to-get-serious-ex-chairman.html.

[521] See A. Ostroukh, *Russia's Aksakov: Law on Cryptocurrencies to Limit Investments in ICOs – RIA*, US News (Dec. 21, 2017), available at: https://www.usnews.com/news/technology/articles/2017-12-21/russias-aksakov-law-on-cryptocurrencies-to-limit-investments-in-icos-ria.

[522] See M. Ross, L. Beyoud, *A Tiny Caribbean Island Looks to Lead in ICO Regulation*, Bloomberg Law (Dec. 19, 2017), available at: https://biglawbusiness.com/a-tiny-caribbean-island-looks-to-lead-in-ico-regulation/.

[523] See FCA, *FCA publishes Feedback Statement on Distributed Ledger Technology*, (Dec. 15, 2017), available at: https://www.fca.org.uk/news/press-releases/fca-publishes-feedback-statement-distributed-ledger-technology.

The evolving landscape

	The US Securities and Exchange Commission ("**SEC**") halts the Munchee ICO due to it being unregistered securities offering[525].
	The US Securities and Exchange Commission ("**SEC**") issues statement regarding cryptocurrencies and ICOs addressing considerations main street investors and market professionals should review before investing[526].
DECEMBER 7, 2017	The Financial Services of Korea bans bitcoin futures trading by securities firms.
DECEMBER 4, 2017	The US Securities and Exchange Commission ("**SEC**") files the first-ever charges against an ICO. An emergency asset freeze was enacted against Canadian company PlexCorps[527].
NOVEMBER 22, 2017	The Royal Bank of Zimbabwe announces that Bitcoin is illegal and would not allow its use in Zimbabwe[528].
NOVEMBER 17, 2017	The Gibraltar Blockchain Exchange ("**GBX**"), announces plans launch the first ICO regulated ICO token exchange in January 2018 pending regulatory approval.
NOVEMBER 15, 2017	The government of Anguilla announces plans for cryptocurrency regulations regarding the registration of ICOs. The AUTO Act, or the Anguilla Utility Token Act, is the world's first registration regulations for ICOs[529].

---

[524] See A. Osipovich, G.T. Rubin, *U.S. Bitcoin Futures Climb in First Day of Trade*, The Wall Street Journal (Dec. 11, 2017), available at: https://www.wsj.com/articles/bitcoin-futures-launch-stokes-fears-of-manipulation-hacks-glitches-1512907201.
[525] See SEC, *Company Halts ICO After SEC Raises Registration Concerns*, (Dec. 11, 2017), available at: https://www.sec.gov/news/press-release/2017-227.
[526] See J. Clayton, *Statement on Cryptocurrencies and Initial Coin Offerings*, (Dec. 11, 2017), available at: https://www.sec.gov/news/public-statement/statement-clayton-2017-12-11.
[527] See SEC, *SEC Emergency Action Halts ICO Scam*, (Dec. 4, 2017), available at: https://www.sec.gov/news/press-release/2017-219.
[528] See M. Neuteboom, *Reserve Bank Of Zimbabwe: 'Bitcoin Is Not Legal'*, Bitcoinist (Nov. 26, 2017), available at: https://bitcoinist.com/reserve-bank-of-zimbabwe-bitcoin-is-not-legal/.
[529] See E. Hobey, *Utility Token Offerings: Anguilla Leads Way with New Cryptocurrency Registration Regulations*, Crowdfund Insider (Nov. 15, 2017), available at: https://www.crowdfundinsider.com/2017/11/124625-utility-token-offerings-anguilla-leads-way-new-cryptocurrency-registration-regulations/.

Singapore issues new guidelines on ICOs which outline securities laws and their relations to token sales[530].

NOVEMBER 14, 2017 The UK Financial Conduct Authority ("**FCA**") issues a warning stating that CFDs (cryptocurrency contracts for differences) are high-risk investments and warned investors against investing in them[531].

India announces plans to develop regulations for Bitcoin and ICOs[532].

NOVEMBER 13, 2017 The European Securities Markets Authority ("**ESMA**") issues a statement on ICOs. ESMA alerted ICO firms to meet relevant regulatory requirements, as well as to adhere to their obligations under EU regulation. ESMA also warned investors about the risks of investing in ICOs[533].

NOVEMBER 9, 2017 The Federal Financial Supervisory Authority of Germany ("**BaFin**") issues a warning to investors about the risk of investing in ICOs[534].

US Securities and Exchange Commission Chairman Jay Clayton says so-called initial coin offerings in many cases looked like securities, raising the prospect the agency will take a more aggressive stance to this red-hot fundraising method.

NOVEMBER 1, 2017 The US Securities and Exchange Commission ("**SEC**") issues a statement on potentially unlawful promotion of ICOs by celebrities[535].

---

[530] See MAS, *A Guide To Digital Token Offerings*, (Nov. 15, 2017), available at: http://www.mas.gov.sg/~/media/MAS/Regulations%20and%20Financial%20Stability/Regulations%20Guidance%20and%20Licensing/Securities%20Futures%20and%20Fund%20Management/Regulations%20Guidance%20and%20Licensing/Guidelines/A%20Guide%20to%20Digital%20Token%20Offerings%20%2014%20Nov%202017.pdf.

[531] See FCA, *Consumer warning about the risks of investing in cryptocurrency CFDs*, (Nov. 14, 2017), available at: https://www.fca.org.uk/news/news-stories/consumer-warning-about-risks-investing-cryptocurrency-cfds.

[532] See *SC seeks govt's response on plea to regulate Bitcoin*, The Hindu (Nov. 14, 2017), available at: https://www.thehindu.com/news/national/sc-seeks-govts-response-on-plea-to-regulate-bitcoin/article20445197.ece.

[533] See ESMA, ESMA Highlights ICO Risks For Investors And Firms, (Nov. 13, 2017), available at: https://www.esma.europa.eu/press-news/esma-news/esma-highlights-ico-risks-investors-and-firms.

[534] See BAFIN, *Consumer warning: the risks of initial coin offerings*, (Nov. 9, 2017), available at: https://www.bafin.de/SharedDocs/Veroeffentlichungen/EN/Meldung/2017/meldung_171109_ICOs_en.html.

The evolving landscape

OCTOBER 27, 2017	New Zealand's FMA claims that any digital currency or ICO-obtained token would be considered as a security. The finance regulator also explains the various means in which token sales will be covered under the country's national law.
OCTOBER 11, 2017	Lithuania's Ministry of Finance publishes new ICO guidelines and states that financial institutions must distance themselves from ICOs and ICO activity[536].
OCTOBER 9, 2017	The Financial Services Regulatory Authority ("**FSRA**") of Abu Dhabi Global Market ("**ADGM**") sets out guidance on ICOs and virtual currencies[537].
SEPTEMBER 29, 2017	The Australian Securities and Investments Commission ("**ASIC**") announces its intent to assist businesses to understand their potential obligations under the Corporations Act by issuing guidance over ICOs.
	South Korea bans raising money through ICOs and token sales[538].
SEPTEMBER 27, 2017	Macau's top financial regulator orders all banks and payment services to not provide services for ICOs and cryptocurrencies[539].
SEPTEMBER 22, 2017	Gibraltar announces that ICOs are to come under regulatory oversight in January 2018[540].
SEPTEMBER 19, 2017	Switzerland and the Swiss Financial Market Supervisory Authority ("**FINMA**") informally voices support for

---

[535] See SEC, *SEC Statement Urging Caution Around Celebrity Backed ICOs*, (Nov. 1, 2017), available at: https://www.sec.gov/news/public-statement/statement-potentially-unlawful-promotion-icos.

[536] See Ministry of Finance, *ICO guidelines*, (Oct. 11, 2017), available at: https://finmin.lrv.lt/uploads/finmin/documents/files/ICO%20Guidelines%20Lithuania.pdf.

[537] See ADGM, *Abu Dhabi Global Market Sets Out Guidance On Initial Coin Offerings And Virtual Currencies*, (Oct. 9, 2017), available at: https://www.adgm.com/mediacentre/press-releases/abu-dhabi-global-market-sets-out-guidance-on-initial-coin-offerings-and-virtual-currencies/.

[538] See C. Kim, *South Korea bans raising money through initial coin offerings*, Reuters (Sept. 28, 2017), available at: https://www.reuters.com/article/us-southkorea-bitcoin/south-korea-bans-raising-money-through-initial-coin-offerings-idUSKCN1C408N.

[539] See AMCM, *Alert to Risks of Virtual Commodities and Tokens*, (Sept. 27, 2017), available at: https://www.amcm.gov.mo/en/about-amcm/press-releases/gap/alert-to-risks-of-virtual-commodities-and-tokens.

[540] See GFSC, *Statement on Initial Coin Offerings*, (Sept 22, 2017), available at: http://www.gfsc.gi/news/statement-on-initial-coin-offerings-250.

	blockchain developments and begins looking into ICOs. FINMA also closes down fake currencies[541].
SEPTEMBER 14, 2017	Thailand announces that ICOs issuing tokens will fall under regulatory jurisdiction of the Thai Securities and Exchange Commission [542].
	The Bank of Indonesia says ICOs will not be legally recognized in the country.
SEPTEMBER 13, 2017	Japan announces plans to introduce oversight on virtual currency exchanges[543].
SEPTEMBER 12, 2017	In the UK, the Financial Conduct Authority ("**FCA**") issues a stern warning over investing in ICOs[544].
SEPTEMBER 5, 2017	Similar to the US, Hong Kong says that ICOs are subject to the securities laws per Hong Kong regulators[545].
	South Korean regulators introduce new regulations on domestic trading of digital currencies[546].
SEPTEMBER 4, 2017	China institutes ICO and token ban. Tokens sold as securities are subject to securities laws in China. Companies who have sold ICO tokens to Chinese investors are directed to refund that money[547].
	Russia prepares to officially legalize ICOs[548].

---

[541] See FINMA, *FINMA closes down coin providers and issues warning about fake cryptocurrencies*, (Sept. 19, 2017), available at: https://www.finma.ch/en/news/2017/09/20170919-mm-coin-anbieter/.
[542] See SEC, *SEC Thailand's Viewpoint on ICO*, (Sept. 14, 2017), available at: https://www.sec.or.th/EN/Pages/FinTech/ICO.aspx.
[543] See *Japan to begin supervision of cryptocurrency exchanges*, Nikkei Asian Review (Sept. 13, 2017), available at: https://asia.nikkei.com/Business/Banking-Finance/Japan-to-begin-supervision-of-cryptocurrency-exchanges.
[544] See FCA, *Consumer warning about the risks of Initial Coin Offerings ('ICOs')*, (Sept. 12, 2017), available at: https://www.fca.org.uk/news/statements/initial-coin-offerings.
[545] See SFC, *Statement on initial coin offerings*, (Sept. 5, 2017), available at: https://www.sfc.hk/web/EN/news-and-announcements/policy-statements-and-announcements/statement-on-initial-coin-offerings.html.
[546] See J. Althauser, *South Korea Moves to Impose Stricter Digital Currency Regulations*, Cointelegraph, (Sept. 5, 2017), available at: https://cointelegraph.com/news/south-korea-moves-to-impose-stricter-digital-currency-regulations.
[547] See W. Zhao, *China's ICO Ban: A Full Translation of Regulator Remarks*, Coindesk (Sept. 5, 2017), available at: https://www.coindesk.com/chinas-ico-ban-a-full-translation-of-regulator-remarks.
[548] See Central Bank of the Russian Federation, *On the use of private "virtual currency"*, (Sept. 4, 2017), available at: https://www.cbr.ru/press/PR/?file=04092017_183512if2017-09-04t18_31_05.htm.

AUGUST 24, 2017	Canadian regulators decide that many ICOs are considered securities under Canadian securities law[549].
AUGUST 11, 2017	The National Bank of Ukraine announces it cannot recognize cryptocurrency as currency and also warns about the risks of fraud in ICOs[550].
AUGUST 5, 2017	South Korean regulators give a break to fintech companies using Bitcoin for currency transfers[551].
AUGUST 1, 2017	In a similar statement to the US, Singapore announces that ICOs and token sales will be regulated by the MAS if the digital tokens are products that are regulated under the Securities and Futures Act[552].
JULY 25, 2017	In the United States, the Securities and Exchange Commission ("**SEC**") rules some ICOs are indeed securities and must follow specific laws, and issues guidance for investors[553].
JUNE 9, 2017	CoinDesk reports that for the first time, blockchain entrepreneurs raised more in ICOs ($327M) than through traditional venture capital funding ($295M) during a similar time period (Jan-June 2017).
JUNE 2016	The Decentralized Autonomous Organization ("**DAO**") code is exploited to steal $50M worth of ETH, causing the collapse of the DAO; however, the success of the DAO token crowdsale does not go unnoticed.
MAY 2016	The Decentralized Autonomous Organization ("**DAO**") is launched; approx. $150M in DAO tokens are sold in a 28-day crowdsale.

---

[549] See CSA, *CSA Staff Notice 46-307 Cryptocurrency Offerings*, (Aug. 24, 2017), available at: http://www.osc.gov.on.ca/documents/en/Securities-Category4/csa_20170824_cryptocurrency-offerings.pdf.

[550] See NBU, *Comments by NBU Governor Oleg Churiy on the Status of Bitcoin in Ukraine*, (Aug. 11, 2017), available at: https://bank.gov.ua/control/en/publish/article?art_id=53613593.

[551] See C. Ji-sung, *Seoul to ease equity capital criteria for bitcoin-mediated foreign currency transfer service*, Pulse (Aug. 5, 2017), available at: https://pulsenews.co.kr/view.php?sc=30800020&year=2017&no=307960.

[552] See MAS, *MAS clarifies regulatory position on the offer of digital tokens in Singapore*, (Aug. 1, 2017), available at: http://www.mas.gov.sg/News-and-Publications/Media-Releases/2017/MAS-clarifies-regulatory-position-on-the-offer-of-digital-tokens-in-Singapore.aspx.

[553] See SEC, Investor Bulletin: Initial Coin Offerings, (July 25, 2017), available at: https://www.sec.gov/oiea/investor-alerts-and-bulletins/ib_coinofferings.

Q4 2015	The Swiss financial market regulator ("**FINMA**") announces guidance that is seen as an encouragement to innovate with cryptocurrency and blockchain technology.
JULY 30, 2015	Ethereum goes live; an earlier crowdsale in July-August 2014 sold 11.9 million coins, called Ether ("**ETH**"), to purchasers using bitcoin ("**BTC**").
MARCH 17, 2015	Isle of Man issues regulations for Bitcoin businesses.
Q4 2015	Swiss law firm MME, together with Ethereum, blockchain startup Monetas, and the Zug Economic Development Office form a crypto-technology cluster in the Swiss Canton of Zug, calling the initiative Crypto Valley.
JULY 31, 2013	The first ICO (Mastercoin) is launched.